AIRCRAFT HYDRAULIC SYSTEMS

AIRCRAFT HYDRAULIC SYSTEMS

THIRD EDITION

by **William A. Neese**

Associate Professor

Embry-Riddle Aeronautical University

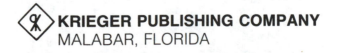
KRIEGER PUBLISHING COMPANY
MALABAR, FLORIDA

Third Edition 1991 (expanded)
Second Edition 1987
First Edition 1984

Printed and Published by
KRIEGER PUBLISHING COMPANY
KRIEGER DRIVE
MALABAR, FLORIDA 32950

Library of Congress Cataloging-In-Publication Data
Neese, William A.
    Aircraft hydraulic systems / by William A. Neese.--3rd ed.
      p.   cm.
    Includes bibliographical refereneces and index.
    ISBN 0-89464-562-5 (alk. paper)
    1. Airplanes--Hydraulic equipment. I. Title.
TL697.H9N39 1991
629.134--dc20   90-23661
                               CIP

10   9   8   7   6   5   4   3

TABLE OF CONTENTS

PREFACE TO THE THIRD EDITION

This textbook was developed and first printed in 1984 for persons preparing for certification as an airframe mechanic. It is intended that this textbook will provide basic information on principles, fundamentals and technical procedures in the subject matter areas relating to the airframe rating. It is designed to aid students enrolled in a formal course of instruction as well as the individual who is studying on his own.

Chapters one through ten contain information on basic hydraulic systems and components, pneumatic systems and components, and typical troubleshooting and repair procedures. The textbook also contains an explanation of the units which make up the various airframe hydraulic and pneumatic systems.

Chapters eleven through fourteen contain information on various types of landing gear systems and components. Several small aircraft and one large aircraft retracting systems are included to familiarize the student with contrasting as well as similar systems and components. Wheel and tire subject matter is included in a condensed manner. Aircraft brakes and brake systems have been included in this section, which includes anti-skid systems and components.

These additional four chapters are designed to aid the student in studying for the landing gear, wheel and brake section of the airframe test.

Chapter fifteen contains systems and components necessary to provide an aircraft with a fully powered flight control system. This high-tech approach to the study of hydraulic systems is designed as an advanced chapter and can be coupled with an electronic flight control course to provide the student with the latest technical subject matter necessary to become more proficient as an airframe mechanic.

The advancements in Aeronautical Technology dictate that an instructional textbook must be brought up to date to be valid. This fifteenth chapter includes systems and components used on a business jet that is just beginning production. Its systems are typical of the current engineering technology for powered flight control systems. The leading edge-trailing edge flap system used is not new, but will serve to represent a typical modern system.

The final chapters are included to describe in detail a typical aircraft system.

The first of these chapters describes the hydraulic power systems of the Canadair Challenger 601 aircraft. Typical system components are discussed in detail. The system operation describes how a typical aircraft system controls the installed hydraulics.

The next chapter also discusses in detail the operation of a typical landing gear hydraulic system. This description of the Canadair 601 aircraft also includes a very detailed explanation of an anti-skid system.

The final chapter is a very detailed description of a powered flight control system. The Canadair 601 system illustrates the mechanical and electronic control for a fully powered flight control system.

There is also a section to explain typical hydraulic and electrical symbols that are currently being used in industry.

The Canadair Challenger represents a very modern, very logical approach to new technology used in a business jet. Most systems used are representative of the same system configuration used on larger, transport jets.

1

FUNDAMENTALS OF HYDRAULICS

General

Hydraulics is that branch of science which deals with the properties of liquids and how they can be used to do work. Hydraulic tools and machines, such as automobile jacks, lifts, door closers, and barber/dentist chairs, are in common use. In aircraft, hydraulic systems are used to operate landing gears, control surfaces, flaps, steering mechanisms, and wheel brakes, to name a few.

The word hydraulics is a derivative of the Greek words hydro (meaning water) and aulis (meaning tube or pipe). Originally, the science of hydraulics covered the physical behavior of water at rest and in motion. This dates back several thousand years ago when water wheels, dams, and sluice gates were first used to control the flow of water for domestic use and irrigation. Use has broadened its meaning to include the physical behavior of all liquids, this includes that area of hydraulics in which confined liquids are used under controlled pressure to do work. This area of hydraulics, sometimes referred to as "power hydraulics," is discussed in this book.

Fluid Flow

When a fluid flows through a tube, it rubs against the walls of the tube. This holds some of the liquid back by resistance. Whenever there is a resistance, there is a loss of energy. As the velocity of a moving liquid increases, the resistence also increases. There are two kinds of fluid flow: laminar and turbulent.

Figure 1.1   Laminar flow.

Laminar flow: (See Figure 1.1) When a liquid is forced through a constant-diameter tube at low velocity, the flow is smooth and even and the fluid's particles tend to move in a parallel stream. The portion of liquid that touches the walls of the tube is slowed down because of friction. This means the fluid near the center of the tube moves at a higher velocity than does the outer portion of the liquid. However, as long as the velocity remains low, the flow will continue smooth because of the low resistance.

Figure 1.2   Turbulent flow.

Turbulent flow: (See Figure 1.2) Resistance to a moving liquid is proportional to its velocity. When the velocity passes a critical point, the resistance increases until turbulent flow results.

The velocity of a liquid in a tube is inversely proportional to the pressure in the tube. Should the liquid pass around a bend or through an orifice or restrictor, or should the tube's diameter suddenly decrease, the pressure decreases and the velocity increases. This increased velocity, in turn, can increase the resistance until turbulent flow results. (See Figure 1.3)

Pascal's Law

The basic principle of hydraulics is expressed in Pascal's Law, formulated by Blaise Pascal, a French mathematician, in the seventeenth century. This law states that a confined body of fluid exerts

Figure 1.3   Fluid flow through orifice.

equal pressure at every point and in every direction in the fluid, and it acts at right angles to the enclosing walls of the container, with any increase in the pressure. (See Figure 1.4)

Figure 1.4   Pressure exerted on a fluid in an enclosed container is transmitted equally and undiminished to all parts of the container and acts at right angles to the enclosing walls.

Hydrostatic Paradox

Before we get into the application of Pascal's Law, we should consider the pressures of static hydraulic fluids. The pressure produced by a column of liquid is directly proportional to the height of the column, and does not depend on the shape of the container. For example, one cubic inch of water weighs 0.036 pound, and a tube that is 231 inches high with a one square inch cross section will hold one gallon of water (one gallon = 231 cubic inches). When the tube is standing straight up, the one gallon of water exerts a pressure of 8.34 pounds per square inch at the bottom of the tube. (See Figure 1.5)

Figure 1.5 The pressure exerted by a column of liquid is determined by the height of the column and is independent of its volume.

It makes no difference as to the size or shape of the container holding the liquid. The volume of the container, likewise, has no effect on the pressure on the bottom. Only the height of the column of liquid has this effect. (See Figure 1.6)

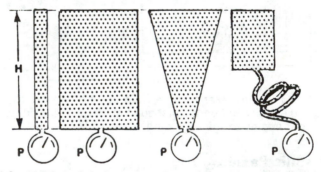

Figure 1.6 Neither the shape nor the volume of a container affects the pressure. Only the height of the column does this.

Characteristics of Liquids

For all practical purposes, liquids are regarded as being incompressible. This means that the volume of a given quantity of a liquid will remain constant even though it is subjected to high pressure. It has been proven that a force of 15 pounds on a cubic inch of water will decrease its volume by only 1/20,000. It would take a force of 32 tons to reduce it 10 percent.

Relationship of Pressure, Force, and Area

In dealing with fluids, forces are usually considered in relation to the areas over which they are applied. The terms force and pressure are used frequently in the discussion of Pascal's Law of fluids. In order to understand how Pascal's Law is applied to fluid power, a distinction must be made between these terms. *Force* may be defined as a push or pull. It is the push or pull exerted against the total area of a particular surface acted upon. In hydraulics, this unit area is expressed in pounds per square inch (psi). This *pressure* is the amount of force acting upon one square inch of *area*.

Computing Force, Pressure, and Area

A formula is used to compute force, pressure, and area in fluid power systems. Although there appears to be three formulas, there is only one formula, which may be written in three variations. In this formula, P refers to pressure, F indicates force, and A represents area. (See Figure 1.7)

FORCE = AREA × PRESSURE   AREA = FORCE/PRESSURE
(A)   (B)

PRESSURE = FORCE/AREA
(C)

Figure 1.7 Relationship between volume, area, and distance.

Force equals pressure times area. Thus, the formula is written $F = P \times A$.

Pressure equals force divided by the area. By rearranging the formula, this statement may be condensed into $P = F/A$

Since area equals force divided by pressure, the formula is written $A = F/P$

Figure 1.8 Device for determining the arrangement of the force, pressure, and area formula.

Figure 1.8 illustrates a device for recalling the different variations of this formula. Any letter in the triangle may be expressed as the product or quotient of the other two, depending upon its position within the triangle. For example, to find area, consider the letter A as being set off to itself, followed by an equal sign. Now look at the other two letters. The letter F is above the letter P; therefore $A = F/P$

In order to find pressure, consider the letter P as being set off to itself, and look at the other two letters. The letter F is above the letter A; therefore, $P = F/A$

Likewise, to find force, consider the letter F as being set off to itself. The letter P and A are side by side; therefore $F = P \times A$. Some examples of this formula application are pressure and force in fluid power systems.

In accordance with Pascal's Law, any force applied to a confined fluid is transmitted in all directions throughout the fluid regardless of the shape of the container. Consider the effect of this in the system shown in Figure 1.9 (force transmitted through fluid) in which the column of fluid is curved back upward to its original level, with a piston at each end. If there is a resistance on the output piston (2) and the input piston (1) is pushed downward, a pressure is created through the fluid, which acts equally at right angles to surfaces in all parts of the container.

Figure 1.9 Force transmitted through fluid.

Figure 1.10   Transmitting force through small pipe.

Referring to Figure 1.9, if the force (1) is 100 pounds and the area of the input piston (1) is 10 square inches, then the pressure in the fluid is 10 psi (100/10). It must be emphasized that this pressure cannot be created without resistance to flow, which, in this case, is provided by the 100 pound force acting against the top of the output piston (2). This pressure acts on piston (2), so that for each square inch of its area it is pushed upward with a force of 10 pounds. In this case, a fluid column of uniform cross section is considered so that the area of the output piston is the same as the input piston. Therefore, the upward force on the output piston is the same as the input piston. All that has been accomplished in this system was to transmit the 100 pound force around a bend.

Since Pascal's Law is independent of the shape of the container, it is not necessary that the tube connecting the two pistons should be the full cross sectional area of the pistons. A connection of any size, shape or length will do, so long as an unobstructed passage is provided. Therefore, the system shown in Figure 1.10 will act exactly the same as that shown in Figure 1.9.

Multiplication of Forces—Mechanical Advantage

If two pistons are used in a fluid power system, the force acting on each is directly proportional to its area, and the magnitude of each force is the product of the pressure and its area. Another consideration is the distance the pistons move, and the volume of the fluid displaced.

Consider the situation shown in Figure 1.11. Here an input piston with a area of 2 square inches travels through a distance to create a movement of the much larger, 20 square inches, output piston. If the input piston is pushed down 1 inch, only 2 cubic inches of fluid is displaced. In order to accommodate these 2 cubic inches of fluid the output piston will have to move only one-tenth of an inch, because its area is 10 times that of the input piston. However, the input force of only 20 pounds will produce a lifting force, the resistance, of 200 pounds. This principle is the basis for the hydraulic jack.

An increase in force can be obtained only by a proportional decrease in distance traveled. This is also if the system is operated in the reverse direction. A distance increase can be obtained, but only at the expense of a force decrease in the same ratio. This leads to the basic statement: Neglecting friction, in any fluid power system, the input force multiplied by the distance through which it moves, is always exactly equal to the output force multiplied by the distance through which it travels. (See Figure 1.12)

Figure 1.11 Multiplication of forces.

Figure 1.12 Relationship of volume, area, and length.

1. Find P: Area = 4 sq. in.
   Force = 100 lbs.
   Pressure = _____ psi

2. Find F: Area = 10 sq. in.
   Force = _____ lbs.
   Pressure = 100 psi

3. Find A: Area = _____ sq. in.
   Force = 200 lbs.
   Pressure = 400 psi

4. Find P: Area = 6 sq. in.
   Force = 150 lbs.
   Pressure = _____ psi

5. Find F: Area = 4 sq. in.
   Force = _____ lbs.
   Pressure = 300 psi

6. Find A: Area = _____ sq. in.
   Force = 500 lbs.
   Pressure = 50 psi

7. Find P: Area = 3 sq. in.
   Force = 150 lbs.
   Pressure = _____ psi

8. Find F: Area = 2 sq. in.
   Force = _____ lbs.
   Pressure = 1000 psi

9. Find A: Area = _____ sq. in.
   Force = 750 lbs.
   Pressure = 1000 psi

10. Find L: Volume = 10 cu. in.
    Area = 5 sq. in.
    Length = _____ in.

11. Find A: Volume = 209 cu. in.
    Area = _____ sq. in.
    Length = 10 in.

12. Find V: Volume = _____ cu. in.
    Area = 20 sq. in.
    Length = 2 in.

13. Find L: Volume = 15 cu. in.
    Area = 5 sq. in.
    Length = _____ in.

14. Find A: Volume = 10 cu. in.
    Area = _____ sq. in.
    Length = 10 in.

15. Find V: Volume = _____ cu. in.
    Area = 5 sq. in.
    Length = 1 in.

16. Find L: Volume = 10 cu. in.
    Area = 2 sq. in.
    Length = _____ in.

17. Find A: Volume = 5 cu. in.
    Area = _____ sq. in.
    Length = 1 in.

For practice exercises 1-9 and 10-17

2

FLUID LINES AND FITTINGS

General

The control and application of fluid power would be impossible without a suitable means of conveying the fluid from the power source to the point of application. Fluid lines used for this purpose must be designed and installed with the same care applicable to the other components of the system. An improperly piped system can lead to serious power loss and/or harmful fluid contamination. The following is a list of some of the most important requirements which must be considered.

1. The lines must be of sufficient strength to contain the fluid at the required pressure and, in addition, must be strong enough to withstand the surges of pressure that may develop in the system.

2. The lines must be of sufficient strength to support components which may be mounted in or on them.

3. Terminal fittings (unions, flanges, etc.) must be provided at all junctions with parts or components that require removal or replacement.

4. Line supports must be capable of dampening shock waves caused by surges of pressure and changes in direction of fluid flow.

5. The lines should have a smooth interior surface to reduce turbulent flow of fluid.

6. The lines must be of the correct size to ensure the required volume and velocity of flow with the least amount of turbulence during all demands of the system.

Lines which provide return flow in hydraulic systems must be large enough so as not to build up excessive back pressure.

7. The interior surface of the fluid lines must be clean upon installation. After installation, lines must be kept clean by flushing or purging the system regularly. Any source of contamination must be eliminated.

To obtain these required results, attention must be given to the various types, materials, and sizes of lines available for fluid power systems. The different types of lines and their application to fluid power systems are described in the first part of this chapter.

Plumbing Materials for Rigid Lines

Many of the fluid lines used in older aircraft and some special installations were made of copper tubing. In flight vibration hardens copper and causes it to crystallize and eventually break. In some cases, these lines are periodically removed from the aircraft, heat treated, quenched in water and returned to service.

As a result of this problem with copper tubing, aluminum alloy and stainless steel have almost completely replaced the copper tubing.

The aluminum-alloy tubing, usually used in low pressure systems, are generally made of alloys such as 1100–H14 half-hard, or aluminum having a small percentage of manganese, 3003–H–14, 2024–T3 and T4, 5052–0 and 6061–T4 and T6. The maximum pressure for these systems is 1500 psi with the exception of 6061–T4 and T6 which can be used in systems where the pressure may reach 3000 psi.

Stainless steel is often used for high pressure hydraulic and pneumatic lines and for exposed hydraulic brake lines on the landing gear.

Most of the (corrosion-resistant) stainless steel tubing used for high pressure systems is of the 18–8 chrome nickel type.

Generally, the material of the fittings is determined by the material of the tubing. Aluminum alloy fittings are used with aluminum alloy tubing, and steel fittings are used with steel tubing while brass or bronze fittings are used with copper tubing.

Application

The material, the inside diameter, and the wall thickness are the three primary considerations in the selection of lines for a particular fluid power system.

The inside diameter is important, since it determines the rate of flow that can be passed through the line without loss of power due to excessive heat and friction.

The wall thickness, the material used, and the inside diameter determines the bursting pressure of a line or fitting. The greater the wall thickness in relation to the inside diameter and the stronger the metal, the higher the bursting pressure.

It is extremely important, when replacing a fluid line, to use a line with the same part number as that originally installed. If a line must be made up in the shop, the aircraft manufacturer will provide information regarding the correct material of which the line is to be made. Aircraft tubing is normally identified with the specification number and the alloy designation stamped on the outside of the tubing.

Sizing

Rigid tubing is identified by both its material and a dash size. The outside diameter of the rigid tubing is identified by the dash number. The dash number is the numerator of the fractional diameter in sixteenths of an inch. (See Figures 2.1 and 2.2) Since the wall thickness of the tube determines its strength, this consideration is very important. To find the inside diameter of the tube, twice the wall thickness must be subtracted from the outside diameter.

Fabricating Rigid Tubing

Fluid power systems are designed as compact as practicable, in order to keep the connecting lines short. Every section of line should be anchored securely in one or more places so that neither the weight of the line nor the effects of vibration are carried on the joints. The aim should be to minimize stress throughout.

Lines should normally be kept as short and free of bends as possible. However, tubing should not be assembled in a straight line, because a bend tends to eliminate strain by absorbing vibrations and also compensates for thermal expansion and contraction. Bends are preferred to elbows, because bends cause less of a power loss. A few correct and incorrect methods of installing tubing are illustrated in Figure 2.3. (See Figure 2.3)

Bends are described in terms of the ratio of the radius of the bend to the inside diameter of the tubing. The ideal bend radius is 2½ to 3 times the inside diameter, as shown in Figure 2.4. (See Figure 2.4) For example, if the inside diameter of a line is 2 inches, the radius of the bend should be between 5 and 6 inches.

Tube OD	Wall thickness	Tube ID
1/8	0.028	0.069
	.032	.061
	.035	.055
3/16	0.032	0.1235
	.035	.1175
1/4	0.035	0.180
	.042	.166
	.049	.152
	.058	.134
	.065	.120
5/16	0.035	0.2425
	.042	.2285
	.049	.2145
	.058	.1965
	.065	.1825
3/8	0.035	0.305
	.042	.291
	.049	.277
	.058	.259
	.065	.245
1/2	0.035	0.430
	.042	.416
	.049	.402
	.058	.384
	.065	.370
	.072	.356
	.083	.334
	.095	.310

Tube OD	Wall thickness	Tube ID
5/8	0.035	0.555
	.042	.541
	.049	.527
	.058	.509
	.065	.495
	.072	.481
	.083	.459
	.095	.435
3/4	0.049	0.652
	.058	.634
	.065	.620
	.072	.606
	.083	.584
	.095	.560
	.109	.532
7/8	0.049	0.777
	.058	.759
	.065	.745
	.072	.731
	.083	.709
	.095	.685
	.109	.657
1	0.049	0.902
	.058	.884
	.065	.870
	.072	.856
	.083	.834
	.095	.810
	.109	.782
	.120	.760

Tube OD	Wall thickness	Tube ID
1 1/4	0.049	1.152
	.058	1.134
	.065	1.120
	.072	1.106
	.083	1.084
	.095	1.060
	.109	1.032
	.120	1.010
1 1/2	0.065	1.370
	.072	1.356
	.083	1.334
	.095	1.310
	.109	1.282
	.120	1.260
	.134	1.232
1 3/4	0.065	1.620
	.072	1.606
	.083	1.584
	.095	1.560
	.109	1.532
	.120	1.510
	.134	1.482
2	0.065	1.870
	.072	1.856
	.083	1.834
	.095	1.810
	.109	1.782
	.120	1.760
	.134	1.732

Figure 2.1 Tubing size designation.

TUBE O.D.	FITTINGS DASH NO.
1/8	– 2
1/4	– 4
3/8	– 6
1/2	– 8
5/8	– 10
3/4	– 12
1	– 16

Figure 2.2 The outside diameter of rigid tubing is identified by its dash number. The dash number is the numerator of the fractional diameter in sixteenths of an inch.

Figure 2.3   Correct and incorrect tubing bends.

Figure 2.4   Ideal bend radius.

The tubing used for aircraft fluid lines has very thin walls and will collapse in the bend if adequate precautions are not taken. Collapsing, or kinking in the bend of the tubing will cause restricting of the fluid flow. Wrinkles in the bend can also cause an opposition to flow and will severely weaken the tube in the bend area.

The bend should be smooth, with no kinks or wrinkles and no marks from the bending tool. Bending tools should be used whenever possible, however, small diameter, thin wall tubing or soft metal can be bent by hand, using a tightly wound steel coil spring that fits around the outside diameter of the tubing to keep it from collapsing. In an emergency, a tube can be bent by first packing it with clean, dry sand and sealing the ends before making the bends. After the bends are completed, the sand must be completely removed before the assembly is installed on the aircraft.

NOTE: THIS BENDER CAN BE SLIPPED OVER PARTIALLY CONNECTED TUBES AS IT IS APPLIED AT DIRECT POINT OF BEND

1 RAISE SLIDE BAR HANDLE UPWARD

RIGHT HAND

2 PLACE TUBE

TUBE

HANDLE

LEFT HAND

3 PREPARE TO RAISE CLIP OVER TUBE

4 DROP CLIP OVER TUBE

NOTE: ZERO MARK COINCIDES WITH MARK ON BLOCK

TUBE

LEFT HAND

5 WITH RIGHT HAND, CONTINUE TO BEND TUBE TO DESIRED ANGLE BY PRESSING SLIDE BAR HANDLE AS SHOWN BELOW

6 TO REMOVE BENT TUBE, LIFT SLIDE BAR HANDLE TO ORIGINAL POSITION AND RAISE CLIP

90° MARK

TUBE

RIGHT HAND

A BEND OF 90° DONE AS SHOWN IN ABOVE STEPS

LEFT HAND

Figure 2.5 Tube bending.

16

Small diameter tubing of most types may be bent with a hand bending tool, as shown in Figure 2.5. The tube is inserted between the radius block and the slide bar and is held in place by the clip. The slide bar handle can then be moved down to bend the tubing to any angle required. The number of degrees of bend is read on the scale of the radius block. It is important to align the incidence mark on the slide bar with the zero mark on the radius block before bending. A hand type bender is available for most sizes of fluid tubing and the proper size should always be used.

Cutting

After the correct length of tubing is determined, the tube should be cut off square with a roller type tubing cutter. (See Figure 2.6) The cutter is rotated around the tubing, the cutting wheel screwed down against the tube, and as the blade cuts into tubing, it is turned down further into the tube. Some burrs may be left on the inside of the tube, which must be removed. These burrs should be removed with a

Figure 2.6 Tube cutting.

reamer, usually attached to the cutter, or a special tube reamer such as the one shown in Figure 2.7. (See Figure 2.7) The end of the tube must be polished so there will be no sharp edges.

If no tubing cutter is available, a fine tooth hacksaw may be used. Be sure there are at least two teeth on each wall of the tube at all times. Cutting stainless steel with a hacksaw is a preferred method as the saw work hardens the stainless steel less than a tubing cutter will.

Figure 2.7   Special type of reamer that can remove burrs from both the inside and the outside of the end of a piece of tubing. One side of the reamer cleans the outside of the cut, and the other side cleans the inside.

Methods of Joining Rigid Tubing

Flared Fittings

A great deal of the tubing assemblies on modern aircraft are joined by flaring the ends of the tubing and using flare-type fittings. There are two types of flared fittings for aircraft use, both of which have essentially the same flare cone angle, but these fittings are not interchangeable. Automotive fittings have a 45 degree flare angle and to prevent these fittings from being interchanged, aircraft fittings use a 37 degree flare cone.

The older aircraft fittings were designed as AC, they were used extensively during WWII, and some of these fittings may still be found. They look a great deal like the more recent AN fittings, except that the threads go all the way to the flare cone on the AC fitting, while on the AN fitting, there is a shoulder between the end of the threads and the cone. The flare cone is slightly different as well, the AC flare cone is 35°, while the AN is 37°, as shown in Figure 2.8. (See Figure 2.8)

The seal for a flared cone fitting is provided by the flare cone of the fitting and the inside of the flare of the tube. Excessive tightening of the nut can distort the flare and cause a leak. Additional torque can intensify a leak. The recommended torque for all flare type fittings should not be exceeded. (See Figure 2.9)

AN	FEATURE	AC
37°	ANGLE	35°
YES	RECESS	NO
COARSER	THREADS	FINER
BLUE OR BLACK	COLOR	GRAY OR YELLOW
LONGER	BODY LENGTH	SHORTER

Figure 2.8   AN and AC fitting differences.

Tubing O.D.	Fitting Size	Aluminum Alloy Tubing, Nut Torque inch-lbs.	Steel Tubing, Nut, Torque inch-lbs.
1/8	– 2	20-30	
3/16	– 3	30-40	90-100
1/4	– 4	40-65	135-150
5/16	– 5	60-85	180-200
3/8	– 6	75-125	270-300
1/2	– 8	150-250	450-500
5/8	– 10	200-350	650-700
3/4	– 12	300-500	900-1000
7/8	– 14	500-600	1000-1100
1	– 16	500-700	1200-1400
1-1/4	– 20	600-900	1200-1400
1-1/2	– 24	600-900	1500-1800
1-3/4	– 28	850-1050	
2	– 32	950-1150	

Figure 2.9   Recommended torque for flare-type fittings.

Before the tube is flared, the B nut and sleeve are slipped over the ends and a flaring tool is used. The flare should be formed so that the outside diameter is at least that of the inside of the toe of the sleeve. (See Figure 2.10) The flare should rest solidly against the flare cone of the fitting before the B nut is tightened.

Two types of connector nuts are used for flared type, 37° AN fittings. The AN 817 nut is a single piece nut that is used only where a straight tubing is being used. Where there is a bend near the end of the tubing, an AN 818 nut and MS20819 sleeve are required. The AN 818 nut is commonly called a B nut.

Single Flare

A single flare can be formed on tubing with either an impact-type flaring tool or one having the rolling action of the flaring cone. Figure 2.11 shows an impact-type flaring tool. (See Figure 2.11) After the end of the tube is cut squarely and polished the halves of the tool are clamped in a vise with about 1/16 inch of the tubing sticking above the blocks. The blocks are tightened by the vise and as few sharp blows of a hammer are used as needed to flare the tube end out against the bevel cut in the blocks. Too many blows will work-harden the tubing.

Figure 2.10 A—Aircraft rigid tubing is flared with a flare angle of 37°. B—The tube must be flared so the outside diameter of the flare is at least the diameter of the toe of the sleeve, but is no larger than the outside diameter of the sleeve.

A rolling type flaring tool (See Figure 2.12) is very popular in maintenance shops. They make a good flare and are completely self contained. To use this tool the dies rotate until the two halves of the correct size are aligned and the tube is inserted in the dies to the stop. The dies are then clamped together and the cone is turned into the end of the tubing. The rollers in the cone burnish the metal as it expands

Figure 2.11   An impact-type flaring tool.

A rolling-type flaring tool.   A hand flaring tool.
Figure 2.12

into the die, resulting in a smooth flare. Reversing the handle, releasing the dies, and the tube is removed from the tool. See Figure 2.13 for the dimensional tolerances used in forming a single flare in both aluminum and steel tubing.

Double Flare

Soft aluminum tubing having an outside diameter of 3/8 inch or smaller may be double-flared to provide a stronger connection.

The procedure to double flare a piece of tubing is to cut off and polish, the same as for a single flare, remove all burrs and insert the tubing into the flare die until the tube contacts the stop pin as shown in Figure 2.14. Clamp the die, insert the upsetting tool, hit the tool a

Tube Size Outside Diameter [Inch]	A - Diameter Steel or Aluminum Alloy Tubing [Inch]		B Radius + -0.010 [Inch]
1/8	0.200	+ 0.000 − 0.010	0.032
3/16	0.302	+ 0.000 − 0.010	0.032
1/4	0.359	+ 0.000 − 0.010	0.032
5/16	0.421	+ 0.000 − 0.010	0.032
3/8	0.484	+ 0.000 − 0.010	0.046
1/2	0.656	+ 0.000 − 0.010	0.062
5/8	0.781	+ 0.000 − 0.010	0.062
3/4	0.937	+ 0.000 − 0.010	0.078
1	1.187	+ 0.000 − 0.015	0.093

Figure 2.13 Dimensional tolerances for a single flare on a piece of aircraft rigid tubing.

(A)   (B)   (C)

Figure 2.14   A—Insert the tube to the stop pin and clamp the dies together.
B—Insert the upsetting tool and strike it with a hammer to upset the end of the tube.
C—Insert the flaring cone and strike it with the hammer to form the flare.

few blows to upset the tubing, then insert the flaring tool and strike it with a hammer to fold the metal down into the tubing forming the double flare. Figure 2.15 shows tolerances for a double flare. (See Figure 2.15)

Tube Beading

When it becomes necessary to join a section of flexible hose to a rigid tubing without the use of a fitting, the tube can be beaded.

A hand beading tool which can be used consists of a split block bored to the size which will clamp the tubing tightly when clamped in a vise. A pin die, to fit the inside diameter of the tube to be beaded, is made with curved cavity to accommodate the bead. The bead is formed by driving the die over the end of the tubing as shown in the illustration. (See Figure 2.16)

A manufactured beading tool as shown in Figure 2.17 consists of a body, a hardened bushing for the inner beading and two rollers that size the outer section of the bead. The tube is placed against the face of the hardened bushing and the tube is then clamped to hold the tubing while the two rollers are turned around the tube. Pressure is applied to the bead-forming roller by means of the hand screw while the tool is being turned.

After the tube is beaded, the hose is slipped over the end and clamped in place. (See Figure 2.18)

TUBE SIZE

Tube Size Nominal Outside Diameter [in.]	A Diameter +0.010 −0.010 [in.	B Radius +0.010 [in.	Wall Thickness [in.	Minimum Inside Diameter [in.]
1/8	0.224	0.032		
3/16	0.302	0.032	0.028	0.114
			0.035	0.100
1/4	0.359	0.032	0.028	0.178
			0.035	0.159
5/16	0.421	0.032	0.035	0.224
			0.049	0.198
3/8	0.484	0.046	0.028	0.310
			0.035	0.288
			0.049	0.261

Figure 2.15   Dimensional tolerances for a double flare on a piece of aircraft rigid tubing.

HOSE CLAMP

Figure 2.16   A—Hand-type tube beading tool.
B—The ends of the tube are beaded before the hose is slipped over them.
C—The hose clamps are centered between the end of the hose and the bead.

Figure 2.17 Using a beading tool.

Fitting   Hose   Tubing

1/16" Max offset

Minimum gap "G" shall be 1/2" or Tube OD/4,
whichever is greater.
Maximum gap "G" is not limited except on
suction lines using other than self-sealing hose.
On such suction lines, maximum G shall be
1-1/2 inch or one tube diameter, whichever
is greater.

Figure 2.18 Flexible fluid connection assembly.

Flareless Fitting (Also called MS)

Because of the difficulty of cone flaring thick wall tubing used in some higher pressure fluid lines, a "bite-type" flareless fitting has been designed.

The tubing end is cut square, all burrs removed and the end polished. Then a ferrule and B nut are slipped over the end of the tube and inserted into a presetting tool as shown in Figure 2.19. (See Figure 2.19) Be sure the tube is square against the bottom of the presetting tool, then screw the nut down by hand until it tightens the ferrule against the tool. Then, using a wrench, TURN the B nut from one to one and

Figure 2.19 Presetting flareless-tube assembly.

Figure 2.20   A—Install the nut and ferrule on the end of the tubing.
B—Seat the end of the tubing firmly against the bottom
of the presetting tool.
C—Turn the nut down until resistance is felt, and then
turn it 1-3/4 turn beyond this point.

three quarters of a turn, depending on the size of the tubing or the
manufacturer's specifications. (See Figure 2.20) A lubricant may be
used during the presetting process. If the tube is going to be used in a
hydraulic system, for example, the lubricant should be the hydraulic
fluid used in the system.

After properly tightening the nut into the presetting tool, the ferrule
(or sleeve as it is sometimes called) cutting edge will grip the tube sufficiently to prevent tube rotation, and is permanently set. The sleeves
cannot be removed from the tubing under any circumstances.

After the presetting process, the nut is backed off and tube removed
from the presetting tool.

The inspection of flareless fittings after the presetting is as follows:

1. Check the cutting edge of the sleeve; it should be embedded into the tube outside diameter.

2. The sleeve should be bowed slightly.

3. The sleeve may rotate slightly but should not move longitudinally more than 1/64 inch.

4. The sealing surface should be smooth and free of burrs, cracks, and scores.

5. The minimum internal diameter of the tube at the point where the sleeve cut is made should be checked.

6. The tube should be proof tested at a pressure equal to twice the intended working pressure.

Swaged Type Fittings

Many modern aircraft utilize swaged type fittings in areas where routine disconnections are not required.

Externally swaged tube fittings are manufactured by the Deutsch Metal Components Division under the trade name of Permaswage. Some typical fittings are shown in Figures 2.21a and 2.21b. Internally swaged tube fittings are manufactured by the Resistoflex Corporation under the trade name of Dynatube. (See Figure 2.22)

Permaswage fittings are made of aluminum, corrosion resistant steel and titanium. The fittings are attached quickly either on or off the aircraft by a hydraulically operated, portable swaging tool. The complete kit for installation of swaged fittings consists of a chipless cutter, a deburring tool, a swaging tool, a marking tool and a hydraulic unit. A go no-go gauge is included for checking the swage. (See Figure 2.23)

Figure 2.21a   Cutaway view of a swaged splice fitting. (Deutsch Metal Products Div.)

Figure 2.21b Checking a swaged fitting. (Deutsch Metal Products Div.)

Figure 2.22 An internally swaged lipseal fitting. (Resistoflex Corp.)

The advantages of the swaged-type tube fittings are a lower original cost than standard AN or MS flareless, less installation time, and substantial weight saved.

HYDRAULIC   CHIPLESS
POWER SUPPLY   CUTTERS   DIE

DEBURRING TOOLS   INSPECTION   MARKING TOOLS
AND PLUNGERS   GAUGES

Figure 2.23   Swaging kit. (Deutsch Metal Components Div.)

Repair of Systems with Swaged Fittings

Repair of tubing with swaged fittings is accomplished by using the manufacturer's manual and following the specifications precisely. A few typical steps are outlined here: (See Figure 2.24)

1. Relieve all systems pressure; cut out the damaged tubing (A).
2. Use the proper size deburring tool (B) from the repair kit; deburr the tube ends.
3. Use the kit marking tool (C) to mark for proper position.
4. Install repair section on marks (D).
5. Position the swaging head; insert die block (E).
6. Apply hydraulic power to tool; advance the knurled nut (F).

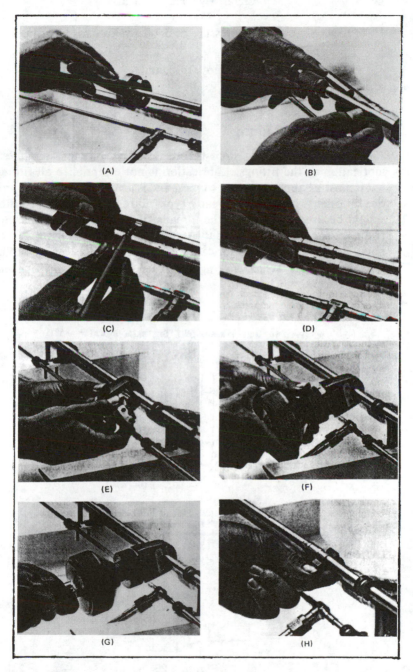

(A) (B)

(C) (D)

(E) (F)

(G) (H)

Figure 2.24 Repair tubing with swaged fittings.(Deutsch Metal Components Div.)

7. Apply hydraulic pressure of 5500 psi to swaged fitting (G).

8. Relieve pressure, remove tool, and test repair with an inspection gauge (H).

Installation of Tubing

One of the important steps before installing tubing assemblies is lubrication of the fittings. Lubrication is not essential to all fittings, but it must be applied for some types, and is a good maintenance practice for others. Normally, the same type fluid that is used in the system should be used to lubricate the threads. It should be used sparingly and none should be applied to the starting threads. See Figure 2.25 for points to be lubricated. Lubricate the outside of the sleeve, coupling nuts, and fittings. When working on oxygen system lines, no petroleum base lubricant may be used.

A. APPLY TO MALE THREADS ONLY OF THREADED MATING PARTS

• ON STRAIGHT THREADS—OMIT FIRST TWO; FILL REMAINING THREADS EVENLY.

ANTISEIZE COMPOUND

• ON TAPERED THREADS—OMIT FIRST TWO THREADS AND NOSE; FILL NEXT THREE EVENLY; OMIT REMAINING THREADS

B. APPLY SPARINGLY TO BACK SURFACES OF FLARED TUBING ENDS AND TO BACK SURFACES OF SLEEVES

ANTISEIZE COMPOUND

Figure 2.25

During installation the tubing should be pushed against the fittings snugly and squarely before starting to turn the coupling nuts. If the tubing is drawn up to the fittings using the B nuts, the flare may be distorted or easily turned off. The most important operation is the proper torquing of the B nuts. Overtorquing causes damage to the flare and fittings and often results in line failure in flight. During installation align the assembly so that the B nut starts freely by hand. The nut should be fitted and started with at least three full turns to prevent cross threading. Each B nut should be tightened until a slight resistance is felt, and from this point, when possible, B nuts should be tightened with a torque wrench. (See Figure 2.26) If flared type connections leak, disconnect the fitting and inspect the sealing surfaces. If no discrepancies exist, check for misalignment of the tube assembly. (See Figure 2.27)

Installing MS flareless tubing assemblies is essentially the same as described for the AN flared assemblies; however, there are some minor differences. The flareless tube and ferrule (sleeve) fit inside the attaching fitting so care must be taken to prevent damage during the installation process. In some cases it may be necessary to install the tube assembly into the fitting before the component is secured. When the tube and sleeve are properly seated in the fitting, screw the B nut down with the fingers until resistance is felt; then, using a wrench, tighten the nut an additional 1/6 to 1/3 turn. Never tighten the B nut on a flareless fitting more than 1/3 turn. If leakage occurs, remove the tube assembly, and check to see that it has been properly preset. Recouple it and once again properly tighten the nut. If it continues to leak, the end of the tube will have to be cut off and a new sleeve pre-

Tube O.D. (inches)	Wrench torque range for tightening tube nuts (inch pounds)	
	Alum. alloy 1100-H14, 5052-0	Steel
3/16		30-70
1/4	40-65	50-90
5/16	60-80	70-120
3/8	75-125	90-150
1/2	150-250	155-250
5/8	200-350	300-400
3/4	300-500	430-575
1-	500-700	550-750
1-1/4	600-900	
1-1/2	600-900	

Figure 2.26 Recommended torque values for tightening tube nuts on aircraft rigid tubing.

DO NOT DEFLECT INTO PLACE;
REPLACE TUBE ASSEMBLY

INCORRECT – WILL DAMAGE
FLARE OR THREADS, OR CAUSE
SLEEVE TO CRACK UNDER
VIBRATION IF TIGHTENED

INCORRECT – MAY PULL OFF OR
DISTORT FLARE IF TIGHTENED

CORRECTLY FITTED
AND TIGHTENED

0.025 CLEARANCE BETWEEN
FLARE AND SHOULDER
BEFORE TIGHTENING

Figure 2.27 Correct and incorrect methods of installing flared fittings.

set into the tube. If this results in a too short tube assembly, an entire new assembly should be made.

Attachment to Components

There are two basic methods to attach a fluid line to a component by tapered pipe threads and by universal bulkhead fittings.

Tapered pipe threads seal by the wedging between the tapered male thread and the tapered female threads. The threads taper 1/16 inch to the inch. These threads are sometimes wrapped with a thin strip of teflon tape or some thread lubricant, to form a complete seal.

Universal bulkhead fittings are installed with an AN 6289 nut which accommodates a back-up ring of either teflon or leather, and an O-ring seal. The AN 6289 nut is screwed above the cutout portion of the threads; a back-up ring (if required) and an O-ring are slipped over the first set of threads. The fitting is then screwed into the boss of the housing until the O-ring contacts the housing. The fitting is then aligned with the tubing or hose. Hold the fitting and turn the AN 6289 nut down until it contacts the housing. (See Figure 2.28)

Note: Hydraulic fittings should never be tightened when the hydraulic system is pressurized.

Inspection and Maintenance

Lines and fittings should be inspected carefully at regular intervals for leaks, damage, loose mounting, cracks, scratches, dents and other damage. Assemblies with damage should either be replaced entirely or repaired. If extensive damage exists, the entire line should be replaced. If the damage is localized, it is permissible to cut out the damaged section and insert a new section with the approved fittings. (See Figure 2.29)

Figure 2.28   Properly installed gasket and back-up ring.

The following defects are not acceptable for metal lines:

1. Cracked flare or sleeve.
2. Scratches or nicks greater than 10% of the tube wall thickness or in the heel of a bend.
3. Severe die marks, seams, or splits.
4. A dent of more than 20 percent of the tube diameter or in the heel of a bend.

It is of the utmost importance that damaged assemblies be replaced with the proper material. Specifications can be obtained from the manufacturer's maintenance manual. If these are not available, it is the technician's responsibility to see that the standards set by the manufacturer are rigidly followed.

Routing, clamping, identification

All fluid lines should be routed through the aircraft so they will have the shortest practical length. However, they should follow the structural members of the aircraft and be properly secured with line clamps at intervals. (See Figure 2.30)

Figure 2.29   A—Repair to a high-pressure rigid fluid line by using a union and two nuts.
B—Repair to a high-pressure fluid line by splicing in a new section of line.

TUBE O.D.	DISTANCE BETWEEN SUPPORTS
1/8 - 3/16	9"
1/4 - 5/16	12"
3/8 - 1/2	16"
5/8 - 3/4	22"
1 - 1-1/4	30"
1-1/2 - 2	40"

Figure 2.30   Spacing between supports for rigid aircraft tubing.

Figure 2.31

Lines should not chafe against any other line, control cable, or portion of the aircraft structure. When lines are routed near electrical wires, the fluid lines should be located below the wire bundles and supported to prevent contact. (See Figure 2.31)

All bends must be located in such a way that they can be supported by clamps, so the stress from vibration, expansion and contraction is not placed on the fitting. All tubing assemblies should have at least one bend between the fittings to allow for thermal expansion and contraction and these stresses. (See Figure 2.32)

Figure 2.32 Correct and incorrect methods of installing tubing.

FUNCTION	COLOR	SYMBOL
Fuel	Red	
Rocket Oxidizer	Green, Gray	
Rocket Fuel	Red, Gray	
Water Injection	Red, Gray, Red	
Lubrication	Yellow	
Hydraulic	Blue, Yellow	
Solvent	Blue, Brown	
Pneumatic	Orange, Blue	
Instrument air	Orange, Gray	
Coolant	Blue	
Breathing Oxygen	Green	
Air Conditioning	Brown, Gray	
Monopropellant	Yellow, Orange	
Fire Protection	Brown	
De-Icing	Gray	
Rocket Catalyst	Yellow, Green	
Compressed gas	Orange	
Electrical Conduit	Brown, Orange	
Inerting	Orange, Green	

Figure 2.33 Functional identification tape data.

38

If the fluid line is routed through a passenger compartment, baggage compartment, or crew compartment where it could be used as a hand hold or if it is installed near an escape or service hatch, the line should be protected with a chafe guard to prevent damage to the assembly. When lines are exposed in a wheel well, they should be protected from damage from rocks and dirt that may be thrown into the wheel well during ground operations.

All fluid lines should be clearly marked with color code to identify the contents of the fluid line.(See Figure 2.33) Each line should have at least one identifying tape or decal installed.

3

FLEXIBLE FLUID LINES

Hose

Hose is used in fluid power systems where there is a necessity for flexibility, such as connections to actuating units that move while in operation, or to units attached to a hinged portion of the equipment. It is also used in locations that are subjected to severe vibrations. For example, flexible hose is often used for connections to and from the pump. The vibration that is set up by an operating pump would ultimately cause rigid lines to fail.

Sizes for Flexible Hose Lines

The size of the flexible hose is identified by a number which refers to the equivalent tubing size. For example, number 8 flexible hose is equivalent to a number 8 tubing. The number 8 tubing has an outside diameter of ½ inch; it will be slightly smaller to allow for wall thickness. The actual inside diameter of both the hose and tubing are the same. As long as the number of the hose corresponds to the number of the tubing, the proper size is being used.

The size, along with other information, is usually stenciled on the outside of the hose. This information includes the military specification of the hose followed by a dash number, which is the size. In addition, the year, quarter of year, and a five-digit manufacturer's code are included. (See Figure 3.1)

Figure 3.1 The lay line printed along a flexible hose provides the needed information about the hose and serves to show whether or not the hose has been twisted when it was installed.

If the hose is factory assembled with end fittings, the length of hose assembly, in inches, will also be included. This information appears at intervals of not more than 9 inches and is connected by a series of dots or dashes. The continuous line of stenciled information and dots or dashes also indicates the natural lay of the hose, commonly called the lay line. In addition to providing the information above, it also provides for installation information by reflecting twist or improper alignment. On some newer types of hose, those with an outer cover of metal braid, or teflon, this information is placed on a metal tag and attached to the hose. In the case of metal outer covered hose where a lay line is not used, twist or improper installation can be checked by looking for a straight line of the metal plaits.

Types of Flexible Hose

There are two basic types of flexible hose used in fluid power systems. These two types of material are rubber and teflon. Although flexible hose made of rubber is the type most commonly used, teflon has many of the desired characteristics for certain applications. The two types of material are described in the following paragraphs.

Rubber

Flexible rubber hose consists of a seamless synthetic rubber tube covered with layers of cotton braid and, in higher pressure hoses, wire braid, and an outer layer of rubber-impregnated cotton braid.

In designing the inner tube, certain requirements must be met if the inner tube is to perform satisfactorily. Some of these requirements are:

1. It must be flexible.
2. It must retain its characteristics when exposed to specific high and low temperature ranges.
3. It must be impermeable to the substance or agent that it has to carry. (Must have minimum porosity.)
4. It must be smooth and offer minimum resistance to flow.

5. It must be made of a material which is chemically compatible with the substance which it is to carry.

There are several different materials which are used in the manufacture of inner tubes. The four most commonly used in aircraft hydraulic systems are:

1. Buna-N
2. Neoprene
3. Butyl
4. Teflon

Some of the characteristics of these are as follows:

Buna-N is a synthetic rubber compound which has an excellent resistance to petroleum based oils.

Neoprene is a synthetic rubber compound which has an acetylene base and is also used for its resistance to petroleum products, although not quite as good as Buna-N.

Butyl is a synthetic rubber compound made from petroleum raw material, and as such, is not suitable for use with petroleum based fluids; however, it is an excellent material for phosphate ester base hydraulic fluid (Skydrol).

Teflon

Teflon is the Dupont trade name for tetra-fluoro-ethylene resin. When compounded and extruded into an inner tube, it provides certain features which are unexcelled in many ways. It is capable of operating under a very wide temperature range (-65°F to 450°F). It is compatible with nearly every substance or agent used. Its surface is wax-like and this provides minimum resistance to flow, and sticky, viscous materials will not cling to it. It has less volumetric expansion than rubber tubes and its service and shelf life are practically unlimited.

Care must be taken in the selection of hose for a particular application. Usually the type of hose will be specified in the maintenance manual. However, there may be instances in which the exact information is not available, and the technician must be able to determine whether the tube is suitable for the system involved. The hose must be selected on the basis of size, pressure rating, temperature rating, and material.

End Fittings—Types of Hose

Flexible hose is available in three pressure ranges: low pressure, which uses a fabric braid reinforcement over the inner tube, and is generally classified as any pressure below 250 psi, (see Figure 3.2); medium pressure, with one wire braid reinforcement which is built to operate with pressures up to 3000 psi in the smaller sizes, however, medium pressure is generally classified as 1500 psi, (see Figure 3.3); and high pressure hose, with multiple wire braid reinforcement. It is available in sizes 4 through 16 and all sizes have a hydraulic working pressure of 3000 psi. (See Figure 3.4)

Aeroquip
Low-pressue hose used for instrument lines, but not for hydraulic systems.

Figure 3.2   Flexible lines — low-pressure hose.

Stratoflex
MIL-H-8794 hose has one steel braid and an outer cover of rough cotton braid.

Figure 3.3   Flexible lines — medium-pressure hose.

Aeroquip
MIL-H-8788 has two steel wire braids for reinforcement and is covered with a smooth outer cover.

Figure 3.4   Flexible lines — high-pressure hose.

Teflon hoses are normally available in either swaged end fittings which are permanent attachment fittings and cannot be reused, and reuseable end fittings which are called lip seal fittings.

The medium pressure teflon hose is constructed with a seamless extruded teflon resin inner tube and is covered with a single layer of stainless steel wire braid. The medium pressure teflon hose is generally used in systems that have a hydraulic working pressure of 1500 psi. (See Figure 3.5)

Parker
Medium-pressure hose of Teflon has a Teflon liner and a single stainless steel braid for reinforcement.

Figure 3.5   Hose of Teflon.

The double wire braid outer shield is used over the teflon extruded inner tube in high pressure applications. These hose assemblies are used when the working pressure is 3000 psi. (See Figure 3.6)

Figure 3.6   High pressure hose of teflon.

There is one additional hose type that is sometimes used on hydraulic system return lines. However, it is used mostly for fuel and oil lines in installations where lightweight, very flexible and fire resistant hoses are needed. This type is Aeroquip 601 hose. It has a seamless, specially formulated synthetic inner tube covered with a partial braid of stainless steel, and a full outer cover of the same material. (See Figure 3.7)

Figure 3.7   Aeroquip 601 hose.

Hose Assembly Procedures

If the hose assembly has a swaged-on fitting installed at the factory that made the hose, it cannot be reused. If the hose is replaced, the entire hose assembly must be discarded and a new hose assembly purchased and installed. (See Figure 3.8)

Hose with reuseable end fittings is generally available in the three piece type. The fittings consist of a socket, a nipple, and a nut. (See Figure 3.9) The A & P may fabricate a flexible hose assembly using this type end fitting. The bulk hose is used and the length determined before the end fittings are installed. The length required will include the distance between the fittings, plus five to eight percent added to this length to compensate for expansion and contraction minus twice the distance between the end of the nipple and the end of the hole in the socket. (See Figure 3.10)

Low pressure hose ends slip over the end of the hose rather than screw on as the medium and high pressure do. Screw a fitting or hose adapter into the nut. (See Figure 3.11) The nipple is turned into the socket until it bottoms and is then backed off from 1/32 to 1/16 inch to allow the nut to turn freely. When the adapter or fitting is removed from the nut, the hose should be blown out with compressed air and the hose hydrostatically tested to a pressure normally twice the working pressure of the hose. (See Figure 3.12)

Medium pressure rubber hose ends are installed in the same basic manner as the low pressure, except the socket is screwed onto the square cut hose end, until it bottoms against the end of the hole. (See Figure 3.13) The adapter used to hold the nut and nipple should be

LIP SEAL

FLARED SKIRT

Fitting for extra-high-pressure hose (Resistoflex Corp.)

SWAGED SOCKET

HOSE COMPRESSED

FLARED SKIRT

A permanent hose fitting (Resistoflex Corp.)

STRAIGHT TO STRAIGHT

000AE 90-SIZE-"L"

STRAIGHT TO 45°

000AE 95-SIZE-"L"

STRAIGHT TO 90°

000AE 96-SIZE-"L"

45° TO 45°

180AE 91-SIZE-"L"

90° TO 45°

180AE 92-SIZE-"L"

90° TO 90°

180AE 93-SIZE-"L"

"L"= Length from seat to seat

Typical hose assemblies to mate with flareless fittings

"L" = Length from seat to seat

Typical hose assemblies to mate with flareless fittings

Figure 3.8

FITTING ASSEMBLED

Figure 3.9 A reusable hose fitting. (Aeroquip Corp.)

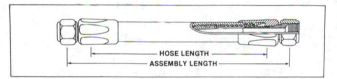

HOSE LENGTH
ASSEMBLY LENGTH

Figure 3.10 The length required for a hose is the distance between the fittings, plus the required 5% to 8% of this length for slack, minus twice the distance between the end of the nipple and the end of the hole in the socket.

A   B

Figure 3.11 A—Low-pressure hose end fittings slip over the end of the hose, rather than screw on as the intermediate- and high-pressure hoses do.
B—A fitting screwed into the nut will hold the nipple so it can be screwed into the socket.

47

Hose size number	Operating pressure (psi)	Proof pressure (psi)	Burst pressure (psi)
4	3,000	6,000	12,000
5	3,000	5,000	10,000
6	2,000	4,500	9,000
8	2,000	4,000	8,000
10	1,750	3,500	7,000
12	1,500	3,000	6,000

Figure 3.12

lubricated before inserting it into the socket. It may be worked in and out and around to open up the inner liner enough to force the nipple into the hose. The nipple is then screwed into the socket until it bottoms out and then backed off from 1/32 to 1/16 inch to allow free rotation of the nut. And the hose should also be blown out with compressed air and hydrostatically tested before use. (See Figure 3.14)

Figure 3.13 A—Screw the end of the hose into the left-hand threads of the socket. Leave a small amount of clearance between the end of the hose and the end of the hole in the socket.
B—Lubricate the assembly tool and work it into the end of the hose to open out the end and force the tube tight into the socket.
C—Screw the nipple and nut onto the assembly tool and force the nipple into the socket. Screw the nut down tight against the socket.
D—Back the nut off about 1/32 to 1/16 inch and remove the assembly tool from the tube.

High pressure rubber hose end installation requires a slightly more detailed procedure due to the unique construction of the bulk high pressure hose itself. The bulk hose should be measured the same as medium pressure, cut off squarely to length using a cut-off machine or fine tooth hacksaw. (See Figure 3.15a) Then using a leather cutting knife, cut around the outer cover of the hose into the wire braid. Use the notch marks on the outer circumference of the socket as a guide. Slit the outer cover lengthwise; be sure to cut down to the wire braid. Using the knife and pliers, pry up the outer corner and twist it off with the pliers. Use a wire brush to remove the rubber particles from the wire braid. Take care that the wire braid is not loosened, frayed or flared when brushing. Apply a sealant to the exposed wire braid (AE 13 696–001 or equivalent). Place the socket in the vise; screw hose into socket until it bottoms. Lubricate the inside of the hose and nipple into socket using a wrench on the nipple hex. Maximum allowable gap between socket and hex is 1/16 inch. Clean the inside of the hose assembly by blowing compressed air through hose and hydrostatically test before installation.

Assembly instructions for 601 flexible hose are essentially the same as for medium pressure rubber hose, with the exception of one important step. When the bulk hose is installed in the socket, make a mark at the rear of the socket with a grease pencil or small painted line to reflect

Figure 3.14 A—Blow out the completed hose assembly with compressed air.
B—Examine the hose for any foreign matter inside of the tube. It is possible for the nipple to shave off thin slices of the inner lines.
C—Hydrostatically test the hose assembly to twice its normal operating pressure, and hold this pressure for between one and five minutes.

Figure 3.15a   A—Strip off the outer cover from the high-pressure hose a distance equal to the inside depth of the socket. B—Twist the hose into the socket, rotating it to the left. C—Lubricate the nipple with oil for black hose or liquid soap for green hose. D—Screw the nipple into the socket and the hose. Leave between 1/32 and 1/16 inch clearance between the nipple hex and the socket.

push out during installation of the nipple into the socket. No push out is allowed in the smaller sized 3 through 10; for sizes 12 through 32, 1/32 inch is allowable. (See Figure 3.15b)

Assembly procedures for teflon hoses will cover only the medium pressure teflon hose; however, the procedure would be essentially the same for the high pressure hose.

Note: The swaged-on hose ends are not reusable and no attempt should be made to salvage them. They should be discarded along with the hose when the hose assembly is replaced.

Cut the teflon hose to the length desired after calculating the cut-off factor as previously described for rubber hose, or by measuring the used length of hose being replaced. (See Figure 3.16) A cut-off wheel is recommended; however, a fine tooth hacksaw may be used. To prevent flare-out of the stainless steel wire ends during cutting, wrap tape around the hose at the cutting point. After the cut is made, remove the tape. Install the sockets on the cut hose, skirt to skirt. (See Figure 3.17) Place nipple hex in vise, push one end of hose onto nipple and work gently in a circular motion to aid in separating the wire braid from the teflon tube. Remove hose from nipple and carefully insert sleeve between braid and tube outside diameter. Be careful that no wires are trapped between the sleeve and the tube. Complete pushing

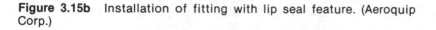

Figure 3.15b Installation of fitting with lip seal feature. (Aeroquip Corp.)

Teflon hose assembly measurements.

MS SWIVEL NUT FITTINGS				MS FLANGE FITTINGS		
	A	B	C		D	E	F
SIZE	ST	45°	90°		ST	45°	90°
-3	0.70	1.08	0.86				
-4	0.74	1.18	0.91				
-5	0.77	1.22	0.97				
-6	0.81	1.29	1.03				
-8	0.93	1.79	1.31		1.27	1.25	1.21
-10	1.05	1.58	1.41		1.35	1.42	1.41
-12	1.13	2.05	1.92		1.55	1.90	1.92
-16	1.30	2.14	2.05		1.61	1.98	2.05
-20	1.44	2.42	2.34		1.69	2.22	2.34

Figure 3.16   Teflon hose cut off factors.

end of sleeve against a flat surface, such as the side of the vise, until tube bottoms against shoulder or sleeve. No lubrication is needed when assembling teflon hose ends. Engage the socket and tighten, using a wrench on the nipple hex, tighten to a gap of 1/32 inch (gap may vary from 0.023 to 0.046 inch). Using dry compressed air, clean the assembly and proof test according to standard hydrostatic test procedures.

Step 1   Step 2   Step 3   Step 4

Figure 3.17

Chafe Guards—Firesleeves

Chafe guards, firesleeves are used to protect the hose and to extend normal service limits. Several types of chafe guards are available for use with any type of hose. Firesleeves are commonly made of asbestos material used to insulate the hose from intense heat. (See Figure 3.18)

Installation of Hose

Before installing a section of hose it should be thoroughly inspected and tested as previously explained. Hoses that have been in service for a period of time may be reinstalled after an inspection of both the external and internal condition. A flashlight can be used to inspect the

AEROQUIP-AE102-SIZE

Silicone Coated Asbestos Fire Sleeve
−65°F. to +450°F.

Heat Shrinkable Polyolefin Abrasion Sleeve
−65°F. to +275°F.

Nylon Spiral Wrap Abrasion Sleeve
−65°F. to +200°F.

FEP100 Teflon Abrasion Sleeve
−65°F. to +400°F.

AEROQUIP AE 138-SIZE

Neoprene Tubing Abrasion Sleeve
−65°F. to +250°F.

Figure 3.18   Protective sleeves for hose. (Aeroquip Corp.)

interior condition. If the hose assembly has elbow fittings that prevent using a flashlight, a steel ball, slightly smaller than the hose ID can be passed through the hose. The ball should roll freely from one end to the other. Hose that is preformed or takes a set on certain installations, should not be straightened out when the assembly is removed. Straightening causes undue stresses, wrinkling inside the hose and other possible defects. To prevent straightening of preformed or set hose, a wire or cord should be attached to each end, pulled taut, to keep the hose in relatively the same set it had when installed. (See Figure 3.19)

Care should be taken when installing a hose assembly to ensure the lay line, or plaits, are correctly aligned and do not reflect twist. (See Figure 3.20) One of the hose ends should be secured first, while the other end is free, then connect the other end, and using two wrenches, one holding the hex nut, tighten the second nut. Slack should be left in the hose to provide for changes in length. When pressure is applied to the system, the hose should be of sufficient length to provide about 5 to 8 percent slack. Hose should be installed with no sharp bends near the fittings, no bends smaller than the minimum bend radii recommended for a particular size hose, and where required, supported with clamps. (See Figure 3.21)

Storage of Hose

Synthetic rubber hose, both bulk hose and hose assemblies, should be stored in a cool, dark, dry area, protected from dust, dirt and ozone.

Storage life of synthetic rubber bulk hose normally does not exceed five years from the cure date stenciled on the lay line, and storage for

SUPPORT WIRE

Figure 3.19 Hose of teflon, once it has been used, takes a set, and if removed from the airplane it must be supported in the same shape it had while it was installed.

hose assemblies does not exceed four years. Teflon hose, both bulk and assemblies, does not deteriorate with age. No age dates have been established for this type hose.

Quick-disconnect Couplings (See Figure 3.22)

Quick–disconnect couplings of the self-sealing type are used at various points in many fluid power systems. These couplings are installed at locations where frequent uncoupling of the lines is required for inspection, test, and maintenance. This provides a convenient method of attaching test and servicing equipment without losing fluid. They also provide a means of quickly disconnecting a line and preventing foreign matter into the system.

Figure 3.20 Correct and incorrect hose installations.

The most common quick-disconnect coupling for hydraulic systems consists of two parts, held together by a union nut. Each part contains a valve which is held open when the coupling is connected, allowing fluid to flow in either direction through the coupling. When the coupling is disconnected, a spring in each part closes the valve, preventing the loss of fluid and entrance of foreign matter.

PLANNING HOSE LINE INSTALLATIONS

1 . . . provide slack or bend in the hose line to provide for changes in length that will occur when pressure is applied.

2 . . . observe linear stripe. The hose must not be twisted. High pressures applied to a twisted hose may cause failure or loosen the nut.

3 . . . relieve sharp bends, avoid strain or hose collapse and make cleaner installations by using Aeroquip elbows or other adapter fittings. Provide as large a bend radius as possible. Never use less than the recommended minimum bend radius specified for the hose.

4 . . . provide additional bend radius when lines are subject to flexing and remember that the metal end fittings are not flexible. Place line support clamps so as not to restrict hose flexing.

Figure 3.21 Flexible hose installation.

(A)

SI HALF   (B)   S4 HALF

1.	Tubular valve.	6.	Protruding nose.
2.	Valve spring.	7.	Poppet valve.
3.	O-ring packing.	8.	Lock spring.
4.	Sleeve.	9.	Mounting flange.
5.	Union nut teeth.		

Figure 3.22   Typical quick-disconnect coupling.

4

HYDRAULIC SEALS AND FLUIDS

Hydraulic Seals

Hydraulic seals are used throughout the aircraft hydraulic systems to minimize internal and external leakage of hydraulic fluid, thereby preventing the loss of system pressure. A seal may consist of more than one component, such as an O-ring and a backup ring, or possibly an O-ring and two backup rings. Hydraulic seals used internally on a sliding or moving assembly are called packings. Hydraulic seals used between non-moving fittings and bosses are normally called gaskets. Most packings and gaskets used in modern aircraft are manufactured in the form of O-rings.

An O-ring is circular in shape and its cross section is truly round, O-shaped. It has been molded and trimmed to extremely close tolerances. An O-ring will form a seal, or stop the flow of fluid, in both directions. When installed it fits into a groove in one of the surfaces being sealed. (See Figure 4.1)

A chevron or V-ring packing and U-shaped packings also get their name from their shape; however, they form a seal in one way only. This means that they will stop the flow of fluid in one direction only. (See Figure 4.2)

To prevent fluid flow in both directions using V- or U-ring seals, two sets of seals must be installed. (See Figure 4.3) The sets of seals are installed with spreaders and backup units between the seals with an accompanying adjusting nut. The apex or point of the seal rests in the groove of a metal or teflon backup ring and when the adjusting nut is tightened, the seals are spread against the wall of the actuating

O -RING
Figure 4.1

V -RING

U -RING

Figure 4.2

BACK-UP —   CHEVRON SEALS

SPREADER

ADJUSTING NUT

Figure 4.3   Proper placement of chevron seals on a hydraulic piston for double action.

cylinder, forming a seal. The direction of fluid flow must be toward the open end of the V- or U-ring seal. The apex is pointing away from the fluid pressure.

Various other cross section shaped seals are designed for specific installations and all manufacturers' service manuals must be rigidly adhered to. Since these specific designs may be very limited in application, the most common type, the O-ring, will be discussed in this manual.

Hydraulic O-rings were originally established under AN (Army-Navy) specification numbers (6227, 6230, 6290) for use in MIL–H–5606 petroleum based fluids, at operating temperatures ranging from –65°F to +160°F. When new designs raised operating temperatures to a possible 275°F, more compounds were developed and perfected.

Recently, newer compounds were developed under MS (military standards) specifications that offered improved low temperature performance without sacrificing high temperature performance. These superior materials were adopted in the MS28775 O–ring, which is replacing AN6227 and AN6230 O–rings, and the MS28778 O–ring which is replacing the AN6290 O–ring. These O–rings are now standard for MIL–H–5606 series systems where the operating temperatures may vary from −65°F to +275°F.

O–rings are manufactured according to rigid standards. Proper selection and use of these small, but very important components, cannot be overemphasized. The materials the seals are made of, the age of the seal, the hardness, and other factors make it very important that the correct part number seal be used for replacement. The preferred method of seal selection is to use the exact part numbers of the seal specified in the manufacturers service manual. Seals are made available in individual hermetically sealed envelopes labeled with the necessary data printed on the envelope. Particular attention should be paid to the part number and the cure date. The cure date is the date the O–ring was manufactured and is stated in the year and quarter year. Normally, rubber goods cure date is considered expired after 24 months.

Some limited use of color coded markings is used on O–ring seals, usually to indicate the type of fluid they are compatible with. For examples see Figure 4.4.

COLOR	USE
Blue dot or stripe	Air or MIL-H-5606 hydraulic fluid
Red dot or stripe	Fuel
Yellow dot	Synthetic engine oil
White stripe	Petroleum-base engine oil or lubricant
White dot preceding usage mark	Nonstandard ring for use as coded
Green dash	Skydrol hydraulic fluid

Figure 4.4   Color code identification for O-rings.

When O–rings (and some other specific installed seals) are used in systems which have operating pressures above 1500 psi, backup rings are used to support the O–rings and to prevent O–ring deformation and resultant leakage. The high pressure of these systems has a tendency to extrude the O–ring into the groove between the two mating surfaces. To prevent this extrusion, backup rings, also called anti-extrusion devices, should be used. (See Figure 4.5)

There are two types of backup rings used in modern aircraft: teflon (single and double spiral) and chrome-retanned leather. Teflon backup rings are generally used with both packings and gaskets. However, leather backup rings may be used with gasket type seals in systems operating up to 1500 psi.

Teflon rings are made from a fluorocarbon-resin material which is tough, friction-resistant, and more durable than leather. They do not deteriorate with age, and are unaffected by any other system fluid or vapor.

THE SEAL OF AN O-RING IS PROVIDED BY PINCHING
THE SEAL BETWEEN THE TWO MOVING PARTS.
(A)

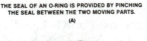

IF THERE IS NO PINCH, FLUID WILL LEAK PAST THE
O-RING.
(B)

IF THERE IS NO BACKUP RING, THE HIGH PRESSURE
WILL EXTRUDE THE O-RING BETWEEN THE MOVING
PARTS.
(A)

EXCESSIVE PRESSURE WILL EXTRUDE THE O-RING
BETWEEN THE TWO PARTS UNLESS A BACKUP RING
IS USED.
(C)

A BACKUP RING PREVENTS THE EXTRUSTION OF
THE O-RING.
(B)

Sealing action of an O-ring.

An O-ring must be backed up in a high-pressure system.

Figure 4.5

Figure 4.6 O-ring with backup washers.

Installation of Backups

Care must be taken during the handling and installation of backup rings. If possible, backup rings should be installed by hand and without the use of sharp tools. Leather backup rings should first be soaked in the recommended fluid (or system fluid) to increase their flexibility for ease of installation. They are installed in such a way that the smooth side (the hair side) is against the O-ring and the rough or cut side of the leather is installed against the fitting. (See Figure 4.6)

When installing teflon backup rings, before reuse, check for evidence of compression damage, scratches, cuts, nicks, and fraying conditions. When teflon spiral rings are being installed in internal grooves, the ring must have a right-hand spiral. Pay particular attention to the scarf cut of the teflon. It is possible for them to be spiraled in such a direction that the scarf will be on the wrong side, which could cause damage to the O-ring. (See Figure 4.7) While the teflon ring is being inserted in the groove, rotate the component in a clockwise direction. This action will tend to expand the ring diameter and reduce the possibility of damage to the ring.

When teflon spiral rings are being installed in external grooves, the ring should have a left-hand spiral. As the ring is inserted into the

THE CORRECT SPIRALING OF THE BACKUP RING
GIVES THIS PLACEMENT OF THE CHAMFERS.
(A)

INCORRECT SPIRALING WILL CAUSE THE RING TO BE
DAMAGED WHEN PRESSURE IS APPLIED.
(B)

WHEN PRESSURE IS APPLIED, THE CORRECTLY
INSTALLED BACKUP RING WILL PROVIDE A SMOOTH
SURFACE ON BOTH SIDES.
(C)

Figure 4.7   Proper spiraling of a teflon backup.

groove, rotate the component in a clockwise direction. This action will tend to contract the ring diameter and reduce the possibility of damage to the ring.

Backup rings may be installed singly, if pressure acts only upon one side of the seal. In this case, the backup ring is installed next to the O-ring, opposite the pressure force. When dual backup rings are installed, in cases where the O-ring is subject to pressure forces from both sides, the split scarf ends should be staggered as shown in Figure 4.8.

Wipers and Scrapers

Wipers and scrapers are used to clean and lubricate the exposed portion of piston shafts. This prevents foreign matter from entering the system and scoring internal surfaces. Wipers may be of the metallic (usually copper base alloys) or felt types. They are used in practically all landing gear shock struts and many actuating cylinders. At times, they are used together, the felt wiper being installed behind the metallic wiper. Normally, the felt wiper is lubricated with system hydraulic fluid from a drilled bleed passage or from an external fitting.

Metallic wipers are formed in split rings for ease of installation and are made slightly undersize to ensure a tight fit.

O–ring Installation

When installing O-rings, use extreme care to prevent damage to the O-ring. It may become cut or nicked either on the sharp edges of the threads, component grooves, or the tools themselves. As mentioned previously, smooth burr free tools should be used for both the removal and installation of the O-rings. If a proper tool cannot be found commercially, one can be made of polished brass and formed to accommodate the particular component. Some typical shapes and sizes of seal tools are shown in Figure 4.9. along with a proper use these tools as demonstrated on Figure 4.11. (See Figures 4.9 and 4.11)

When installing O–rings over a sharp edge or threaded section, you should cover the sharp area with paper, aluminum foil, brass shim stock, or a piece of plastic. (See Figure 4.10)

Figure 4.8   Teflon backup ring installation (external).

Inspecting O-rings for Defects

After removal of all O-rings from the parts affected, clean all areas which will receive new O-rings. Each O-ring removed must either be replaced with a new O-ring of the exact same part number, or ensure the removed O-ring is flawless before reusing it. One method of inspecting O-rings for reuse is to use a 4-power magnifying glass with adequate lighting to inspect each ring. By rolling the ring on an inspection sizing cone or dowel the inner diameter surface can be checked for small cracks, particles of foreign matter, and other irregularities that will cause leakage. A slight stretching of the O-ring with fingers only when it is rolled inside out, will help detect defects on both the inner and outer diameter. Care should be taken not to exceed the elastic

Figure 4.9 Typical O-ring installation and removal tools.

EXTERNAL O-RING INSTALLATION
(USING PAPER COVER TO AVOID O-RING DAMAGE FROM SHARP EDGES OR THREADS)

Figure 4.10 O-ring installation.

A) INTERNAL O-RING REMOVAL
(USING PULL TYPE EXTRACTOR AND HOOK TYPE REMOVAL TOOLS)

BACKUP RINGS
O-RING
EXTRACTOR TOOL
CYLINDER MOUTH
PULL
CYLINDER
REMOVAL TOOL
PULL

REMOVAL TOOL (HOOK TYPE)
EXTRACTOR TOOL (PULL TYPE)

B) INTERNAL O-RING REMOVAL
(USING PUSH TYPE EXTRACTOR AND HOOK TYPE REMOVAL TOOLS)

BACKUP RINGS
EXTRACTOR TOOL
CYLINDER
O-RING
PUSH
BACKUP RINGS
CYLINDER MOUTH
REMOVAL TOOL
O-RING
PULL

REMOVAL TOOL (HOOK TYPE)
EXTRACTOR TOOL (PUSH TYPE)

C) DUAL INTERNAL O-RING REMOVAL
(USING PUSH TYPE EXTRACTOR AND HOOK TYPE REMOVAL TOOLS)

BACKUP RING
O-RING
BACKUP RING
O-RING
PULL
REMOVAL TOOL
PUSH
EXTRACTOR TOOL (INSERTED UNDER O-RINGS)

REMOVAL TOOL (HOOK TYPE)
EXTRACTOR TOOL (PULL TYPE)

D) INTERNAL O-RING REMOVAL
(USING WEDGE TYPE EXTRACTOR AND HOOK TYPE REMOVAL TOOLS)

BACKUP RING
O-RING
BACKUP RING
PUSH
O-RING EXTRACTOR TOOL
PULL
O-RING REMOVAL TOOL

REMOVAL TOOL (HOOK TYPE)
EXTRACTOR TOOL (WEDGE TYPE)

E) EXTERNAL O-RING REMOVAL
(USING SPOON TYPE EXTRACTOR REMOVAL TOOLS)

REMOVAL SPOON

F) EXTERNAL O-RING REMOVAL
(USING WEDGE TYPE EXTRACTOR AND HOOK TYPE REMOVAL TOOLS)

PULL
REMOVAL TOOL
PUSH
EXTRACTING TOOL
REMOVAL TOOL (HOOK TYPE)
EXTRACTOR TOOL (WEDGE TYPE)

limits of the rubber. After inspection and prior to installation, immerse the O–ring in clean hydraulic fluid.

Hydraulic Fluids

Liquids are used in hydraulic systems primarily to transmit and distribute forces to the various units to be actuated. Liquids are able to do this because they are almost incompressible. Pascal's Law states that when a force is applied to any area of the enclosed liquid it is transmitted equally throughout the enclosure. Thus, if a number of passages exist in a system, pressure can be distributed through all of them by means of a liquid.

Manufacturers of hydraulic devices usually specify the type of liquid best suited for use on their equipment. Their recommendations are based on the working conditions, temperature expected both inside and outside the system, pressures the liquid must withstand, the possibility of corrosion, etc.

Viscosity

One of the most important properties of a liquid to be used in a hydraulic system is its viscosity. Viscosity is the internal resistance of a fluid which tends to prevent it from flowing. A liquid, such as gasoline, has a low viscosity, and a liquid, such as tar, which flows slowly has a high viscosity. The viscosity of a liquid is affected by changes in temperature. This is, a liquid flows more easily when hot than when cold. A good hydraulic fluid will have a low viscosity at all temperatures.

Chemical Stability

Chemical stability is another property which is exceedingly important in the selection of a hydraulic fluid. It is defined as the liquid's ability to resist oxidation and deterioration for long periods.

Flashpoint

Flashpoint is the temperature at which a liquid gives off vapor in sufficient quantity to ignite momentarily or flash when a flame is applied. A high flashpoint is desirable for hydraulic fluid because it provides a good resistance to combustion.

Firepoint

Firepoint is the temperature at which a substance gives off vapor in sufficient quantity to ignite and continue to burn when exposed to a spark or flame. Like flashpoint, a high firepoint is required of desirable hydraulic fluids.

Types of Hydraulic Fluids

Many different liquids have been tested for use in hydraulic systems. The liquids that are presently in use include mineral oil, vegetable oil, and phosphate esters. Hydraulic liquids are usually classified according to their type of base. Reference the table in Figure 4.12, which includes the fluid base, color, mil-spec number, compatible seals and packings, and an approved flushing agent should the system become contaminated. (See Figure 4.12)

Contamination

There are many different types of contamination which are harmful to hydraulic fluids. The classes of contamination are as follows:

1. Abrasives, including such particles as core sand, machine chips, and rust.
2. Nonabrasives, including those resulting from soft particles worn or shredded from seals and other organic components. The origin of contamination can be traced to four major areas as follows: (a) particles originally contained in the system from fabrication and storage of system components; (b) particles introduced from outside sources, such as reservoir or breather vents or openings; (c) particles created within the system during operation, such as frictional wear or contact in components, pumps, cylinders, etc; and (d) particles introduced by foreign liquids. One of the most common is water which normally settles to the bottom of the reservoir.

Contamination Control

System filters (discussed in Chapter 6) provide adequate control of the contamination problem. During normal hydraulic system operations, precautions must be taken to ensure that contamination is held to a minimum during service and maintenance.

Note: Some peculiar safety considerations are required when aircraft systems utilize the phosphate ester (Skydrol) hydraulic fluids. In addition to using the specific seals that are compatible with these fluids, the precautions listed in Figure 4.12 should be followed.

MIL. SPEC OR MFR's NO.	COLOR	BASE	FLUSHING AGENT(s)	SEALS & PACKINGS	REMARKS
MIL-H-7644	Blue (usually) Sometimes: Blue-Green Almost Clear White	VEGETABLE (castor oil) & alcohol)	Same Fluid (clear new) Alcohol (de-natured)	Natural Rubber ONLY Metal "Crush washers"	Not used in modern aircraft, but may be found in older independent brake systems and pneudraulic shock struts. Unstable; due to alcohol evaporation. Pungent Odor (alcohol content) Disadvantage: FLAMMABLE - HIGHLY
MIL-H-5606	Red (Clear)	MINERAL (petroleum derivative)	Preferred: Stoddard Solvent (Dry-cleaning solvent) MIL-PS-661	Neoprene Rubber (Synthetic) BUNA-N Rubber (Synthetic) Leather Backup rings	Wide temperature/chemical stability operating range. Widely-used Excellent lubricating and anti-erosion/corrosion qualities Disadvantage: FLAMMABLE (Especially when spraying/atomized)
MIL-H-6083 Hydraulic Component and system preservative fluid	Slightly Darker Red (Clear)	"VARSOL"	Solvent Naptha	"Teflon" Backup rings Metal "Crush washers"	
MIL-H-83282A Fire resistant		Synthetic hydro—carbon	Alternatives: Same fluid (Clean new) Mixture: 50% Benzine and 50 % Nitrate Dope Lacquer Thinner	Same as for 5606	Disadvantages: Can be irritating to skin/eyes/breathing. Use skin and eye protection. Contains tricresyl phosphate (tcp)
MIL-H-8446 SKYDROL 7000 SKYDROL 500 SKYDROL 500A SKYDROL 500B SKYDROL 500C SKYDROL "LD" Chevron Hyjet IV	Light Green (clear) Amber (clear) Light Purple (clear) (Ditto) (Ditto) (Ditto) (Ditto)	PHOSPHATE ESTER (Synthetic)	Trichlorethylene (spec. P-D-680) ANY no. skydrol fluid (clean, new)	7000 + 500A + 500: BUTYL RUBBER 500B/500C/"LD" Ethylene Propylene Rubber (EPR seal) May use teflon backup rings. Permissible to replace "old" butyl rubber seals with newer ethylene propylene seals, not visa-versa. (sez Monsanto)	NON FLAMMABLE Wide sustained operating temp. range (up to 270° continuous) Needs no special preservative fluid for "spares" or stored systems. All Skydrol fluids can be intermixed in A/C with no special precautions or maintenance (flushing, etc.) In fact, addition of 500C or 500LD to system being 500B will improve stability. Disadvantages: Irritating to skin/eyes/breathing. Attacks many plastics and all paints except epoxy and polyurethane. Readily absorbs containing moisture from atmosphere.

Figure 4.12

5

BASIC HYDRAULIC SYSTEMS

The most basic form of hydraulic system is that used by a hydro-electric power plant. Large dams block streams of water which form lakes storing billions of tons of water. This is the power source, as the water flows downward through pipes to the turbine, the power of the water flowing from the lake drives the turbines, the generator uses the energy to produce electricity.

The most basic hydraulic system using fluid, as discussed in Chapter One, uses the mechanical advantage of the two sizes of piston areas to create a lifting force to raise an automobile or an airplane. (See Figure 5.1)

Another example of a very basic hydraulic system is that of the hydraulic brake system. (See Figure 5.2) This system was among the first use of hydraulic systems on airplanes. In its simplest form it consists only of a rubber expander tube in the brake housing connected to a diaphram type brake master cylinder. When the pilot depresses the brake pedal he forces fluid into the expander tube. The tube expands

Figure 5.1   Hydraulic jack.

forcing the brake linings to contact the rotating brake drum. When the pilot releases the pedal, the diaphram moves back and the brake return springs between the brake blocks in the wheel press the fluid out of the tube, back to the housing. (See Figure 5.3)

It is a totally enclosed system, which has its limitations. If the fluid expands due to heat, it may cause the brakes to drag, and if any fluid is lost due to external leakage, there is no way to replenish the fluid automatically.

A simple hydraulic system incorporating a vented reservoir connected to the brake master cylinder, using a piston, spring returned and wheel cylinders instead of an expander tube is illustrated in figure 5.4. (See Figure 5.4) The master cylinder builds up pressure by the movement of the piston inside the sealed fluid filled master cylinder. The resulting pressure is transmitted to the fluid line which is connected to the brake wheel cylinder. A return spring in the brake assembly returns the fluid from the wheel cylinder to the master cylinder. In this simple system, if fluid heats and expands, it is sent to the vented reservoir. If a slight amount of fluid is lost, the reservoir can replenish it automatically.

Figure 5.2   An automobile brake system.

Figure 5.3   A simple closed hydraulic system.

Figure 5.4 Hydraulic brakes may be operated by one of the simplest hydraulic systems used in modern aircraft.

Hydraulic Power Systems

The systems we have just discussed are the most basic systems, and are limited to just applying the brakes. As the aircraft have become more complex, the demand for hydraulically operated devices has increased. Some very simple systems are used for light aircraft while extremely complex systems have been designed for large jet aircraft.

The power system is sometimes called the heart of the system and the subsystems are known as the muscle. The power system includes all the components normally installed in the system, from the reservoir to, but not including, the selector valve. In pressurized reservoir systems, this also includes all components used to control and direct the pressurizing agent to the reservoir.

Before discussing the construction, function, and location of the hydraulic system components, let us examine a few basic different types of hydraulic systems and see how the jack and brake system evolves into a typical system.

All hydraulic systems must have fluid flowing through the system, a reservoir, previously mentioned, to store the fluid, a pump of some sort to move the fluid throughout the system, and an actuating unit to convert the fluid into a mechanical force to perform work. We must have flow control valves to direct the fluid flow and pressure control valves to control the system pressure. Of course we must also have fluid lines and fittings to carry the fluid throughout the system. These lines were discussed in Chapter Two.

Simple Hand Pump System—Single-acting actuator

A basic hand pump system using a hand operated pump and a single-acting actuating unit is illustrated in Figure 5.5. The four units needed to complete this system and their relationship are shown.

Figure 5.5   A simple hydraulic system with a hand pump operating a single-acting actuator.

The reservoir is needed to store the fluid for operation of the system. The pump is provided to create a flow of fluid. The pump in this system is hand operated. The selector valve is needed to direct the fluid flow. The purpose of the actuating cylinder is to convert the fluid pressure into useful work. The fluid forces the piston out, doing the work, and a spring inside the actuator returns the piston when the selector is positioned to return the fluid to the reservoir.

Double-Acting Actuator—(See Figure 5.6)

The basic system can be slightly modified by replacing the selector valve and the actuator, to perform work on both strokes of the actuator piston. By installing a four port, four way selector and a double-acting cylinder that uses hydraulic fluid on both sides of the piston, the system has now been improved to provide more useful work.

To improve even further on this basic system, we now install an engine-driven pump to replace the hand pump. (See Figure 5.7) The pump is coupled directly to the engine, using very little engine power and at the same time allowing the pilot more freedom by not being required to hand pump the actuator. To control the pressure when it is not needed, a pump control valve is installed and can be controlled. When pressure is not required, fluid flows from the bottom of the reservoir through the pump, through the pump control valve, back to the top of the reservoir. The fluid circulates through this section of the system freely with almost no restriction, and the pump uses very little power from the engine.

Figure 5.6 A simple hydraulic system using a double-acting actuator.

Figure 5.7 A basic hydraulic system using an engine-driven pump with a pump control valve.

When the system is actuated, the pilot puts the selector valve in the desired position and closes the pump control valve. The pump now directs the fluid flow to the selector valve where it is ported into the actuator to do its work. Inside the pump control valve is a relief valve feature, (which will be discussed in more detail in a later chapter) which will return the fluid to the reservoir when the piston reaches the end of its travel. Fluid on the opposite side of the piston returns to the reservoir throu.'1 the return port of the selector valve. In the off or neutral position, the selector valve will trap the fluid in the actuator.

Some systems designed in this type are automatic in their action. When the pilot positions the pump control valve and the selector valve, the build up of pressure on the pressure side of the selector valve, or in some cases, the pump control valve will return to neutral thereby taking the load off the pump and engine.

System with a Pressure Regulator or Unloading Valve

In Figure 5.8, we now have added a device called an accumulator into the pressure manifold. The construction, function and types of accumulators will be discussed in detail in a later chapter. In this system, its basic function is to dampen pressure surges and to store an amount of fluid under pressure to aid the engine driven pump. We have also added an automatic, pressure operated unloading valve. The basic function of this device is to unload the pump, direct fluid output back to the top of the reservoir, and trap pressure within the pressure manifold when system pressure has been reached, a term called "kicked-out" or cut-out in some aircraft systems. As systems fluid is used to operate a subsystem, the accumulator supplies fluid down to a specific pressure where the unloading valve "kicks-in" or cuts-in putting the pump back on the line until the kick-out pressure is reached. The shock-absorbing feature of the accumulator prevents the pressure surges from causing damage to the system.

We have added a separate system relief valve which is installed between the pressure and return manifold to prevent damage to the system from excessive system pressure, should the unloading valve fail to "kick-out" at the proper pressure. If we add one more component, that of our hand pump, (See Figure 5.9) we now have a typical small aircraft hydraulic system. The hand pump is used to provide pressure before the engine is started. By connecting the engine-driven pump suction line in the reservoir to a standpipe, the hand pump also

becomes an emergency pump should the system develop a leak sufficient enough to deplete the fluid level below the stand pipe pick-up.
There will be enough fluid left below the stand pipe to operate our
subsystems at least one time.

Figure 5.8 Hydraulic system using an engine-driven pump and a
system pressure regulator or unloading valve.

Figure 5.9 Hydraulic power system using an engine-driven pump and
a hand pump as a back-up.

Another small item, which will also be discussed in more detail later, is the system return filter. To keep the fluid in the system clean, we need a filter through which all the fluid will pass. This typical location will effectively trap all foreign particles from both subsystems, the relief valve as well as the unloading valve.

You will notice that in a typical system of this type, when the selectors are closed or at neutral there is not fluid flow in the power section. In addition, the selectors for the subsystems are arranged in parallel between the pressure and return manifold. These systems are commonly called "closed center systems," referring to the flow of fluid. Figure 5.10 completes a closed center basic system.

Figure 5.10 Complete basic aircraft hydraulic system using both an engine-driven pump and a hand pump.

Open Center Systems—(See Figure 5.11)

Many light aircraft use a hydraulic system that contains several subsystems. The basic system components, the pump, reservoir, relief valve and actuators operate the same as they do in a closed center system. The main difference in the open center system is the construction of, and arrangement of, the selector valves. In an open center system the selectors act both as flow control devices and as system pressure control devices. We will see the principle upon which this type of valve operates in a later section on selector valves.

Figure 5.11   Open-center hydraulic system.

When the selector handle is in neutral there is an unrestricted fluid flow through the valve on to the next subsystem. In this arrangement the valves are installed in series, which means that only one subsystem can be operated at a time. When system back pressure builds as the actuator pistons bottom out, the resulting pressure automatically shifts the selector valve to neutral or "kick-out" position. When all the selectors are shifted to neutral, the fluid is routed through the selectors to the reservoir. If the selectors should fail to return to neutral the system is protected from over pressurization by the system relief valve. (See Figure 5.12)

Hydraulic Power Pack System

Another simplified hydraulic system, used by many manufacturers of light airplanes, is the electric motor driven pump, contained in a unit called a power pack. A typical power pack system for a light twin-engine airplane is illustrated in Figure 5.13 and Figure 5.14.

Figure 5.12   Basic open-center hydraulic system.

In this type system, the hydraulic pump is driven by a reversible DC motor in one direction of rotation to lower the landing gear (as shown in Figure 5.13), while reversing the direction of the DC motor raises the gear (as shown in Figure 5.14).

The operation of these power pack systems and their components will be discussed more in detail in the later chapter covering typical aircraft hydraulic systems.

At this point, it should be pointed out, that the unique feature of the power pack system is that many of the systems power section components are contained in one compact unit, commonly called the power pack. They incorporate the system reservoir, control valves, relief valves, shuttle valve, as well as the pump and other auxiliary valves into one unit.

Figure 5.13 Power-pack type hydraulic system. In this condition, the landing gear is being lowered.

Figure 5.14 Power-pack type hydraulic system. In this condition, the landing gear is being retracted.

6
HYDRAULIC SYSTEM COMPONENTS

Reservoirs

The reservoir is a tank in which an adequate supply of fluid for the system is stored. Fluid flows from the reservoir to the pumps where it is forced through the system, and eventually returns to the reservoir.

The reservoir not only supplies the operating needs of the system, but also replenishes fluid lost through leakage. Furthermore, the reservoir serves as an overflow basin for excess fluid forced out of the system by thermal expansion (the increase of fluid volume caused by temperature changes), by the accumulators, and by piston and rod displacement. The reservoir also furnishes a place for the fluid to purge itself of air bubbles which may enter the system. Foreign matter picked up in the system may also be separated from the fluid in the reservoir, or as it flows through the filters.

Nonpressurized Reservoirs

Most nonpressurized reservoirs are used in aircraft that fly in lower altitudes. These reservoirs must be large enough to hold all the fluid for any condition of the hydraulic system and the actuators, including an additional supply to replace fluid lost through minor leakage. The reservoir is constructed to have a space above the fluid level, even when they are full, to allow the fluid to purge itself of air bubbles normally picked up as it makes its way to the reservoir.

In unpressurized reservoirs the air port on top serves as an overboard vent which allows the reservoir to "breathe." This is to prevent a vacuum from being formed as the fluid level in the reservoir is lowered, and also to allow the air that has entered the system to escape. (See Figure 6.1)

The reservoir will incorporate a filter to maintain the hydraulic fluid in a clean state, free from foreign matter. Filters are usually located in filler necks and internally within the reservoir. The filler neck filter may be a screen mesh type (finger strainer). (See Figure 6.2)

All reservoirs containing filters are designed to permit easy removal of the filter element for cleaning or replacement. The sight glass gives a visual indication of the amount of fluid in the reservoir. A reservoir

Figure 6.1   Hydraulic reservoir.

Figure 6.2

instruction plate is usually attached to the reservoir, or adjacent air-craft structure near the filler opening. Information on the instruction plate will usually include the following:

1. Simple instructions for filling.
2. Full level indication.
3. Reservoir capacity at full level.
4. Refill level indication.
5. Specification number and color of fluid.
6. Position of operating cylinders during filling.
7. System pressure (accumulator charged or discharged).

Additional information may be added, such as:

1. Safety precautions.
2. Filter element information.
3. Total capacity information.

In addition to the above information being readily available on or near the reservoir, the airplane service manual will contain a more detailed description of the reservoir and its servicing. (See Figure 6.3)

Figure 6.3 Hydraulic reservoir instruction plate.

Many unpressurized reservoirs are designed so that the returning fluid is swirled into the reservoir through a filter, around baffles, and fins, to prevent vortexing of the fluid in the reservoir.

When an aircraft utilizes an emergency pump in addition to the engine-driven pump, a second outlet is installed to provide for a reserve supply of fluid, should the engine pump lose all its fluid. This device or feature is called a stand pipe and may be installed sticking up inside the reservoir, with the outlet to the engine pump. When the engine pump loses all its fluid, due to a break in the system, the emergency or hand pump can still pick up enough fluid to provide for emergency operations. A variation of this feature is shown in Figure 6.4 where the pick up or supply line to the engine-driven pump is located higher on the reservoir. (See Figure 6.4)

Figure 6.4   Hydraulic reservoir pressurized with air.

Pressurized Reservoirs

The reservoir on aircraft designed for high altitude flying is usually pressurized. Pressurization assures a positive flow of fluid to the pump(s) at high altitudes when low atmospheric pressures are encountered. Additionally, there are some aircraft designed with the inlet of the installed hydraulic pump physically higher than the reservoir. To assure that an adequate supply of fluid, free from foaming (air bubbles which can cause pump cavitation) is always available at the pump inlet, three different methods of pressurization are used.

One method of pressurization uses an aspirator in the return line from the main system to the reservoir. This system is employed on the Douglas DC-8 aircraft, and since the aircraft uses a variable displacement pump (which will be discussed later), a continuous flow of fluid back to the reservoir is always there. As the fluid flows through the aspirator, it pulls in air from the cabin or ambient by jet action and mixes it with the returning fluid. A pressure regulator or relief valve maintains reservoir pressure at a predetermined range.

A variation of this aspirator—jet pump method of pressurization is employed using fluid from the main pressure manifold, a pressure sensitive diaphram which can open or close the flow of fluid through the aspirator as required to maintain a predetermined reservoir pressure. (See Figure 6.5)

Figure 6.5 Hydraulic reservoir pressurized with an aspirator.

A second method of air pressurization currently used in many high performance aircraft, including the Boeing 727 and other Boeing models, is accomplished using engine bleed air to maintain a pressure of up to 40-45 psi in the main system reservoirs. (See Figure 6.6)

Figure 6.6 Air-pressurized reservoir schematic.

An air pressure regulator is used to control the engine bleed air to a desired range within the reservoir. It will normally incorporate a relief valve to relieve excessive pressure. (See Figure 6.7)

Some designs of air-pressurized reservoir systems maintain this pressure for long periods of time, even when the engines are shut down and no bleed air is being supplied. Caution must be exercised before servicing any pressurized reservoir. In some cases it is necessary to release all the air pressure before servicing or performing maintenance on the system.

A third type of reservoir pressurization system uses fluid pressure from the main system to pressurize the reservoir. This reservoir is divided into two chambers by a floating piston. (See Figure 6.8) This is an airless type pressurization system. The floating piston is forced downward in the reservoir by a compression spring within the pressurized cylinder and by system pressure entering the pressurized port of the cylinder. Pressure ratios between the inlet piston (from system pressure) are nearly 50:1. This means that a 3000 psi inlet pressure is reduced to about 60 psi on the outlet side of the reservoir. This low pressure to the pump prevents pump cavitation by

Figure 6.7 Reservoir air pressure regulator.

Figure 6.8 Typical fluid-pressurized reservoir.

effectively maintaining its pressure throughout the supply part of the system. The reservoir is incorporated with a relief feature to prevent excessive pressure. An indicator index mark on the small end of the piston provides for fluid level readings while some aircraft, such as the Douglas DC-9, as shown in Figure 6.9, also include a remote transmitter to provide fluid level information to the flight crew. (See Figure 6.9) These reservoirs are normally serviced by using a servicing stand employing a hand pump to overcome the spring pressure, forcing the fluid into the large (low pressure) end of the reservoir. (See Figure 6.10)

Figure 6.9 Hydraulic system reservoir.

Due to the fact that the reservoir is pressurized, either by air or fluid, it can be installed in any attitude and still maintain a positive flow of fluid in the pump(s).

The vent (air breather) line usually contains a filter to purify the air that enters the reservoir.

Figure 6.10   Fluid-pressurized reservoir schematic.

Filtration and Cooling of Hydraulic Fluids

Many malfunctions in fluid power systems can be traced to some type of contamination in the fluid. Because of the extremely close clearances between component parts in many hydraulic pumps and valves, the importance of keeping the hydraulic fluid clean and free of contaminants cannot be overemphasized. Foreign matter in the system can cause excessive wear, clog valves and other components, and substantially increase maintenance and replacement costs. Although great care is taken while servicing, maintaining and operating hydraulic systems, it is impossible to prevent some foreign matter from entering the system. Some contaminants are built in: that is, small particles of core sand, metal chips, lint, and abrasive dust, resulting from the manufacturing process. Also, tiny particles of metal and sealing material are deposited in the fluid as a result of normal wear on valves, pumps, and other components.

Pressure and return line filters are usually constructed like the one illustrated in Figure 6.11. (See Figure 6.11) This particular filter consists of the following major parts: filter case, head, filter element, and

Figure 6.11 Hydraulic filter assembly.

by-pass or relief valve. The case contains the element; the case screws into the head which contains the "in" port and "out" port and relief/bypass valve. The normal fluid flow through this filter is through the "in" port, around the outside of the element, through the element to the inner chamber, and out through the "out" port. (See Figure 6.12) The filter element is made of a specially treated cellulose paper and is commonly referred to as a micronic type; however, other elements may be made of sintered metal (bronze) a woven wire, or a one-piece corrugated wire mesh of stainless steel.

Figure 6.12   Full flow hydraulic filter.

The elements listed have a range generally between a minimum rating of about 5 microns to maximum range of about 40 microns. The micron rating is based on the size particles the element will remove from the fluid. To get an idea of the relative size of these microns, the unaided eye can see something only as small as 40 microns, while white blood cells are about 25 microns. (See Figure 6.13)

The paper cellulose element, and some of the stainless steel woven mesh elements are wrapped around a spring type frame to prevent collapsing of the element as the fluid flows through.

Should these filters become clogged, the by-pass or relief valve in the filter head will open allowing a flow of unfiltered fluid. (See Figure 6.14)

RELATIVE SIZES

LOWER LIMIT OF VISIBILITY (NAKED EYE).........40 MICRONS
WHITE BLOOD CELLS...25 MICRONS
RED BLOOD CELLS..8 MICRONS
BACTERIA (COCCI)..2 MICRONS

The relative size of these particles may be used to help visualize the effectiveness of a hydraulic filter.

Figure 6.13 Micronic-type filter, using a paper element.

Figure 6.14 Micronic hydraulic filter.

The cellulose element is discarded at regular intervals and replaced with new elements. The micronic stainless steel type element, being very expensive, is normally removed, cleaned using ultrasonic cleaning methods, tested and repaired as necessary before returning it to service. It should be well protected and packaged to prevent contamination and damage after it is cleaned, inspected and awaiting re-use.

Some hydraulic filter units use a by-pass indicator to alert the operator of a by-pass (a clogged element) or differential pressure situation. The pin on top of the filter head will protrude from the filter housing. Then the element should be removed and cleaned, or replaced and the element and the fluid downstream checked for contamination. (See Figure 6.15)

A filter strong enough to be used on the pressure side of the system using a stack is called a Cuno filter. The Cuno is made up with a stack

Figure 6.15   Metal type filter assemblies.

of discs as shown in Figure 6.16 and spacers mounted on a rod, with a cleaner blade between each disc. (See Figure 6.16) The assembly is inside the bowl with a handle to rotate the rod protruding through the top of the filter housing. The rod can be rotated and the cleaner blades will scrape away any dirt trapped between the discs. The dirt will fall to the bottom of the bowl where it can be removed by taking out the drain plug, at periodic inspection intervals.

Since most filtering devices are replaced at periodic time intervals, the applicable service manual of each aircraft manufacturer should be consulted when maintenance is performed and should be followed closely.

Figure 6.16   Buildup of a Cuno-type hydraulic filter.

Temperature Control/ Cooling of Hydraulic Fluid

Hydraulic systems operate most efficiently when the fluid temperature is held within a specific range. Temperatures higher than the desired level reduce the lubricating characteristics of the fluid and also cause the fluid to break down, forming a sludge or other contaminants. In most systems, cold fluid may cause sluggish action of the fluid when the system is first operated; however, the friction resulting from the flow of fluid through the system will usually increase the temperature to the desired level.

The component used to cool the hydraulic fluid is usually referred to as a heat exchanger. Figure 6.17 illustrates one type of fluid heat exchanger using finned tubing. (See Figure 6.17) The exchanger is immersed in one of the aircraft fuel cells. Fluid enters the inlet coupling, flows through the fin wall tubing, through the outlet coupling, and then returns to the reservoir. The heat of the fluid is absorbed by the fins and the fuel.

Another type, similar in design to an automobile radiator in which the fluid flows through small tubes in the core, and air or fuel is forced through the honeycomb material around the core to cool the fluid is shown in Figure 6.18. (See Figure 6.18)

Figure 6.17   Fin tubing heat exchanger.

FUEL FILTER ELEMENT

ENGINE FUEL
SUPPLY HOSE

SYSTEM #1 HYDRAULIC COOLING COIL

FILTER BYPASS RELIEF VALVE

STRAP

SUPPORT BRACKET

SYSTEM #2
HYDRAULIC OUTLET
LINE TO RESERVOIR

SYSTEM #1
HYDRAULIC INLET LINE

SYSTEM #2
HYDRAULIC COOLING COIL

FUEL RELIEF VALVE SPRING

FUEL HOSE

LEGEND
→ INDICATES DIRECTION
OF FLUID FLOW

HYDRAULIC OUTLET LINE TO RESERVOIR

SYSTEM #2 HYDRAULIC INLET LINE

Figure 6.18 Radiator type heat exchanger.

7

HYDRAULIC PUMPS AND FLOW CONTROL VALVES

Hydraulic Pumps

All aircraft hydraulic systems have one or more power-driven pumps and may have a hand pump as an additional source of power. Fluid power is available in an aircraft hydraulic system when fluid is moved under pressure. Pumps are simply fluid movers; they generate the flow of fluid. Pressure will only be generated when there is a restriction to the flow.

Power driven pumps are the primary source of energy and may be either engine driven or electric motor driven. As a general rule, motor driven pumps are installed for use in emergencies, that is, for operation of actuating units when the engine driven pump is inoperative. Hand pumps are generally installed for testing purposes as well as for use in emergencies.

In this section, the various types of pumps used in aircraft, both hand and power driven, are described and illustrated.

Hand Pumps

Hand pumps are used in hydraulic systems to supply fluid under pressure to subsystems such as landing gear, flaps, and to charge system accumulators.

Most hand pumps used in aircraft hydraulic systems are of the double-action type. Double action means that a flow of fluid is created on each stroke of the pump handle instead of every other stroke, as in the single-action type, commonly used in jacks and maintenance stands. There are several versions of the double-action hand pump, but all utilize the reciprocating piston principle, and operation is similar to the one shown in Figure 7.1. (See Figure 7.1)

This pump consists of a cylinder, a piston containing a built in check valve (A), a piston rod, an operating handle, and a check valve (B) at the inlet port. When the piston is moved to the left in the illustration, check valve (A) closes and check valve (B) opens.

Fluid from the reservoir then flows into the cylinder through the inlet port (C). When the piston is moved to the right, check valve (B) closes. The pressure created in the fluid then opens check valve (A), and fluid is admitted behind the piston. Because of the space occupied by the piston rod, there is room for only part of the fluid, therefore, the remainder is forced out port (D) into the pressure line. If the piston is again moved to the left, check valve (A) again closes. The fluid behind the piston is then forced through outlet port (D). At the same time, fluid from the reservoir flows into the cylinder through check valve (B). Thus, a pressure (flow) stroke is produced with each stroke of the pump handle.

Figure 7.1 Double action hydraulic hand pump.

Power Driven Pumps

As previously mentioned, power pumps are generally driven by the aircraft engine, but may also be electric-motor driven, such as the light airplane power pack type system. Power pumps are classified according to the type of pumping action utilized, and may be either the gear type, or piston type. Power pumps may be further classified according to whether they are designed for constant displacement or variable displacement.

A constant displacement pump is one that displaces or delivers a constant fluid output for any rotational speed. For example, a pump might be designed to deliver 3 gallons of fluid per minute at a speed of 2,800 revolutions per minute. As long as it runs at that speed, it will continue to deliver at that rate, regardless of the pressure in the system. For this reason, when a constant displacement pump is used in a system, a pressure regulator or unloading valve must also be incorporated in the system to unload the pump.

A variable displacement pump has a fluid output that varies to meet the demands of the system. For example, a pump might be designed to maintain system pressure at 3,000 psi by varying its fluid output from 0 to 7 gallons per minute. When this type of pump is used, no pressure regulator or unloading valve is needed, since no pumping action takes place except when pressure (fluid flow) is required by the system.

Constant Displacement (Volume) Pumps

Gear Type Pump

A gear type pump consists of two meshed gears which revolve in a housing. (See Figure 7.2) The drive gear in the installation is turned by a drive shaft which is driven by the engine accessory section, or an electric motor. The clearance between the gear teeth is very small between the teeth and the pump housing minimizes slippage of fluid from the discharge side back to the suction side.

The inlet port is connected to the reservoir lines and the outlet port is connected to the pressure line. In the illustration, the drive gear is turning in a counterclockwise direction, and the driven (idle) gear is turning in a clockwise direction. As the teeth pass the inlet port, fluid is trapped between the teeth and the housing. This fluid is carried around the housing to the outlet port. As the teeth mesh again, the fluid between the teeth is displaced into the outlet port. This action produces a positive flow of fluid under pressure into the pressure line. A shear pin or shear section that will break under excessive loads is incorporated in the drive shaft. This is to protect the engine accessory drive if pump failure is caused by excessive loads or jamming of parts.

All gear type pumps are constant displacements commonly used in systems with operating pressures in the low to medium pressure range, that is, normally below 1500 psi, and with relatively low fluid flow.

Figure 7.2   Gear type rotary pump.

Gerotor Pumps

Another design of internal gear pump is the gerotor, sometimes called a "missing tooth" type. (See Figure 7.3) This pump consists of a pair of gear-shaped elements one within the other, located in the pump chamber. The inner gear is connected to the drive shaft of the power source. (To simplify the explanation of the gerotor pump, the teeth of the inner gear and the spaces between the teeth and the outer gear are numbered.) (See Figure 7.4) Note that the inner gear has one less tooth than the outer gear. The tooth form of each gear is related to that of the other in such a way that each tooth of the inner gear is always in sliding constant with the surface of the outer gear. As the drive gear

Figure 7.3 The gerotor pump is a special form of gear pump, producing up to about 1500 psi pressure with a moderate flow.

Figure 7.4 Principles of operation of the internal gear pump.

rotates and pulls the driven gear around, the volume of the cavity increases to its maximum. During the rotation the expanding cavity is under the inlet port and fluid is drawn into the pump. As the gears continue to rotate, the cavity formed by the missing tooth moves under the outlet port. As the gear rotates past the outlet port the cavity decreases forcing the fluid into the discharge or pressure port.

Vane Type Pump

When a large volume of fluid is required but system pressure is relatively low, a common pump used is the simple vane type. (See Figure 7.5) It is also classed as a positive or constant displacement pump because of its positive action in moving fluid. This pump uses a rotor which is attached to the drive shaft and is rotated by the power source.

The rotor is slotted and each slot is fitted with a rectangular vane. These vanes, to some extent, are free to move outward in their respective slots. The rotor and vanes are enclosed in a housing, the inner surface of which is offset with the drive axis.

Figure 7.5 The vane pump is constant displacement and moves a relatively large volume of fluid under relatively low pressures.

As the rotor turns, centrifugal force keeps the vanes snug against the wall of the housing. The vanes divide the area between the rotor and housing into a series of chambers. The chambers vary in size according to their respective positions around the shaft. The inlet port is located in that part of the pump where the chambers are expanding in size so that the partial vacuum formed by this expansion allows fluid to flow into the pump. The fluid is trapped between the vanes and is carried to the outlet side of the pump. The chambers contract in size on the outlet side, and this section forces the fluid through the outlet port and into the system.

Although some rotary (vane) pumps are capable of operating in high-pressure systems (above 1500 psi), their use is usually limited to systems which operate at pressures of 1500 psi or below.

Piston Type Pumps (Constant Displacement)

Piston type constant displacement pumps consist of a circular cylinder block with either seven or nine equally spaced pistons. Figure 7.6 is a partial cutaway view of a seven-piston pump manufactured by Sperry Vickers Corp. (See Figure 7.6)

The main parts of the pump are the drive shaft, piston, cylinder block and valve plate. There are two ports in the valve plate. Those ports connect directly to openings in the face of the cylinder block. Hydraulic fluid is sucked in one port and forced out the other port by the reciprocating (back-and-forth) motion of the pistons.

There is a fill port in the top of the cylinder housing. This opening is normally kept plugged, but it can be opened for testing the pressure in the housing or case. When installing a new pump or newly repaired one, this plug must be removed and the housing filled with fluid

Partial cutaway view of axial piston pump.

Cutaway drawing of
an axial piston pump.

A fixed-delivery piston pump.

Figure 7.6

before the pump is operated. There is a drain port in the mounting flange to drain away any leakage from the drive shaft seal.

When the drive shaft is rotated, it rotates the pistons and cylinder block with it. The offset position of the cylinder block causes the pistons to move back and forth in the cylinder block while the shaft, pistons, and cylinder block rotate together. As the pistons move back and forth in the cylinder block, they draw fluid in one port and force it out the other. Since each one of the pistons will be performing the same operation in succession, fluid is constantly being taken into the cylinder bores through the inlet port and expelled from the cylinder bores into the pressure line of the system. This action creates a steady, non-pulsating flow of fluid. Certain models of this pump are capable of developing up to 3000 psi working pressure.

The constant flow of fluid through the pump, with a small amount leaking past the rotating group (cylinder block-drive shaft) into the case of the pump provides lubrication of the bearings.

Another (fixed) constant displacement type pump is illustrated in Figure 7.7. This is a stratopower pump, sometimes called a cam type piston pump. Two major functions are performed by the internal parts of the fixed displacement stratopower pump. These functions are mechanical drive and fluid displacement. (See Figure 7.7)

Figure 7.7   Fluid flow—stratopower pump (fixed displacement).

The mechanical drive mechanism is shown in Figure 7.8. Piston motion is caused by the drive cam displacing each revolution of the shaft. By coupling the ring of pistons with a nutating (wobble) plate supported by a fixed center pivot, the pistons are held in constant contact with the cam face. As the drive cam depresses one side of the wobble plate (as pistons are advanced), the other side of the wobble plate is withdrawn an equal amount, moving the pistons with it. (See Figure 7.8)

Figure 7.8   Mechanical drive—stratopower pump.

Fluid is displaced by the axial motion of the pistons. As each piston advances in its respective cylinder block bore, pressure opens the check and a quantity of fluid is forced past. Combined back pressure and check spring tension closes the check when the piston advances to its foremost position. The low-pressure area occurring in the cylinder during the piston return allows atmospheric pressure (or reservoir positive pressure) to force fluid to flow from the intake loading groove into the cylinder. Fluid is circulated through the back of the pump for cooling and lubricating purposes by the centrifugal action of the drive cam. (See Figure 7.9)

Figure 7.9   Fluid displacement—stratopower pump.

Variable Displacement Pumps

The internal features of the variable displacement stratopower pump are illustrated in Figure 7.10. This pump operates similarly to the fixed displacement stratopower pump; however, this pump provides the additional function of automatically varying the volume output. (See Figure 7.10)

Figure 7.10   Internal features of stratopower variable displacement pump.

This function is controlled by the pressure in the hydraulic system. For example, assume that a pump of this type, rated at 3000 psi, is providing flow to a 3000 psi system. When system pressure reaches 3000 psi and there is no demand on the system, the pump unloads (delivers no flow to the system). The pressure regulation and flow are accomplished by an internal bypass which automatically adjusts delivery of fluid to the demands of the system.

Flow cutoff actually begins before the fluid reaches system pressure. For example, in a 3000 psi system, flow cutoff begins at approximately 2850 psi and reaches zero flow (unloads) at 3000 psi. When the pump is operating in the unload condition, the bypass system provides circulation of fluid internally for cooling and lubrication of the pump. Four major functions are performed by the internal parts of the variable displacement stratopower pump. These features are mechanical drive, fluid displacement, pressure control, and by-pass. Two of these functions—mechanical drive and fluid displace-ment are identical to those performed by the fixed displacement stratopower pump.

A schematic diagram of the pressure control mechanism is shown in Figure 7.11. Pressure is bled through the control orifice into the pressure compensator cylinder when it moves the compensator piston against the force of the calibrated control (compensator) spring. This motion, transmitted by a direct mechanical linkage, moves sleeves ax-ially on the pistons, thereby varying the time during which the relief holes are covered during each stroke. (See Figure 7.11)

Figure 7.11 Pressure control mechanism—stratopower variable displacement pump.

Fluid flows through the hollow pistons during the forward stroke, and escapes out the relief holes until they are covered by the piston sleeves. The effective piston stroke (delivery) is controlled by the piston sleeve position. During nonflow requirements, only enough fluid is pumped to maintain pressure against leakage.

During normal pump operation, three conditions may exist: full flow, partial flow, and zero or no flow. During full flow operation, fluid enters the intake port and is discharged to the system past the pump checks by the reciprocating section of the pistons. (See Figure 7.12) Piston sleeves cover the relief holes for the entire discharge stroke.

During partial flow, system pressure is sufficient (as bled through the orifice) to move the compensation stem against the compensator spring force.

If system pressure continues to build up, as under nonflow conditions, the stem will be moved further until the relief holes are uncovered for practically the entire piston stroke. The relief holes will be

Figure 7.12 Fluid flow—stratopower variable displacement pump.

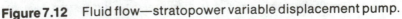

covered only for that portion of the stroke necessary to maintain system pressure against leakage and to produce adequate bypass flow.

The bypass system is provided to supply self-lubrication, particularly when the pump is in nonflow operation. The ring of bypass holes in the pistons is aligned with the bypass passage each time a piston reaches the very end of its forward travel. This pumps a small quantity of fluid out of the bypass passage back to the supply reservoir and provides a constant changing fluid in the pump. The bypass is designed to pump against a considerable back pressure for use with pressurized reservoirs.

The Sperry Vickers variable displacement pump (as shown in Figure 7.13) varies its output from full flow to zero or no flow by changing the alignment of the rotational axis of the cylinder block. The pumping action of the Sperry Vickers variable displacement pump is identical with that of the fixed or constant displacement Sperry Vickers pump. (See Figure 7.6) However, the variable pump is designed so the angle can be varied. By changing the angle of the rotational axis, the stroke of the piston is decreased or increased; hence the volume of fluid pumped during each stroke of the pistons is reduced or increased. If the axis of the cylinder block is parallel to the axis of the drive shaft, no fluid will be delivered because there will be no back and forth movement of the pistons within their respective cylinders. (See Figure 7.13)

Figure 7.13   A variable-delivery pump.

Staring with zero pressure in the system, the cylinder block and yoke are in the extreme angle position as shown in Figure 7.14. As the pump builds up pressure in the outlet port, and the system, it acts on the pressure control valve (sometimes called a compensator valve) (H), through a small interconnecting line (G). Pressure moves the control pilot valve (J) down against the spring to the position shown in Figure 7.15, zero flow. This opens the passageway (F), allowing pressure to enter against the rod side of the control piston (L). The piston moves to the left, compressing the spring, and thus causing the yoke (C) to be swiveled upward until the cylinder block makes a zero angle with the drive shaft (zero flow). At this point the fluid output from the pressure port is zero, since the cylinder block and the drive shaft are in alignment.

FULL FLOW

ZERO FLOW

A. DRIVE SHAFT	J. PILOT VALVE
B. BEARINGS	K. ADJUSTING SCREW
C. YOKE	L. PRESSURE CONTROL PISTON
D. CYLINDER BLOCK	M. HOLLOW CENTER (CONTROL
E. VALVE PLATE	PISTON)
F. PASSAGEWAY	N. PISTON
G. CONNECTING LINE	O. PIVOT PIN
H. PRESSURE CONTROL VALVE	

Figures 7.14 and 7.15   Variable volume, stroke reduction pump.

Maintenance of Pumps

Most hydraulic pumps are removed and replaced and sent to an authorized repair station when extensive repair or overhaul is required. However, some minor maintenance may be performed at all locations. Replacement of O-rings on external fittings and plugs is permissible; when the shaft seal leaks beyond allowable limits, depending on the pump model, it may be replaced. As long as the shaft seal can be removed without disassemble of the rotating group, this is a relatively simple repair.

All pump cases should be filled with the system fluid before they are installed to prevent cavitation on initial pump start up.

When leak checking hydraulic pumps, it is usually recommended that normal operating temperatures be established before testing.

Flow Control Valves – General

Flow control valves, as applied to fluid power systems, are used for controlling the flow of the fluid, and the direction of fluid flow.

These valves may be controlled manually, electrically, mechanically, hydraulically, or by combinations of two or more of these methods. In some systems the entire sequence of operation of the most complicated equipment may be automatic. The method of control depends upon many different factors. The purpose of the valve, the design and purpose of the system, the location of the valve within the system, and the availability of the source of power are some of the factors that determine the method of control.

Classification of Valves

The most common method of classifying valves is according to their purpose, flow control, pressure control, and directional control. All the types of valves available for fluid power systems are too numerous to describe within the scope of this book.

Most valves, however, are variations of these three fundamental classes—flow control, pressure control, and directional control. Flow control and directional control valves are discussed in this chapter, while pressure control valves are covered in Chapter 8.

Flow Control

A typical example of a valve used to control flow is the ordinary water faucet. It is normally in the closed position allowing no flow. It can be fully opened allowing full flow. The rate of flow is varied by turning the faucet handle clockwise or counter-clockwise, which changes the size of the opening of the faucet.

Gate Valves

In the gate valve, flow is controlled by means of a wedge or gate, the movement of which is usually controlled by a handle. (Figure 7.16 illustrates the principal element of the gate valve.) They permit straight flow and offer little or no resistance to the flow of fluid when the valve is completely open. Gate valves are usually intended for use as fully opened or fully closed valves. (See Figure 7.16)

Figure 7.16 Operation of gate valve.

Directional Control Valves

Directional control (selector) valves are designed for the specific purpose of directing the flow of fluid, at the desired time, to the point in a fluid power system where the fluid is applied to accomplish work. It may be desired, for example, to perform a work operation by driving a piston back and forth in its cylinder. A directional control valve, which functions alternately to admit fluid to and from each end of the cylinder, is used to make this operation possible. It is also used in some of the flow control valves and pressure control valves which will be discussed in later chapters.

Figure 7.17 illustrates the operation of a simple poppet valve. The valve consists primarily of a moveable poppet which closes against a valve seat. (See Figure 7.17)

Directional control valves may be operated by differences of pressure acting on opposite sides of the valving element, or they may be positioned manually, mechanically, or electrically. Often two or more methods of operating the same valve will be utilized in different phases of its action.

Directional control (selector) valves may be classified in several ways. Some of the different methods are the type of control, the number of ports in the valve housing, or the specific function of the valve. The ball, cone or sleeve, poppet, rotary spool, and sliding spool or piston are the most common type of valving elements. The basic operations principal of the poppet, rotary spool, and sliding piston are described in the following paragraphs.

Figure 7.17 Operation of a simple poppet valve.

Poppet

It should be noted that the use of the poppet valving element is not limited to directional control. It is also used in some of the flow control valves and pressure control valves which will be discussed in later chapters.

Figure 7.18 illustrates the operation of a typical poppet valve for an open center system. It is a four way, four port valve. As the cam rod is moved to the gear down position, fluid enters through the "P" pressure port and passes through open valve 4 and on to the actuating cylinder. As the piston moves, return fluid flows through the open

"I" poppet and return "R" port. When the handle is moved to the neutral position, cam lobe 8 will open valve 3 which allows flow through to return and since all the other poppets are closed, the fluid will be trapped in the actuating cylinder. This opening of poppet 3 effectively reduces the load on the pump, and if the airplane has another sub-system, such as the flap system on the Piper aircraft, fluid can flow on to the next sub-system. (See Figure 7.18) When the gear handle is placed in the up position, poppets 2 and 5 will open and all the others will close. Fluid now flows through poppet 2 and out port "B" and moves the actuator to the right. Return fluid is forced through port "A" around poppet 5 to return.

Figure 7.18   Poppet type four-way valve.

Three- and Four-Way Poppet Valves

Poppet valves used in the closed center hydraulic system are illustrated in Figures 7.19 and 7.20. Figure 7.19 shows a cam operated, spring closed double poppet selector valve used to operate a single acting actuator. The first view shows the upper poppet (b) being lifted off its seat by the inside cam (e) opening fluid flow from the pump pressure line (c) to the actuator, while the lower poppet (a) is closing the return flow. When the cam is rotated 180° (bottom view) the (b) poppet at the top closes the pressure line and the outside cams (f) lift the lower poppet (a) off seat allowing the fluid to return to the reservoir through port (d). The spring inside the actuator returns the piston. (See Figure 7.19)

By adding another poppet, double lobe cam, and another working line, we can use this type valve to operate a double acting actuator.

A. LOWER (RETURN) POPPET   D. RETURN LINE
B. UPPER (PRESSURE) POPPET   E. INSIDE CAM
C. PRESSURE LINE   F. OUTSIDE CAM

Figure 7.19 Three-way poppet type selector valve.

(See Figure 7.20) This becomes a four-way, four port valve typical for a closed center system. When the cam shaft is rotated to an intermediate position, all four ports are blocked and there is no flow in the valve. Blocking the working ports will create a liquid lock preventing movement of the actuator.

Figure 7.20   Four-way poppet selector valve.

Rotary Spool

The rotary spool type selector valve has a round center section, with ports connecting pressure, return, and the working ports. A rotary four way, four port valve, as shown in Figure 7.21, is illustrated to show the fluid flow necessary to extend and retract an actuator. In figure A, the fluid is flowing from the pressure source through the valve into the right side of the actuator; as the actuator extends, return fluid flows through the valve out of the reservoir. Figure B shows the opposite position of the rotary selector which will retract the actuator piston. In the neutral or off position, all four ports are blocked, effectively holding the actuator stationary and blocking fluid flow.

Figure 7.21a A rotary four-way valve.

Four-way radial selector valve.

A. POPPET	E. POPPET
B. PRESSURE PORT	F. RETURN PORT
C. POPPET	G. POPPET
D. ALTERNATING LINE PORT	H. ALTERNATING LINE PORT

Figure 7.21b Four-way rotary selector valve.

Spool or Piston Selector Valve

The sliding spool selector valve is shown in Figure 7.22. The three positions of the valve illustrate passages for fluid in the up, down and off or neutral position. When the valve is in the neutral position there is no flow through the valve. Figure A shows the spool lands blocking the working ports A and B, since the area of both the spool lands is

Figure 7.22a   A piston-type selector valve.

Figure 7.22b   A spool-type selector valve.

equal; pressure entering from the system pump through the P pressure port is blocked. Figure B shows the spool moved to the left which opens working port A to pressure; as the actuator moves, return fluid flows into port B and out to the reservoir through port R. In the opposite operating position the spool is moved to the right which opens port B to pressure thus moving the actuator in the opposite direction. At the same time return flow is in through port A, through the drilled passage in the rod to port R and on to return. (See Figure 7.22)

The movement of the spool in the valve described above is controlled or actuated manually by the attachment of a control handle, or by use of push pull rods to a remote location. However, this type valve lends itself to operation by electrical solenoids as shown in Figure 7.23. A very reliable, simple operating directional control can now be provided by energizing either of the solenoids. (See Figure 7.23)

Figure 7.23 Solenoid-operated sliding spool directional control valve.

An open center sliding spool (piston) selector is illustrated in Figure 7.24. This type selector is designed to provide a means of directing fluid and automatically returning to the neutral or open position. When the actuator reaches the end of its stroke, the fluid output of the pump is then directed through the open center of the valve to unload the pump. (See Figure 7.24)

In the illustration, the valve is moved manually to the right and held in this position by the spring loaded cam mechanism. Fluid flows from

Figure 7.24   An open-center system selector valve.

the inlet port "A" through port "D" to one side of the actuator, moving the actuator, by extending the piston. Fluid returning from the opposite side of the actuator enters through port "B" and on to the reservoir through the cut out groove in the piston and out port "C".

The valve is automatically returned to neutral by the build up of system pressure when the actuator bottoms out. Pressure opens the relief valve (check) through the pressure inlet side, when full system pressure is reached. The pressure forces the valve piston back to the neutral position. This action takes place for either working position of the valve.

Servo Valves

The four-way directional control valves discussed in the preceding section are positioned by the operator, either with a control handle, or in the case of the solenoid-operated valves, with an electrical switch. This usually provides positive movement of the actuating unit, that is, full movement in either direction. If partial movement of the actuating unit is desired, the operator must control this movement by manually controlling the control handle or switch. This method of control satisfies the requirements of many fluid power systems, but it does not provide an exact and automatic method of control. The servo valve is often used to provide such control.

A servomechanism is a device in which the output quantity, such as the rotation of a motor or the distance of travel of a piston in a cylinder, is monitored and compared with a desired quantity. By way of a feedback system, the difference between the two quantities (the error) is used to actuate the system and to generate a rate of change of the output. The feedback signal may be provided by fluid pressure, mechanical linkage, electrical signals, or a combination of the three. The feedback signal positions a servo valve which, in turn, corrects any errors in the movement of the actuator.

One simple type of servo valve is illustrated in Figure 7.25. The valve is controlled by the two solenoids which receive the electric feedback signals through the follow-up system from the actuating unit. With neither of the windings energized (or balanced current through both) the magnetic reed is centered as shown in the illustration. In this condition, high pressure fluid from the input line cannot pass to the actuator, since the center land of the spool valve blocks the inlet port. The pressurized fluid flows through the alternate routes, through the two fixed orifices, passes through the two nozzles, and returns to the reservoir without causing any movement of the actuator.

If the right-hand solenoid is energized, the magnetic reed will move to the right, blocking off the flow of high pressure fluid through the right-hand nozzle. Pressure will build up in the right-hand pressure chamber. This will move the valve to the left. In moving left, the

Figure 7.25   Servo valve.

center land will open the high pressure inlet and permit fluid to flow directly to the right-hand side of the actuator. This process will cause the actuator movement to the left. By energizing the left-hand solenoid, the magnetic reed will move to the left, and the entire process will be reversed, the actuator then being moved to the right. (See Figure 7.25)

Check Valves

Some authorities classify check valves as flow control valves. However, since the check valve permits flow in one direction and prevents flow in the other direction, most authorities classify it as a one-way directional control valve.

Check valves are available in various designs. The ball and the cone or sleeve are common as shown in Figure 7.26 and Figure 7.27, while some installations will also use a gate or swing type as shown in Figure 7.28. (See Figures 7.26, 7.27, 7.28)

BALL-TYPE CHECK VALVE
(A)

Figure 7.26

CONE-TYPE CHECK VALVE
(B)

Figure 7.27

SWING-TYPE CHECK VALVE
(C)

Figure 7.28

The force of fluid in motion opens the check valve allowing free flow. It will be closed by fluid attempting to flow in the opposite direction aided by the spring. (See Figure 7.29)

The cone type check, when opened, exposes several passage ways around the face of the cone to allow for free flow of fluid. The ball simply moves off the seat of the check with fluid flow.

Figure 7.29 Typical check valve.

It is important for the technician to note the arrow on the body of the check valve during installation. The arrow represents free flow of fluid.

We have previously discussed the use of some of these types of check valves in hand pumps, selectors, etc.; however, they are used throughout the hydraulic system where control of fluid flow is required.

Restrictor/Orifice Check Valves

A restrictor/orifice check valve is a combination cone type restrictor that also includes a check valve. (See Figure 7.30) It will allow normal speed of operation (fluid flow) in one direction, the direction of the free arrow, and limited speed (flow) in the other, repesented by a restricted arrow on the valve body. One of the most common applications of this valve is in the up line of a landing gear. Since the landing gear is usually quite heavy, it tends to fall too rapidly when lowered. By installing a restrictor-check in the up line, free flow up retracts the

(A)

(B)

1. Outlet port.   4. Inlet port.
2. Cone.   5. Orifices.
3. Orifice.   6. Orifice.

Figure 7.30   Orifice check valves.

RESTRICTING ORIFICE

FULL
FLOW

RESTRICTED
FLOW

DETAIL OF ORIFICE CHECK VALVE

(A)

PRESSURE

RETURN

ORIFICE CHECK VALVE

LOCATION OF AN ORIFICE CHECK VALVE IN A
LANDING GEAR SYSTEM.

(B)

Figure 7.31

gear at full speed. However, when the gear is lowered, return flow of fluid through the restricted path will effectively slow down the rate of fluid flow and thus the speed of gear extension. (See Figure 7.31)

Metering Check Valve

A metering check valve, sometimes called a one way restrictor, serves the same function as the restrictor check valve. However, this type valve can be adjusted to change the speed of operation by allowing more or less fluid to pass through the restricted path. (See Figure 7.32)

Figure 7.32   A metering check valve.

The pin holds the ball check partially off seat to provide for the speed of fluid flow. Fluid flows into port A, around the offset ball and out through port B as a restricted flow. When flow is reversed, fluid flows in port B off seats the ball check and free flows out port A.

Orifices or Restrictor Valves

Restrictors, sometimes referred to as orifices, are used in fluid power systems to limit the speed or movement of certain actuating devices. They do so by serving as restrictions in the line, thereby limiting the rate of flow. Figure 7.33 shows an example of a typical restrictor. This type is referred to as a fixed restrictor, or a fixed orifice. (See Figure 7.33)

Figure 7.33   Drawing of an orifice.

Some types of restrictors are constructed so that the amount of restriction can be varied. One type of variable restrictor is illustrated in Figure 7.34. This type can be adjusted to conform to the requirements of a particular system. (See Figure 7.34)

Figure 7.34   A variable restrictor.

Sequence Valves

A sequence valve is sometimes called a timing valve or a load and fire valve, because it times the operation of certain hydraulic subsystems in a proper sequence. A common use of this valve is in a landing gear door subsystem where the doors must open before the gear can extend and the gear must be retracted before the doors are closed. Figure 7.35 shows the construction of a typical sequence valve. It is essentially a mechanically operated check valve. There is a free flow of fluid from port A through the check valve to port B when the valve is in the return part of the system. However, when it is used as a "load and fire" timing device, fluid pressure is trapped by the check valve when it enters port B. When the landing gear retracts and the strut mechanically depresses the plunger pushing it up, fluid can now flow freely from port B out port A and on to close the door actuators. (See Figure 7.35 and Figure 7.36)

Figure 7.35 A sequence valve.

Figure 7.36 Mechanically operated sequence valve.

Figure 7.37 illustrates the typical landing gear system using a sequence valve to control the fluid flow.

Figure 7.37   Illustrates the typical landing gear system.

Manually Operated Check Valves

The check valve illustrated in Figure 7.38 is one that can be used as a typical one way check valve in the top illustration with free flow of fluid from port (c) through the valve, compressing the spring and lifting the poppet (b) off seat, and blocking flow from port (a). When the control handle (d) is rotated, the cam lobe lifts the poppet off seat, allowing free flow in both directions. (See Figure 7.38)

Priority Valves

The pressure operated sequence valve, also called a priority valve, looks like a check valve externally. Like a check valve, the installation position is indicated by an arrow. Figure 7.39 is a schematic of this valve. (See Figure 7.39) They are used in such subsystems as wheel well doors, which must operate first, requiring a lower pressure than the main gear.

This completely automatic valve consists of a body containing a spool, seat, poppet, related springs, seals and an end cap.

Figure A shows insufficient pressure to unseat the spool. When gear door actuators have completed their travel (located upstream of the priority valve) system pressure builds until it overcomes spring tension and causes the poppet to unseat and allow fluid to flow through the valve.

A. NORMAL OUTLET PORT
B. POPPET
C. NORMAL INLET PORT
D. CONTROL HANDLE SHAFT

Figure 7.38   Manually operated check valve.

THERE IS INSUFFICIENT PRESSURE TO OPEN THE
VALVE, AND THERE IS NO FLOW OF FLUID
THROUGH IT.

(A)

THE PRESSURE IS SUFFICIENT TO HOLD THE VALVE
OPEN, AND THERE IS FLOW THROUGH THE VALVE.

(B)

FLUID FLOW THROUGH THE PRIORITY VALVE IN
THE RETURN DIRECTION

(C)

Figure 7.39   Priority valve.

133

Shuttle Valves

All aircraft incorporate emergency systems which provide alternate methods of operating essential systems required to land the aircraft safely. To allow operating pressure to the actuating unit and still not enter the other system, a shuttle valve is installed in the working line to the actuating unit.

The main purpose of a shuttle valve is to isolate the normal system from the emergency. These emergency systems may be hydraulic or pneumatic. Shuttle valves are located as close to the actuating unit as possible. This reduces the number of units to be bled and isolates as much of the normal system as possible. In some installations, the shuttle valve is an integral part of the actuator.

A typical shuttle valve is shown in Figure 7.40. (See Figure 7.40) The body contains three ports—the normal port, the emergency inlet port and the unit inlet port. Enclosed in the body is a sliding part called the shuttle. it is used to seal one of the two inlet ports. A shuttle seat is installed at each inlet port, and during operation, the shuttle is held against one of these seats sealing off that port. When a shuttle valve is in its normal position, fluid has a free flow from the normal inlet port to the unit inlet port. When emergency fluid, air or gas is released under pressure by a control valve, the pressure at the emergency inlet port forces the shuttle to shift, sealing the normal inlet port and allowing free flow from the emergency inlet port to the unit port.

A. SHUTTLE
B. POSITION RETAINING BALL
C. NORMAL SYSTEM INLET PORT
D. CYLINDER PORT
E. EMERGENCY SYSTEM INLET PORT

Figure 7.40   Shuttle valve.

Hydraulic Fuses

Fuses are located in many brake, flap and thrust reverser systems to prevent the complete loss of fluid when a hydraulic leak occurs downstream of the fuse. If a line should break or an excessive external leak develop, the fuse will stop the flow of fluid.

There are two basic types of hydraulic fuses in use on modern aircraft. One type of fuse shuts off the flow when a specified volume of fluid flows through the fuse. This type is a quantity measuring fuse. (See Figure 7.41) The fuse piston slides inside the sleeve suspended between the sleeve valve and the metering orifice housing. The fuse operates on the ratio of the flow through the main passage and the metered orifice. Metered flow through the orifice is created by the pressure drop of the main flow around the sleeve valve at the outlet. Metered flow moves the valve at the outlet. Metered flow moves the piston toward the control plug seat. When there is no leak downstream, of the fuse, the piston will not seat, as the required quantity of fluid will not flow through the fuse. When flow through the fuse is reversed, the piston moves in the opposite direction, and since there is virtually no restriction to reverse flow, the piston quickly returns to the start position.

Figure 7.41 Hydraulic fuse operating on the principle of the quantity of flow needed to isolate the line.

When there is a large leak downstream, the piston is closed to the seat in the sleeve valve after the required volume of fluid has passed. The fluid flow will stop and no more fluid will be lost.

Another type hydraulic fuse is the pressure drop or pressure sensing fuse. (See Figure 7.42) This fuse will shut off the flow of fluid when a sufficient pressure drop across it occurs. When the pressure through outlet port drops due to line breakage downstream, and the pressure at the inlet port remains high, the loss of pressure at the outlet port causes the piston to be shifted to the right and over the flow holes. The fluid flow in the reverse will not restrict it in any way and will return the piston to its normal flow condition.

NORMAL FLOW THROUGH THE FUSE
(A)

FLOW IS STOPPED. THE PRESSURE DROP ACROSS
THE FUSE HAS MOVED THE PISTON OVER SO THAT
IT COVERS THE HOLES THROUGH WHICH THE FLUID
MUST FLOW.
(B)

Figure 7.42 Hydraulic fuse operating on the principle of pressure drop across the fuse.

Fire Shutoff Valve   (See Figure 7.43)

The fire shutoff valves are manually operated, two-position, ball type, one for each engine, and usually mounted on the firewall or the bulkhead.

They are operated by cables, by the flight crew, to stop the flow of hydraulic fluid, and fuel. When these valves are operated, after a fire warning is received, they will shut off the fuel flow to the engines, as well as the hydraulic fluid flow to the pumps, and the engine will stop.

Figure 7.43   A fire shutoff valve.

8

PRESSURE CONTROL VALVES

Pressure Regulators

As the term implies, pressure regulators are used in fluid power systems to regulate the system pressure.

Pressure regulators, often referred to as unloading valves, are used in hydraulic systems to unload the pump and to maintain and regulate system pressure between the maximum and minimum. All systems do not require pressure regulators. The open-center system, with its "return to neutral" selector valves, does not require a pressure regulator. Many systems are equipped with variable displacement pumps which contain a built in pressure or flow regulating device as described in Chapter 7. Although manufacturers are leaning more toward the use of variable displacement pumps, especially, in larger aircraft, there are many closed-center hydraulic systems that utilize constant displacement pumps and, therefore, require a pressure regulator.

Pressure regulators (unloading valves) are made in a variety of types by various manufacturers; however, the basic operating principles of all regulators are similar to the one illustrated in Figure 8.1. View A shows the regulator in the kicked-in (or cut-in) position and view B in the kicked-out (cut-out) position. (See Figure 8.1)

A regulator is said to be in the kicked-in position when it is directing fluid under pressure into the system. In the kicked-out position, the fluid in the system downstream of the regulator is trapped at the desired pressure, and the fluid from the pump is bypassed into the return line and back to the reservoir.

Referring to Figure 8.1, assume that the piston (5) has an area of 1 square inch, the steel ball of the bypass valve (1) has a cross sectional area of one fourth square inch, and the piston spring (6) provides 600 pounds of force pushing the piston down. When the system pressure is less than 600 psi, fluid from the pump enters the in port (2), flows to the top of the regulator, and to the check valve (3). When the pressure of this input fluid increases, the check valve opens and fluid flows into the system and to the bottom of the regulator against the piston (5), until the pressure is great enough to force the piston upward and unseat the ball, directing the fluid through the system port (4) to the system. The regulator is then in the kicked-in position, (as shown in view A of Figure 8.1).

1. Bypass valve.   5. Piston.
2. Pressure input.   6. Spring.
3. Check valve.   7. Line to
4. System connection.   reservoir.

Figure 8.1 Hydraulic pressure regulator.

When the pressure on the piston builds up to 600 psi, the force applied on the piston builds up to 600 psi; the force applied on the piston face will be 600 pounds (force equals pressure times area = F = P × A). In this case, the pressure is 600 and the area of the piston is 1 square inch; therefore, the force is 600 pounds. Since the spring pushes down on the piston with a force of 600 pounds, the two forces on either side of the piston are balanced. However, the force holding the ball in place must be considered. This force, 600 × ¼ square inch, equals 150 pounds. This force allows the fluid to continue to build up pressure in the system.

When the pressure in the system increases to 800 psi, there is 800 pounds of force pushing upward on the piston; spring force is constant (600 pounds); therefore, the resultant force is 200 pounds pushing the piston upward (800 pounds minus 600 pounds). However, the force applied to the steel ball will also be 200 pounds (800 × ¼). At this point the regulator is in a balanced state as both the upward and downward forces are equal. Any pressure in excess of 800 psi will move the piston up and push the ball off its seat. Since the fluid will always follow the path of least resistance, it will pass through the regulator and back to the reservoir through line (7).

When the fluid from the pump is suddenly allowed a free path to return, the pressure on the input side of the check valve (3) drops and the check valve closes. The fluid in the system is then trapped under pressure. The regulator is now in the kick-out position, as shown in Figure 8.1 B. This fluid will remain pressurized until a unit is actuated, or until pressure is slowly lost through normal internal leakage in the system.

The pump continues to operate, although it does not have to force the fluid against pressure. Therefore, the pump is not constantly under a load and will operate under trouble-free conditions for a longer period.

With the regulator in the kicked-out position, there is very little pressure acting on the steel ball and this pressure acts on the entire surface area of the ball. Therefore, the 600 pound force of the spring (6) is the only force pushing downward on the piston (5). When the system pressure decreases to a point slightly below 600 psi, the spring (6) forces the piston (5) down and closes the bypass valve (1). When the bypass is closed, the fluid cannot flow to return. This causes the pressure to increase in the line between the pump and the regulator. This pressure opens the check valve (3), and the fluid will then enter the system and build up the pressure to 800 psi. Therefore, when the system pressure lowers a certain amount, the pressure regulator will kick-in, thus sending fluid into the system. When the pressure increases sufficiently, the regulator will cut out allowing the fluid from the pump to flow through the regulator and back to the reservoir. As stated previously, the difference between the regulator kick-in pressure and kick-out pressure is the differential or operating range. This prevents the regulator from kicking in or out with small changes in pressure. The pressure regulator serves to take the load off the pump and to regulate system pressure. See Figure 8.2 for a typical

Figure 8.2 Balanced type unloading valve in system.

Figure 8.3a Bendix balanced type regulator.

Figure 8.3b Bendix pressure regulator in the "kicked-out" position.

system location, and Figure 8.3 for an illustration of a Bendix balanced regulator.

Pressure Switch

Electrically operated pressure switches are used in hydraulic systems with electrically driven pumps to maintain system pressure within set limits. The pressure switch is set to open an electrical circuit to the pump motor when system pressure builds up to correct value, causing the pump to stop. As pressure drops to a lower value, the pressure switch closes the circuit to start the pump operating again. Pressure switches are also used in hydraulic systems to control the operation of warning and protective devices. The switch may turn on a light to warn the pilot of insufficient pressure, or it may turn off a pump to avoid dumping fluid through a broken line.

There are various types of hydraulic pressure switches. However, the Bourdon tube type as shown in Figure 8.4 will be discussed here. (See Figure 8.4)

A typical Bourdon tube type pressure switch is used to control the operation of a motor-driven pump. The flexible steel finger, attached to the small end of the Bourdon tube, moves outward as the tube (A) begins to uncoil. This finger presses against the toggle plate (B) until the desired pressure is reached, at which time it will cause the toggle to

A. BOURDON TUBE
B. TOGGLE PLATE

C. HYDRAULIC FLUID
   CONNECTION
D. TOGGLE PLATE OPPOSITE
   INNER SURFACE

Figure 8.4 Bourdon tube pressure switch.

pivot rapidly, thereby opening the contact points, completing the circuit to the motor. Again, the pump sends fluid into the system to build up pressure.

Pressure Reducer

Pressure reducing valves are used in hydraulic systems where it is necessary to lower the normal system operating pressure to a specified amount.

Figure 8.5 is an operation schematic diagram of a pressure reducing valve. (See Figure 8.5) View (A) shows system pressure being ported to a subsystem through the shuttle and sleeve assembly. Subsystem pressurized fluid works on the large flange area of the shuttle, which causes the shuttle to move to the left after reaching a specified pressure, thus closing off the normal system. The valve will stay in this position until the subsystem pressure is lowered, at which time the shuttle will move to its prior position and allow the required amount of pressurized fluid to enter the subsystem. During normal operation of the subsystem, the pressure reducing valve continuously meters fluid to the subsystem.

Figure 8.5   Pressure reducing valve operational schematic.

Also incorporated within the pressure reducer valve is a relief valve. When pressurized fluid builds up to an excess amount within the subsystem, the shuttle assembly overcomes spring tension and moves farther to the left, as shown in view (B). This movement causes a passage to be opened to return and all excess fluid is relieved. When pressure is lowered to an acceptable amount, the shuttle assembly returns to a balanced position.

Relief Valve

Relief valves are pressure limiting or safety devices commonly used to prevent pressure from building to a point where it might blow seals, burst or damage components within the hydraulic system.

Main system relief valves are designed to operate within certain specific pressure limits and to relieve complete pump output when in the open position.

In systems designed to operate at 3,000 psi, normal pressure, the relief valve might be set to be completely open at 3,650 psi and reseat at 3,190. The pressure where the valve just begins to open is called the cracking pressure. The cracking pressure is usually somewhere between full flow and reseat. When the relief valve is in the open position, it directs excessive pressurized fluid to the reservoir return line. (See Figure 8.6)

The main system relief valve is set to relieve any pressure above the normal system regulator kick-out pressure and only in the event of a malfunction of the regulating device.

A. COMPRESSION SPRING   C. BALL SEAT SLEEVE
B. PRESSURE ADJUSTMENT   D. BALL

Four port relief valve.   Four port relief valve relieving fluid.

Four port relief valve.   Four port relief valve relieving fluid.
Figure 8.6

Several types are used as main system relief valves. A simple ball-type, as shown in Figure 8.7, includes the housing, an inlet (pressure) port, a return port, and a coil spring holding the ball check on its seat. (See Figure 8.7) When the pressure in the system reaches the cracking pressure (counteracting spring tension), the ball is forced off its seat allowing fluid flow from the pressure port through to the return port. As pressure continues to build, the spring will continue to compress until the entire pump output is relieved to return. When system pressure returns to normal, the spring once again closes the ball seat.

Figure 8.8 shows a typical "in line" type relief valve. Stamped on the housing are the words "Press" (Pressure) and "RET" (Return) to aid in installation of the valve. The principle of operation is identical to the relief valve described previously. (See Figure 8.8)

Relief valves are adjusted to a specific pressure setting recommended by the manufacturer. To change the manufacturer's adjustment, a return port can be disconnected, the system pressurized and the valve examined at the return port. The valve can be adjusted to crack at a specific pressure but should not be adjusted while it is installed on an

A. PRESSURE-ADJUSTING SCREW   D. RETURN PORT
B. ADJUSTING SCREW CAP   E. BALL
C. COMPRESSION SPRING   F. PRESSURE PORT

Figure 8.7 Two-port relief valve.

aircraft. A test stand should be used to prevent damage, from over pressure, to the aircraft system.

Thermal Relief Valves

Thermal relief valves are usually smaller as compared to system relief valves. They are used in systems where a check valve or selector valve prevents pressure from being relieved through the main system relief valve.

Figure 8.9 illustrates a typical thermal relief valve. (See Figure 8.9) As pressurized fluid in the line in which it is installed builds up to an

PRESSURE

END CAP

PROBE

SEAT

POPPET

SLEEVE

RETAINER NUT

SPRING GUIDE

NAME PLATE

SPRING

SPRING ADAPTER

ADJUSTING SCREW

BODY

RETURN

Figure 8.8   Pressure relief valve.

excessive amount, the valve poppet is forced off its seat and allows a small amount of fluid to flow to the reservoir. When system pressure decreases, spring tension overcomes system pressure and closes the poppet. Thermal relief valves normally are set to crack at a pressure slightly above main system relief valve cracking settings.

Figure 8.9 Typical thermal relief valve.

Wing Flap Overload Valve (Flap blow-up valve)

A wing flap overload valve, designed much the same as a main system relief valve, is installed in the flap down line to prevent lowering of the flaps at too high an airspeed, which could damage the flaps. The pressure on the down line rises to a specified level (the cracking pressure of the valve) because of the airload on the flap surface at too high an airspeed. The valve will open and allow excess pressure to be relieved, thus causing the flap's movement to stop. (See Figure 8.10)

When several relief valves are installed in a hydraulic system, they should be adjusted in a sequence which will permit each valve to reach. its cracking pressure. Therefore, the valve with the highest setting should be adjusted first, the others in decending order according to the pressure setting of each valve.

Accumulators

The accumulator serves a two-fold purpose. It serves as a cushion or shock absorber by maintaining an even pressure in the system, and it stores enough fluid under pressure from emergency operation of certain actuating units. It is designed with a compressed air chamber

Figure 8.10 Flap blow-up valve.

separated from the fluid by a flexible diaphragm, flexible bladder, or moveable piston. In addition to the two-fold purpose of dampening pressure surges and supplying emergency fluid, the accumulator also supplements the pumps output under peak loads by storing energy in the form of fluid under pressure.

Diaphragm-Type Accumulator

The diaphragm accumulator shown in Figure 8.11 is constructed in two halves which are bolted or screwed together. A synthetic rubber diaphragm is installed between the two halves, making two chambers. The top opening may be fitted with a screen disc or button type protector to prevent the diaphragm from extruding through the fluid opening when system hydraulic pressure is depleted.

The bottom opening provides a means for installation of an air filler valve. This valve allows servicing of the air/nitrogen and traps it within the accumulator. (See Figure 8.12)

Figure 8.11 Spherical accumulator.

High pressure air valves that seal
with a metal-to-metal seal.

Figure 8.12

Bladder-Type Accumulator

Figure 8.13 illustrates a bladder-type accumulator which consists of a metal sphere in which a bladder is installed to separate the air and the hydraulic fluid. The inside of the bladder serves as the air/nitrogen chamber with an air servicing valve in the bottom port. When fluid under pressure is forced into the accumulator through the top port, the bladder collapses to the extent necessary to make space for the fluid, depending upon the fluid pressure.

SYSTEM PRESSURE

AIR VALVE

BLADDER-TYPE ACCUMULATOR

Figure 8.13   Spherical accumulator.

Piston-Type Accumulator   (See Figure 8.14)

Cylindrical shape accumulators consist of a cylinder and piston assembly. Attached to both ends of the cylinder are end caps. The internal piston separates the fluid and air/nitrogen chambers. This type accumulator is widely used on modern aircraft hydraulic systems because they use less space than the spherical type.

Maintenance of Accumulators

As an example of accumulator precharge or preload, that is, the initial charge of air or nitrogen, let us assume that the cylindrical accumulator in Figure 8.15 is designed for a preload of 1,300 psi in a 3,000 psi system. (See Figure 8.15)

When the initial charge of 1,300 psi is introduced into the unit, hydraulic system pressure is zero. As air pressure is applied through the air pressure port, it moves the piston toward the opposite end until

FLUID INLET

PISTON

AIR VALVE

Figure 8.14 Piston-type accumulator.

PRESSURE LINE

SCREEN DISC

DIAPHRAGM

FLUID CHAMBER

AIR CHAMBER

AIR VALVE CAP

GASKET   SEALS   PISTON

BLEED

FLUID CHAMBER   AIR CHAMBER   AIR VALVE CAP

Figure 8.15 Pressure accumulator, spherical and cylindrical types.

152

it bottoms. If the air behind the piston has a pressure of 1,300 psi, the hydraulic system pump will have to create a pressure within the system greater than 1,300 psi before the hydraulic fluid can actuate the piston. Thus at 1,301 psi, the piston will start to move within the cylinder, compressing the air as it moves. At 2,000 psi it will have moved several inches. At 3,000 psi the piston is to its normal operating position, compressing the air until it occupies a space less than one-half the length of the cylinder.

In the spherical type accumulator, the diaphragm/bladder will be flexible enough to allow the same action as described for the cylindrical type accumulator.

When installing the accumulator, the air chamber should be downward. Sometimes the air charge is placed in the accumulator before it is installed. In all cases, the manufacturer's instructions should be followed. Great care must be taken due to the high pressure involved. All system pressure must be relieved before the accumulator is removed.

Hydraulic Actuators

An actuator is a device which converts fluid power into mechanical force and motion. Cylinders and motors are the most common types of devices used in fluid power systems.

The first part of this section will be devoted to the various types of actuating cylinders and their application to fluid power systems. The next part of the section covers fluid motors used in fluid power systems.

Cylinders

An actuating cylinder is a device which converts fluid power to linear or straightline force and motion. Since linear motion is a back and forth motion along a straight line, this type of actuator is sometimes refered to as reciprocating. Actuating cylinders are normally installed in such a way that the cylinder is anchored to a stationary structure and the ram or piston is attached to the mechanism to be operated.

Ram—Single and Double Acting

A ram is usually one in which the cross-section area of the piston is more than one half the cross-section area of the moveable element. It is sometimes referred to as a plunger, and is usually used for push function rather than pull.

The single acting ram applies force in only one direction. (See Figure 8.16) There is no provision for retracting the ram with fluid power; however, the force area to extend the ram is much greater in the "push" travel. A double acting ram is one that is both extended and retracted with fluid power. (See Figure 8.17) One other type ram could be classified as a telescoping ram. (See Figure 8.18) A series of rams are nested in the telescoping assembly. With the exception of the smallest ram, each ram is hollow and serves as the cylinder housing for the next ram. This telescoping action provides a relatively long stroke from a small space. An example of this type ram would be used in a dump truck and some hydraulic jacks. (See Figure 8.19)

Figure 8.16   Single-acting ram type actuating cylinder.

Figure 8.17   Double-acting ram type actuating cylinder.

Figure 8.18 Telescoping ram type actuating cylinder.

Piston Type Cylinders

An actuating cylinder in which the cross sectional area of the piston rod is less than one-half the cross sectional area of the moveable element is referred to as a piston type cylinder.

Figure 8.20 illustrates a single-acting, spring loaded piston type actuating cylinder. This cylinder utilizes fluid pressure to extend the piston rod. Since the force of the fluid acts only to extend the piston a return spring is utilized to return the piston to the retracted position. A three way selector valve is normally used to control the operation of this actuator. (See Figure 8.20)

A Double-Acting Cylinder

Figure 8.21 illustrates a double-acting type actuating cylinder, which means that fluid under pressure can be applied to either side of the piston to provide movement in both directions. This type cylinder is referred to as an unbalanced actuating cylinder; that is, there is a difference in the effective working areas on the two sides of the piston. The diameter of the piston rod on the retract side of the piston reduces the area by the diameter of the rod and thus the effective force that can be developed. (F = A × P). A four-way selector valve is normally used to operate this type of actuator. (See Figure 8.21)

Three-Port Cylinder

Figure 8.22 illustrates a three-port, double-acting piston type actuating cylinder. This type is used where it is necessary to move two mechanisms at the same time. Fluid entering port A will extend both pistons, while in the reverse position of the four-way selector, fluid enters ports B and C at the same time, retracting both piston rods. (See Figure 8.22)

Figure 8.19   Jack hydraulic system schematic.

Figure 8.20 Single-acting linear hydraulic actuator. Hydraulic pressure moves the piston to the right, and a spring returns it when the pressure is released.

UP
PORT   DOWN
                                                  PORT

Figure 8.21 Double-acting unbalanced linear hydraulic actuator.

Figure 8.22 Three-port, double-acting actuating cylinder.

Figure 8.23 Double-acting balanced linear hydraulic actuator.

Balanced, Double-Acting

Balanced, double-acting piston type actuating cylinders, as shown in Figure 8.23, are used in mechanisms where equal force is required in both directions of piston rod travel. The piston rod shaft extends through the piston and out through both ends of the cylinder. The balanced double-acting cylinder is commonly used in servo-mechanisms. (See Figure 8.23.)

Tandem Cylinders

Some fluid power applications require two or more independent systems. For example, most flight control systems on modern aircraft require two independent systems. On these aircraft two systems are operating a moveable control surface at the same time.

A tandem cylinder is illustrated in Figure 8.24. The tandem cylinder consists of two cylinders arranged one behind the other, but designed as a single unit. This example shows two balanced, double-acting piston type cylinders connected to a common shaft. Both system (A and B) and (C and D) can effectively operate the cylinder. Failure of either system does not render the actuator inoperative. Use of this type cylinder permits doubling the output force with no change in piston area. (TF =A1 + A2 × P1 + P2 of both cylinders of a tandem cylinder). (See Figure 8.24)

Figure 8.24   Tandem actuating cylinder.

Cushioned Cylinders

In order to slow the action and prevent shock at the end of the piston stroke, some actuators are constructed with a cushioning device to slow (cushion) the movement of the piston during part of its stroke. The cushion is usually a metering device built into the cylinder to restrict the flow at the outlet port, thereby slowing down the movement of the piston. Figure 8.25 shows an actuator with a built in metering rod in the piston which slows the last movement of the retracting piston by blocking the return fluid, through the orifice, to slow the landing gear movement into the wheel-well. On the extend stroke, once the metering rod moves past the orifice, the cylinder extends at full speed. (See Figure 8.25)

Internal Lock Actuators

Some aircraft incorporate internal locking actuators to lock the landing gear, or other devices, after the actuating cylinder has reached

Figure 8.25

the end of its stroke. Figure 8.26 (A) illustrates a ball lock actuator. It locks the gear down when the cylinder retracts. The locking pin holds the locking ball in the groove so the piston cannot move out of the cylinder in (B); as fluid enters the gear-up port, the pressure moves the locking pin back, allowing the balls to drop out of the groove in the piston, and the piston moves with fluid pressure. The collar is extended with spring force, holding the balls in place while the piston is extended. (See Figure 8.26)

Figure 8.26 Mechanism for locking the piston of a linear hydraulic actuator at the end of its stroke.

Rack and Pinion Rotary Actuators

A simple form of rotary actuator is the rack and pinion actuator used on some of the Cessna aircraft main landing gear. (See Figure 8.27) The actuator is in reality a linear actuator, double-acting unbalanced type. However, there is a noticeable difference. The piston rod is designed with a rack of teeth cut in its shaft, and these teeth mesh with those in a pinion gear that rotates a pinion shaft. As the piston moves in and out the pinion gear rotates the pinion shaft which raises or lowers the landing gear. (See Figure 8.27)

Figure 8.27   Rack and pinion type linear hydraulic actuator, having a rotary output.

Servo Actuators

A servo actuator is designed to provide hydraulic power to move various aircraft controls. These servo actuators usually include an actuating cylinder, single or tandem type, a flow control valve, check valves and relief valves. (Servo valve is described in Chapter 7). The input to move the servo actuator may be an input from the mechanical linkage, electronic autopilot signals, or pitch and yaw dampeners. When the force from any of these inputs is applied, the flow control valve moves the actuator. The piston moves the control mechanism which normally contains a device called a follow-up linkage, which will return the control valve to a neutral position. Each movement of the servo actuator accomplishes the same sequence of events, that is, the input moves the flow-control valve, the flow control valve moves the actuating cylinder, and the follow-up linkage returns the flow-control valve to neutral. (See Figure 8.28)

Figure 8.28 Elevator control system—functional schematic.

Hydraulic Motors

Figure 7.6 (Piston type hydraulic pump)

A fluid power motor is a device which converts fluid power energy to rotary motion and force. Basically, the function of the motor is just the opposite as that of a pump. The design and operation of fluid power motors are very similar to pumps; in fact, some hydraulic pumps can be used as motors with little or no modifications.

The motor, however, uses fluid pressure from the system, entering through the inlet port, which forces the pistons down in the cylinder block. As they move down, they rotate the drive shaft. As the pistons move down, in turn, they provide smooth rotating force, while expelling the fluid back to return.

Piston or vane type motors (pump) may be used; however, the piston type is used when more torque is desired.

The speed and torque of the motor can be controlled. The speed is varied by controlling the amount of fluid entering the inlet port. The

Figure 8.29 Modular unit. (Boeing Co.)

torque can be varied by controlling the pressure of the incoming fluid. However, the majority of the motors used in fluid power systems are of the fixed displacement type.

Modular Unit

A modular unit, as shown in Figure 8.29, is used on some aircraft to contain several smaller components into one housing, thus reducing weight and simplifying maintenance. (See Figure 8.29)

Typical components included within the modular unit (sometimes called a manifold) are filters, check valves, a relief valve, a bypass valve, and pressure warning switches. A schematic flow diagram of the modular unit is shown in Figure 8.30. (See Figure 8.30)

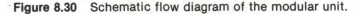

Figure 8.30 Schematic flow diagram of the modular unit.

9

HYDRAULIC SYSTEMS – TROUBLESHOOTING

General

Aircraft fluid power systems have been designed in many different configurations for many different aircraft from some very simple systems used on light airplanes to the very complex systems used on large jet aircraft, both military and civilian. On light airplanes, the fluid power system may consist of one or two sub-systems, landing gear and flaps, as an example. On large transport type aircraft the sub-systems may include landing gear, flaps, ground and flight spoilers, control surfaces, brakes, leading edge devices, and possible other devices.

In this chaper we will examine a few typical systems used on both light and large aircraft.

Expanding on the brief description of light aircraft systems in Chapter 5, we can now understand the function of each component and how it relates to the other components of the hydraulic system.

A Pump-Control Valve System (Temporary System)

A basic hydraulic system used on light airplanes that have only one or two sub-systems (landing gear, flaps) called a temporary system is illustrated in Figure 9.1. (See Figure 9.1)

Figure 9.1   Power control valve.

This system uses an engine driven pump which runs all the time the engine is running. However, to prevent the pump from robbing the engine of power by maintaining hydraulic pressure on the system when it is not needed, a manually operated pump control valve is used.

The pump control valve is closed by the pilot when he moves the selector valve to raise or lower the landing gear. This action closes the flow of fluid between the pressure and return line and routes fluid under pressure to the inlet port of the selector. When the actuating cylinder bottoms out the resulting build up of pressure acts against a piston inside the pump control valve counteracting a bias spring. When full system pressure is reached, fluid pressure overcomes the bias spring pressure and the pump control valve opens allowing free flow of fluid from the pump outlet back to the reservoir. This bias spring action also acts as the system relief valve, to prevent damage to system components. To determine the setting, or system pressure, when the system relief valve opens, it is necessary to physically hold the pump control valve in the closed position until maximum pressure is reached and the relief valve opens.

When the pump control valve is open and fluid flow is from the pump, through the pump control valve, back to the reservoir, all the sub-system selector valves will be positioned to neutral, and there will be no load on the pump. The pump only moves fluid through the system; no pressure is developed. The pump is normally a constant displacement gear type.

Pressure Regulator/Unloading Valve Light Airplane System

With the addition of an automatic, pressure operated unloading valve installed between the pump outlet and the return manifold, we now have an improved system. (See Figure 9.2) This automatic unloading valve accomplishes essentially the same function that the manual pump control valve did in the temporary system. However, this improvement frees the pilot from engaging and disengaging the system manually.

We have also added an accumulator to the system to dampen the pressure shocks and surges of the kick-in and kick-out action of the unloading valve, and to help replace any fluid lost through the normal internal leakage when the unloading valve is in the kick-out position.

In addition, to these changes, we can also add a system filter to keep the system fluid clean. A typical location for the filter is in the return line to the reservoir.

Figure 9.2 Hydraulic system using an engine-driven pump and a system pressure regulator or unloading valve.

Complete Basic Closed Center System

With the addition of a standpipe in the system reservoir, as shown in Figure 9.3, designed to reserve a supply of fluid for a hand pump, our system now includes a means of providing fluid flow should the engine-driven pump fail. If a line breaks somewhere in the system, the engine-driven pump can exhaust the fluid level in the reservoir only down to the top of the standpipe. If the broken line is isolated (not used), there will still be enough fluid left to operate the hand pump so the landing gear can be lowered.

Figure 9.3 Complete basic aircraft hydraulic system using both an engine-driven pump and a hand pump.

Hydraulic Power Pack System

Illustrated in Figure 9.4 and Figure 9.5, is a typical power pack system for a light aircraft. This system utilizes a reversible DC motor to drive the gear type pump. Most of the system components are contained within the pack itself, with the exception of gear actuators, lines, free fall valve, a pressure switch, and thermal relief valves.

The operation of this system will be discussed in greater detail in the landing gear section, since the pack, in this installation, operates only the landing gear.

Figure 9.4 Power-pack-type hydraulic system. In this condition, the landing gear is being retracted.

Figure 9.5 Power-pack-type hydraulic system. In this condition, the landing gear is being lowered.

Open Center Systems

Many of the light aircraft used an open center system to power several sub-systems. Illustrated in Figure 9.6 is a typical open center system using fluid power to operate the landing gear and flap sub-system.

Figure 9.6   A simple, open-center system.

The reservoir, constant displacement pump, filter, and system relief valve all function the same as they do in a closed center system. The big difference is that the two selector valves are connected in series, while the closed center system selector valves are connected in parallel.

The open center selector valves serve as both flow control devices and as unloading valves. They are designed to permit free flow of fluid through the valve in the off or neutral position, thus unloading the pump and directing fluid from the pump through both selector valves to the reservoir.

The selector valves on most open center systems are designed so that they will automatically return to the neutral position when the sub-system actuator(s) bottom out and pressure builds to a predetermined setting. (See open center selector valve in Figure 7.24).

The other difference between open and closed center systems is that in the open center system, only one sub-system can be operated at a time. The pilot must wait until the landing gear selector returns to neutral before there is fluid pressure available for the flap selector.

Systems Using a Variable Displacement Pump

The controlling feature of the variable displacement pump (Chapter 7, Figure 7.12) depends on system pressure to control the flow of fluid into the system. An example is the angle of rotation in the Vickers pump controlled by system pressure. Therefore, the variable displacement pump will be used on closed center systems where there is controlling pressure available at all times when the system is in operation.

Figure 9.7   Closed-center system (*variable*-displacement pump)
1. Reservoir
2. Engine driven pump
4. Filter
5. Hand Pump
6. Accumulator
6A. System pressure gage
7. Landing gear selector
8. Main gear actuators
9. Nose gear actuator
10. Flap selector
11. Flap actuator
12. Relief valve

Figure 9.7 illustrates a typical closed center system using a variable displacement pump. The main difference in system components is the pump itself, and an additional return line from the pump case drain to the reservoir to provide for the cooling and lubrication fluid flow. (See Figure 9.7)

The pressure, (flow control device) is inside the pump, which may be driven by the engine accessory section, an electric motor, or on some larger turbine powered aircraft, by an air driven motor. The air driven motor normally receives its power from the turbine engine bleed air system.

The following examples of different configurations of hydraulic systems represent an overview of these aircraft, and the information is not intended to be a complete detailed description of any of them.

Gates Lear Jet 25

The hydraulic system supplies fluid under pressure of 1500 psi to the brake, landing gear, flap and spoiler systems. The constant displacement engine driven pumps supply fluid through a filter and pressure regulator to the hydraulic system upon demand. An electrically operated auxiliary hydraulic pump, provided for ground operation and standby power, is cycled by a pressure switch connected to the fluid side of the accumulator. System pressure is maintained at 1250 to 1500 psi (kick-in and kick-out) by the pressure regulator. The system relief valve is set to crack at 1700 psi. The Lear 25 uses an air pressurized reservoir, incorporating an aspirator to provide the 10 psi reservoir air pressure. (See Figure 9.8 and Figure 6.5.)

Canadair Challenger

Three independent systems provide hydraulic power to operate the ailerons, elevators, rudder, flight and ground spoilers, wheel brakes, nose wheel steering and landing gear extension and retraction.

All systems operate at a working pressure of 3000 psi, and use synthetic hydraulic fluid SKYDROL 500B.

The three systems—designated as No. 1, No. 2 and No. 3—are continuously operating and supply power to their respective sub-systems. (See Figure 9.9)

No. 1 system derives primary power from an engine driven pump (1A PUMP) mounted on the left engine. Additional power is provided by an

Figure 9.8 Gates Lear Jet Model 25.

electric pump (1B PUMP).

No. 2 system is similar, except that the EDP 2A PUMP is mounted on the right engine, and the electric pump is designated as 2B PUMP.

No. 3 system derives power from a continuously operating electric pump (3A PUMP), with a second electric pump available for additional power (3B PUMP).

172

Figure 9.9 Hydraulic system schematic.

Cessna Citation

The hydraulic system is an open-center type system. Two engine driven constant displacement pumps (one on each engine) supply a continuous flow of hydraulic fluid as long as the engine(s) is operating. Hydraulic pressure is provided by closing (energizing) of the bypass (open center) valve upon demand during the operation of the landing gear, speed brake, and optional thrust reverser subsystems. A pressure relief valve permits pressure build up in a selected sub-system to its opening pressure of 1350 psi; it is fully open at 1500 psi. In a no demand condition, the bypass valve is open (de-energized) and fluid flows from pressure to return. It is possible in this design open center system to operate more than one sub-system simultaneously due to the selector valves installation, which is in parallel to the pressure manifold. (See Figure 9.10) The system reservoir is pressurized by fluid pressure tapped from the main system pressure manifold upstream of the system bypass valve.

SUPPLY

LOW PRESSURE (OPEN CENTER)

RETURN (OPEN CENTER)

AMBIENT

Figure 9.10 Cessna Citation.

Boeing 727 Hydraulic Systems

Hydraulic power is supplied by three independent systems; system 'A', system 'B' and the stand-by system.

System 'A' is pressurized by engine driven pumps mounted on engines one and two. System 'B' is pressurized by two electrically driven pumps. The stand-by system is pressurized by one electrically driven pump. Each system delivers 3000 psi.

System 'A' operates the trailing edge flaps, leading edge devices, outboard flight spoilers, ground spoilers, ailerons, elevators, lower rudder, landing gear, steering and nose brakes, and can be used as an alternate source of pressure to the main brakes through the brake interconnect.

System 'B' operates ailerons, elevators, inboard flight spoilers, upper rudder, aft stairs, main landing gear brakes and the cargo door. System 'B' can pressurize system 'A' on the ground before engine starting through the ground interconnect.

The stand-by system is powered from the essential AC bus and will supply pressure to operate the stand-by rudder actuator and to power the hydraulic motor-pump assembly which extends the leading edge devices when system 'A' pressure is lost. (See Figure 9.11)

The systems described here represent the installation in one particular model of the different airplanes. It should be emphasized that modifications are made from time to time and this information may not be current. The student is also reminded that maintenance and repair on any hydraulic system must be done in accordance with the aircraft manufacturer's instructions.

Hydraulic Power, DC-9 All Series

Hydraulic power is used for the operation of the elevator boost, rudder, flaps, slats, spoilers, ventral stairway, engine thrust reversers, landing gear, brakes, and nose wheel steering. It is provided by hydraulically separate right and left systems operating at a nominal pressure of 3000 psi, reduced to 1500 psi during cruise flight.

The main source of power for each system is an engine driven pump. Backup means of pressurizing both systems are provided by an electrically driven auxiliary pump.

Each system is provided with separate ground power pressure and suction connections for applying external hydraulic power and for filling the reservoirs. The external power can be provided by a hydraulic test stand having a variable displacement pump capable of delivering 9 U.S. gallons per minute at 3000 psi, using hydraulic fluid filtered to 15

HYDRAULIC POWER SYSTEM

Figure 9.11 Boeing Model 727.

microns absolute. The maximum operating temperature should not exceed 200 °F. There is also a ground service hand pump in each main gear wheel well that can be used to fill the reservoirs or provide pressure to actuate various systems for maintenance.

There are several configurations of pressure, suction, and reservoir fill connections to be found on DC-9 aircraft, although all DC-9s have an access door on each side of the aircraft just ahead of the main landing gear doors. (See Figure 9.12)

Approved fire resistant hydraulic fluids meet Douglas Material Specification (DMS) 2014C. Currently approved fluids are Monsanto Skydrol 500-B, LD, LD-4, and 500B-4, and Chevron Hyjet IV.

Ground Servicing of Hydraulic Systems

Servicing instruction for each hydraulic system is usually available at or near the system reservoir. The instruction plate will specify the type of fluid to be used, the capacity of the reservoir, and the procedure and conditions for servicing.

It is extremely important for the technician to service the reservoir with the proper type of fluid. Fluid servicing equipment and containers should be kept clean and free of dust, dirt, and lint.

A pressurized reservoir should be serviced with a hand pump type servicing device to permit the entry of new fluid while the reservoir remains under pressure. If this equipment is not available, the reservoir must be carefully depressurized before removing the cap to pour in fluid. Fluid containers should always be closed except when fluid is being used.

When inspection of the filters indicates that the fluid is contaminated, or the wrong type fluid is inadvertently used for servicing, the system should be flushed. If the improper fluid was circulated throughout the system, all the affected seals may have to be replaced. The flushing procedures, and changing of seals should be done according to the aircraft manufacturer's instructions.

Inspections

Hydraulic systems are inspected for evidence of external leakage, worn or damaged tubing or hoses, security of mounting of all units, proper safetying and other specified conditions as specified in the service manual.

Figure 9.12 Douglas DC-9—Hydraulic system schematic.

178

External leakage from stationary connections must be repaired. None is permitted. A small amount of leakage may be permitted at piston rods, rotating shafts, or other locations, which will be specified in the service manual.

Fluid lines cannot be nicked, dented, or otherwise damaged beyond the limits explained in Chapter 2.

Internal leakage beyond allowable limits must be repaired according to the manufacturer's instructions. One method for isolating internal leakage is to pressurize a component, then remove an opposite port line. Example, extend an actuating cylinder and remove the line to the retract port. Any leakage under pressure through the return port should be cause for further testing. The same technique can be used to isolate leakage through closed selector valves, relief valves, and one way check valves.

Lack of system pressure can be caused by several failures. A sheared pump shaft, a defective (open) relief valve, a pressure regulator stuck in the kicked-out position, a check valve installed backwards, or lack of fluid in the system.

If the system operates normally using a ground test stand, the system pump is normally replaced because the test stand eliminates all system components except the pump.

If the system fails to maintain pressure in the pressure manifold, the check valve in the pressure regulator, or the unloading valve itself may be leaking internally.

High system pressure could be caused by an improper adjustment of the pressure regulator. Spongy or jerky movement of an actuating unit is usually the result of air entrained with the fluid. This problem can normally be solved by several normal cycles of the actuating unit which will bleed the air back through the return manifold to the reservoir where it will be separated from the fluid.

If the fluid level inside the system reservoir falls below the pick-up point of the pump, the pump will force air into the system. This will cause the conditions just described and in addition may cause failure of the pump due to lack of a cooling flow of fluid. Pumping of air, which leads to cavitation of the pump may produce a banging or chattering noise in the hydraulic system.

A loud hammering noise in systems having an accumulator usually indicates an insufficient pre-load in the accumulator. This lack of compressible air will cause the pump to kick-in and kick-out as soon as the pump goes on or off the line. This kicking in and out without any air to compress and cushion the shock causes the heavy hammering.

Some systems do not use air gages on the air side of the accumulator. To determine the air pre-load, pump the hand pump slowly and watch the hydraulic pressure gage. It will not rise at first, but then it will suddenly jump up and, as you continue to pump, will rise slowly again. The pressure jump where the hydraulic gage first indicated a reading, was the point where the fluid pressure was opposed by the air pressure. This indication is the amount of air pre-load in the accumulator.

Another simple method for determining air pre-load is to pressurize the system with either the hand or engine driven pump. Then operate a slow moving sub-system, such as the flaps, with the pump off and observe the system pressure gage. The point where the gage reads hydraulic pressure, then suddenly falls to zero, will be the pre-load.

Troubleshooting procedures are similar in practically all applications. The aircraft mechanic uses the basic seven distinct steps to successful troubleshooting. They are as follows:

1. Conduct a visual inspection. This includes inspecting for external leaks, security of components, proper servicing, all lines and mechanical linkage.

2. Conduct an operational check. This check is normally accomplished with ground support equipment to determine the proper operation of each sub-system.

3. Classify the trouble. Malfunctions usually fall into four basic categories—hydraulic, pneumatic, mechanical, and/or electrical.

4. Isolate the trouble. This step calls for sound reasoning, a full and complete knowledge of hydraulic theory, as well as a complete understanding of the affected hydraulic system.

5. Locate the trouble. This step is used to eliminate unnecessary parts removal, thus saving money, valuable time, and manhours.

6. Correct the trouble. This step is accomplished after the trouble has definitely been located.

7. Conduct a final operational check. The affected system must be actuated a minimum of five times or until a thorough check has been made to determine that its operation and adjustments are satisfactory.

   Note: Always check the applicable maintenance manual for CAUTION, WARNING, and SAFETY notes concerning maintenance procedures.

10

PNEUMATIC SYSTEMS

Back-Up Pneumatic Systems

In the event of failure of the aircraft hydraulic system, there must be some provision for emergency extension of landing gear and the application of the brakes. A very effective and simple system to provide this is the back-up pneumatic system. (See Figure 10.1)

A steel storage bottle usually containing approximately 3000 psi of compressed air or nitrogen is installed with a shuttle valve in the line to separate the normal hydraulic system from the back-up system. The control valve vents the air side of the shuttle valve until the system is put into operation. In the event of a hydraulic system failure, (example: wing flap), the wing flap handle is put in the down position to provide a return for the hydraulic fluid from the retract side of the actuators, and the emergency control valve is opened (down position). This directs high-pressure air into the shuttle valve, shifting the shuttle valve, and extends the actuating cyclinder, lowering the flaps.

Full Pneumatic System

The pneumatic system supplies compressed air for various normal and emergency pneumatic actuating systems. The compressed air is stored in storage bottles until required for actuation of the system. These bottles are normally charged with compressed air from an external source on the ground and are kept full in flight with an air compressor.

The system as shown in Figure 10.2, a typical pneumatic power system, is powered by the hydraulic system. The air compressor hydraulic actuating system consists of a solenoid-operated selector valve, flow

Figure 10.1 Emergency pneumatic system.

regulator, hydraulic motor, and two check valves. When the solenoid is energized, this allows hydraulic pressure to operate the hydraulic motor. When solenoid is deenergized, the selector blocks fluid flow, stopping the motor. (See Figure 10.2)

The flow regulator prevents excessive speeds of the hydraulic motor, and overspeed of the compressor. The selector check valve prevents return system pressure from entering the selector valve. The case line check valve prevents return pressure entering and stalling the motor through the case.

The air compressor is a four-stage radial piston compressor which means that the air is compressed through four progressively smaller cylinders. Figure 10.3 illustrates a two-stage compressor. (See Figure 10.3) The air used for compression is supplied from the engine air system through the equipment air supply, and air filter, through the absolute air pressure regulator. The absolute pressure regulator is located in the compression inlet line and regulates the pressure of the air entering the compressor. This stabilizes the pressure of the air for the compressor.

Figure 10.2   Pneumatic power system.

The moisture separator is the regulator and relief valve for this pneumatic system. (See Figure 10.4) It removes up to 95 percent of the moisture from the air compressor discharge line. The automatically operated condensation dump valve purges the separator oil-moisture chamber by means of a blast of air (3000 psi) each time the compressor shuts down. (See Figure 10.4)

The pressure switch controls system pressure by sensing the pressure between the check valve and relief valve. It electrically energizes the air compressor solenoid-operated selector valve when system pressure reaches 3100 psi. (See Figure 10.5)

The relief valve protects the system against over-pressurization. It opens when the system pressure reaches 3750 psi and resets at 3250 psi. (See Figure 10.6)

Figure 10.3 Schematic of two-stage air compressor.

Figure 10.4 Moisture separator.

Figure 10.5 Pneumatic system check valve.

Figure 10.6 Pneumatic system relief valve.

A chemical dryer further reduces the moisture content of the air emerging from the moisture separator. (See Figure 10.7)

Figure 10.7 Chemical drier.

Figure 10.8 is a closed-center, high pressure pneumatic system used on the Fairchild F-27 airliner. (See Figure 10.8)

The two compressors are driven from the engine accessory drive as shown in Figure 10.9. (See Figure 10.9) Air is taken into the first stage through an airduct and compressed through four stages. The discharge air from the fourth stage is routed through an intercooler and a bleed valve to the unloading valve. The bleed valve is actuated by engine oil pressure, and in the event of oil pressure loss, will open and relieve the compressor of any load.

The unloading valve maintains system pressure between 2900 and 3300 psi. When the pressure rises to 3300 psi, a check valve traps it and dumps the output of the compressor overboard. When the pressure drops to 2900 psi (kick-in), the output is directed back into the system. Normal system pressure (kick-out) is maintained at 3300 psi.

A shuttle valve is used for ground charging of the system. When ground charging is complete and the engine is started, the shuttle valve slides over and the compressor provides airflow.

Moisture is removed from the air by a moisture separator which will effectively remove about 98 percent of the moisture as it flows into the system. After the moisture separator the air passes through a dessicant, (chemical dryer) which removes the last traces of moisture.

The air is filtered through a 10 micron sintered metal filter.

The system is equipped with a back pressure valve which is essentially a 1700 psi relief valve in the supply line of the right engine only. This valve does not open until the pressure from the compressor or ground charging system is above 1700 psi, thus assuring the most efficient operation of the moisture separator.

There are three air storage bottles in this system. A 750 cubic inch bottle for the main system, a 180 cubic inch bottle for emergency operation, and a third 180 cubic inch bottle for normal brakes. Figure 10.10 illustrates a typical air storage bottle. (See Figure 10.10) Both of the brake bottles are isolated by check valves so that the air in these bottles cannot be used for any other sub-system operation.

The majority of the sub-system operates with a pressure of 1000 psi, so a pressure-reducing valve is installed between the isolation valve and the supply manifold for operation of the landing gear (normal), passenger door, propeller brake, and nose wheel steering.

A manually-operated isolation valve allows a mechanic to close-off the air supply which allows for servicing of the system without draining the storage bottle.

An emergency system stores compressed air under the full system pressure of 3300 psi and is available to both the landing gear extension system and energency brake application.

While most airplanes built use hydraulic or electric power for heavy duty applications, there are some advantages in using compressed air over other systems. These are:

1. Air is universally available in an inexhaustible supply.

2. The components in a pneumatic system are simple and lightweight.

Figure 10.8 Full pneumatic system for a twin-engine turboprop airplane.

RELIEF AND
UNLOADING VALVE

COMPRESSOR-
AIR-DISCHARGE
FITTING

INTER COOLER

INTER-STAGE
PRESSURE-
RELIEF
VALVE

BLEED LINE

LINE BLEED
VALVE

OVERBOARD AIR FOR
LINE BLEED VALVE

INTER-STAGE PRESSURE-
RELIEF VALVE

AFTER COOLER AND
FOURTH-STAGE BLEED
VALVE—UNLOADER VALVE
INTERCONNECT LINE

PRESSURE SENSING

STAGE # 1
CYLINDER

MOUNTING FLANGE

STAGE # 1
PISTON

STAGE # 2
PISTON

STAGE # 2
CYLINDER

CAM ASSEMBLY

STAGE # 3
CYLINDER

CRANKSHAFT
BEARING

CRANKSHAFT

STAGE # 4
CYLINDER

Figure 10.9   Four-stage pneumatic compressor.

Control valve

Charging
valve

Figure 10.10   Steel cylinder for high-pressure air storage.

3. Pneumatic systems are lighter, since no return system is required; as air is used to perform work it is dumped overboard.

4. The system is relatively free of temperature problems.

5. There is no fire hazard. However, the systems are not without their disadvantages. The biggest problem is the lack of lubrication for components. While compressed air is an excellent medium (fluid) for power systems, it does not provide any form of internal lubrication.

11

LANDING GEAR STRUCTURES AND RETRACTION SYSTEMS

General

Every aircraft is equipped with a landing gear system. The landing gear is that portion of the aircraft which supports the weight of the aircraft while it is on the ground. It contains components which are necessary for taking off and landing the aircraft safely, such as landing gear struts which absorb landing and taxiing shocks, brakes which are used to stop and in some cases steer the aircraft, nosewheel steering for steering the aircraft and shimmy dampers which absorb vibrations, and aircraft wheels, tires and tubes. All of these components will be discussed in this section of the Aircraft Hydraulic Systems text.

Landing Gear Arrangement

The landing gear of a fixed-wing aircraft consists of main and auxiliary units, either of which may or may not be retractable. The main landing gear forms the principal support of the aircraft. The auxiliary landing gear consists of tail or nose wheel installations.

Many aircraft are equipped with a tricycle gear arrangement, (Figure 11.1). This is almost universally true of large aircraft, the few exceptions being older model aircraft. This older arrangement is usually referred to as a conventional arrangement rather than the more popular tricycle arrangement.

Components parts of the tricycle gear arrangements are the nose gear and the main gear. Nose gear equipped aircraft are protected at the fuselage tail section with a tail skid or bumper. There are several advantages to the nose gear arrangement, they are: (1) it allows more forceful application of the brakes at higher speeds without nosing over; (2) it provides better visibility for the pilot during taxiing; and, (3) forces acting on the c.g. (center of gravity) tends to prevent aircraft ground looping.

The conventional landing gear is becoming rare and many pilots have never flown an airplane with this arrangement of the wheels, (figure

Figure 11.1 An aircraft with a tricycle landing gear

Figure 11.2 An airplane having a tailweel-type landing gear.   This   configuration   is   often   called   a "conventional" landing gear.

11.2). The main problem with the tail wheel type of landing gear is it's tendency to cause the airplane to ground-loop. The pilot must be careful to keep the airplane rolling straight. Steering on the ground is done by moving the tail through rudder pedal connections or by the differential use of the brakes. The tail wheel is uaually locked in line with the fuselage for take-off.

On other arrangement of the landing gear is the tandem landing gear, however, it is seldom used on civilian aircraft, but some heavy bombers do use it. The main wheels are located in line under the fuselage and the wings are supported by outrigger wheels.

All aircraft must contend with one type of aerodynamic drag; that produced by the friction of the airflow over the structure called parasite drag. Parasite drag increases as speed increases, slower aircraft loose little efficiency by using the lighter weight fixed landing gear, but faster aircraft retract the landing gear into the structures and thus gain efficiency even at the cost of slightly more weight. By retracting the landing gear into the structure the parasite drag is greatly reduced.

Some fixed landing gear may have its parasite drag decreased markedly by enclosing the wheels in streamlined fairings, called wheel pants, (Figure 11.3).

Figure 11.3 Streamlined wheel fairings called "wheel pants" are used to decrease the wind resistance of a fixed landing gear.

Retractable Gear

Some small aircraft use a single mechanical retraction mechanism incorporating a roller chain and sprockets operated by a handcrank. One other older mechanical method uses a simple hand operated lever, sometimes called a Johnson Bar, named for it's designer, to raise and lower the landing gear. Many aircraft use an electrical system consisting of electric motors and mechanical linkage while some European-built aircraft use a pneumatic system.

The simplest hydraulic landing gear system uses a hydraulic power pack (see figure 5.15, 5.14, 9.4, 9.5). Referring to these figures, to raise the landing gear, the gear selector is positioned to the GEAR UP position. This starts the hydraulic pump, forcing fluid into the gear-up side of the three gear actuating cylinders, raising the gear. The initial movement of the pistons unlocks the gear down locks so the gear can retract. When all three wheels are completely retracted, the up limit switch stops the pump operation. The landing gear is held in the up position by trapped hydraulic fluid in the up lines. The pressure switch stops the pump at a predetermined pressure (approximately 1500-1800 psi), but if the pressure drops enough to allow any one of the wheels to drop away from the up-limit switch, the pressure drop in the switch will once again turn the pump on and restore the pressure back up to cut-out. The check valve in the gear up line at the outlet of the pump will then close and trap fluid throughout the gear up side of the system. Should pressure build to an undesirable value in the up line (about 2200 psi), the relief valve will open preventing excessive line pressure.

To lower the landing gear, the selector switch is placed in the GEAR DOWN position, which reverses the direction of rotation of the motor-pump assembly, this also releases the pressure on the gear up side of the cylinders. The shuttle valve moves over and fluid flows through the power pack, allowing the gear to free-fall and lock down. The pump continues to build up pressure until all gears are down and locked. When all down lock switches are actuated in the down and lock position, power to the reversible motor is removed and the pump stops.

To provide for lowering the landing gear in case of power failure, either hydraulic or electric, the pack system incorporates a free-fall valve which connects the hydraulic gear up line to the hydraulic gear down line. This allows the fluid to be dumped from one side of the actuating cylinders to the other. The landing gear free-falls to the down position, over center springs will pull the down lock in place.

Figure 11.4

The free-all valve is a simple two port valve normally closed to fluid flow between port A and port B. When the pilot desires emergency extension of the landing gear, he simply pulls the cable operated handle and the valve opens permitting a free flow of fluid from port A and port B, which allows transfer of fluid from the gear actuating cylinders up lines to the gear down side.

Another electrical landing gear system using a reversible electrical motor and no hydraulic components is also used on some light aircraft.

Manual control
torque tube

Manual control
gearbox

Gearbox

Retracting
mechanism

Universal joints

Landing
gear motor

Drag strut

Trunnion
support

Shock strut

Drag strut

Figure 11.5 Electrical retraction system

Such a system, as shown in figure 11.4 has the following features: (1) a motor for converting electrical energy into rotary motion, (2) a gear reduction system for decreasing the speed and increasing the force of rotation, (3) other gears for changing rotary motion (at a reduced speed) into push-pull movements, (4) linkage for connecting the push-pull movement to the landing gear shock struts.

Basically, the system is an electrically driven jack for railing or lowering the gear. When a switch in the cockpit is moved to the "UP" position, the electric motor operates. Through a system of shafts, gears, adapters, and actuator screw, and a torque tube, a force is transmitted to the drag strut linkage. Thus, the gear retracts and locks. If the switch is moved to the "DOWN" position, the motor reverses and the gear moves down and locks. The sequence of operation of door and gears is similar to that of a hydraulically operated landing gear system. Some installations use mechanical sequencing of doors and gear in some cases the doors are attached directly to the landing gear strut. A hand crank mechanism is provided for emergency extension should the electrical system fail. (See Figure 11.5).

Some aircraft use an open center hydraulic system rather than the pack type system. Figure 9.6 illustrates an open center system that powers the landing gear retracting system as well as hydraulically operated trailing-edge flaps. This system employs an engine driven pump which operated continuously and the fluid flow to the landing gear is controlled by the landing gear selector valve. When the landing gear is up and locked the selector valve senses system pressure build-up and will automatically return to the neutral or open center position, (see Figure 7.24). As the landing selector valve goes to the neutral position, fluid flow goes through the valve to the flap selector while the lines to the gear actuators (port B-D figure 7.24) remain closed trapping fluid in the up side of the retracting system. This sequence of events takes place on landing gear extension, trapping fluid in the down lines. The system pressure reduces to "0" while the selector valve is in neutral.

Closed center hydraulic systems on both large and small aircraft, are very popular and while the aircraft vary greatly in size and complexity, the landing gear components in themselves, are very similar. The primary difference would be in the overall size of the components, the operating pressure range, and the volume of fluid which must be used. One typical small and one typical large aircraft closed center system will be discussed here to represent most aircraft. The small aircraft landing gear system illustrated is that of the Lear 25. See figure 11.6 and 11.7. The normal landing gear is retracted or extended by operating the landing gear selector switch. Setting the switch to "gear up" initiates a sequence of all three gear systems. The inboard main doors are opened, the gear is retracted, and the doors are then closed. The nose gear doors are attached by linkage to the nose gear and close when the gear retracts. Setting the switch to "gear down" reverses the sequence.

In the event of main hydraulic system failure, landing gear selector system malfunction, or electrical system failure, the gear can be extended pneumatically. Emergency extension is initiated by depressing the "energency gear extension" handle (with the normal landing gear selector switch in "gear down" to avoid subsequent accidental retraction of the gear) located on the left side of the center pedestal. Air under pressure is then directed from the emergency air bottle through lines and shuttle valve to: (1) the nose gear uplatch actuator, (2) the down side of the nose gear actuator, (3) the main gear inboard door uplatch actuators, (4) the down side of the main gear inboard door actuators, (5) the down side of the main gear actuators, (see Figure 11.8).

The McDonnell Douglas DC-9 and MD-80 landing gear systems described in limited detail here represents a typical system used on a large jet liner. However, because of the complexity of these systems no attempt will be made to describe these systems in great detail.

The landing gear extension and retraction system is composed of two major systems designated as the mechanical control and the hydraulic control system. (Figure 11.9).

The mechanical control system is divided into four sections. These are: (1) the landing gear control valve cable system, (2) the main gear inboard door sequence follow up valve system, (3) the alternate, or bypass, valve system, and (4) the sub system.

The landing gear control valve cable system is a dual cable system that runs from the landing gear control lever, cable drum in the flight compartment to the landing gear control valve for normal operation.

The main gear door sequence valve follow-up system is made up of

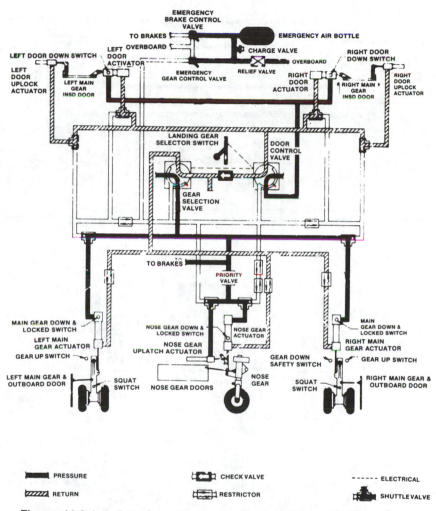

Figure 11.6 Landing Gear Hydraulic System Schematic-Gear Down Cycle

two push pull cables to open and close the main inboard doors. The alternate/bypass valve is used as a back up system to free-fall the gear in case of hydraulic failure. It is also used on the ground to manually open the doors for ground maintenance.

When the landing gear control lever is placed in the "up" position, the cable system positions the control valve to port fluid to the retract side of the main and nose gear cylinders. The cable system unlocks the main door latch and the gear retracts. After the gear retracts the follow-up system closes the main gear doors.

Figure 11.7 Landing Gear Hydraulic System Schematic-Gear Up Cycle

To extend the gear the sequence of events is reversed. In the event of hydraulic power failure the gear can be extended by free-fall. When the alternate landing gear extension lever is pulled up a cable releases the nose gear uplock, the main gear door is unlocked and the by-pass valves open to return. The gear will then free-fall and the lock in the down position. The spring in the bungee cylinders assure the locked condition in the down position.

GEAR DOWN OPERATION SEQUENCE - EMERGENCY AIR

1. Emergency Gear Control Valve to down position.

Note

Air pressure moves all system shuttle valves to positions shown.

2. Emergency air pressure moves door control valve and gear selector valve to down position.
3. Door uplock actuators release and main gear inboard doors open.
4. Nose gear uplatch actuator releases and gear extends. Inboard doors will remain open.

Figure 11.8 Landing Gear Emergency Air System Schematic

In some aircraft, design configurations make emergency extension of the landing gear by gravity and airloads alone impossible or impractical. In such aircraft, provisions are included for forceful gear extension in an emergency. Some installations are designed so that either hydraulic fluid, or compressed air, provides the necessary pressure, while others use a manual system for extending the landing gears under emergency conditions.

Figure 11.9 Mechanical and Hydraulic Control Systems

Hydraulic pressure for emergency operation of the landing gear may be provided by an auxiliary hand pump, and accumulator, or an electrically powered hydraulic pump, depending upon the design of the aircraft.

Accidental retraction may be prevented by such safety devices as mechanical downlocks, safety switches and ground locks.

Figure 11.10 Main Landing Gear for a Light Twin Airplane

1.	Support fitting, aft	16.	Actuating cylinder
2.	Bearing	17.	Support bracket
3.	Retainer, tube assembly	18.	Upper side brace link
4.	Hinge, gear door	19.	Downlock hook
5.	Upper torque link	20.	Downlock pin
6.	Space washer	21.	Lower side brace link
7.	Lower torque link		
8.	Gear door	22.	Safety switch (squat switch)
9.	Nut	23.	Safety switch actuator
10.	Strut housing		
11.	Hydraulic fluid plug	24.	Gear door rod
12.	Air valve assembly	25.	Gear fork
13.	Forward support fitting	26.	Brake hose
14.	Downlock spring	27.	Brake housing
15.	Retraction fitting	28.	Brake disk

Gear Structural Supports, Alignment

The main landing gear consist of several components that enable it to function; typical of these are the torque links, trunnion and bracket arrangements, drag strut linkage, electrical and hydraulic gear retraction devices, and gear indicators. (Figure 11.10).

Alignment

Torque links (figure 11.11) keep the landing gear pointed in a straight ahead direction; one torque link connects to the shock strut cylinder, while the other connects to the piston. The links are hinged at the center so that the piston can move up or down in the strut. (Figure 11.12).

Figure 11.11 Torque Links

Figure 11.12 The torque links limit the extension of the oleo strut and keep the wheel in alignment.

Figure 11.13 Trunnion and Bracket Arrangement

Support

To anchor the main gear to the aircraft structure, a trunnion and bracket arrangement (figure 11.13) is usually employed. This arrangement is constructed to enable the strut to pivot or swing forward or backward as necessary when the aircraft is being steered or the gear is being retracted. To restrain this action during ground movement of the aircraft, various types of linkages are used, one being the drag strut. The upper end of the drag strut (figure 11.14) connects to the shock strut. The drag strut is hinged so that the landing gear can be retracted. This drag strut may also contain an over-center linkage arrangement which acts as a mechanical down lock.

Some designs of main gear shock struts employ a side brace arrangement to help support the main strut assembly in the down and lock position. (Figure 11.15).

In addition to providing support for the strut assembly, the side brace often contains the main gear down lock over-center linkage to provide positive, mechanical, down lock action. The side brace upper end is

Trunnion bearing surface

Drag strut

Retracting mechanism

Figure 11.14 Drag Strut Linkage.

usually attached to the aircraft wing or main fuselage structure while the lower end is attached to the upper outer cylinder. The brace is hinged in the middle to provide for a retracting mechanism, and the main gear retracting cylinder may be attached directly to the side brace as indicated in figure 11.16. The mechanical down lock, sometimes called a link, jury strut, or a bungee, operates the over-center mechanism. A spring in the over-center mechanism holds the linkage in the locked position. When the landing gear is retracted, the drag or side brace over-center mechanism is sequenced to unlock first enabling the brace to hinge and permit the gear to retract.

Landing gear up locks may sometimes be incorporated into the drag or side brace to provide a mechanical gear up lock device. Some gears are held in the up position by trapped hydraulic fluid (see figure 9.4) while others use a hydraulically operated seperate up latch mechanism sequenced on gear retraction. (See figure 11.17). The use of main gear door up locks to hold the main gear up is employed in the DC-9 system. (See figure 11.18).

Sequencing

A typical hydraulic sequencing system is shown in a schematic detail in figure 11.9. First, consider what happens when the landing gear is retracted. As the selector valve is moved to the UP position, pressurized fluid is directed into the gear up line. The fluid flows to each of eight

Up and locked

Inboard

In transit

Downlock
bungee

Gear actuator

Jury strut
(upper and lower)

Upper
side
strut

Downlock actuator

Lower
side strut

Drag brace
(ommitted
for clarity)

Down and locked

Figure 11.15 Wing Landing Gear Operating Sequence

units: to sequence valves C and D, to the three gear down locks, to the
nose gear cylinder, and to the two main actuating cylinders.

Notice what happens to the fluid flowing to sequence valves C and D
in figure 11.19. Since the sequence valves are closed, pressurized fluid
cannot flow to the door cylinders at this time, plus, the doors cannot
close. But the fluid entering the three down lock cylinders is not
delayed; therefore, the gear is unlocked. At the same time, fluid also

UPPER OVER
CENTER LINK

LOWER OVER
CENTER LINK

UPPER-SIDE
BRACE LINK

LOWER-SIDE
BRACE LINK

DOOR-SEQUENCE
DRIVE ARM

BUNGEE CYLINDER

OUTBOARD-DOOR
ACUATING ROD

BUNGEE
SPRINGS

BUNGEE-
SPRING
BRACKET

BRAKE
HOSES

TORQUE
LINKS

Figure 11.16 Main Landing Gear for a DC-9 Airplane

enters the up side of each gear-actuating cylinder and the gear begins to
retract. The nose gear completes retraction and engages it's uplock first,
because of the small size of its actuating cylinder. Also, since the nose
gear door is operated soley by linkage from the nose gear, this door
closes. Meanwhile, the main landing gear is still retracting, forcing fluid
to leave the downside of each main gear cylinder. This fluid flows
unrestricted through an orifice check valve, opens the sequence check
valve A or B, and flows through the landing gear selector valve into the
hydraulic system return line. Then, as the main gear reached the fully
retracted position and engages the spring-loaded uplocks, gear linkage
strikes the plungers of sequence valve C and D. This opens the sequence
check and allows pressurized fluid to flow into the door cylinders,
closing the doors.

(A) Latch roller clearance

(B) Latch roller support adjustment

Figure 11.17 Landing Gear Door Latch Installation

Figure 11.18 Main-Gear Doors

Figure 11.19 Hydraulic Landing Gear Retraction System Schematic

ACTUATOR BEARING
ATTACHED TO STRUCTURE

UPPER
SIDE-STRUT   CAM
ACTUATOR WALKING BEAM   STRUCTURAL
UP GEAR PORT   BEARING
BEAM
GEAR ACTUATOR   SUPPORT   SIDE-
LINK   STRUT
DOWN GEAR PORT   ACTUATOR
SIDE-STRUT
UPPER
TRUNNION   SEGMENT
BEARING
(STRUCTURE)   TRUNNION   HOOK
BEARING   ASSEMBLY
(STRUCTURE)
DOOR   DOWN-LOCK
TRUNNION   OPERATOR   ROLLER
CRANK

DRAG STRUT   SIDE-STRUT
LOWER SEGMENT
SHOCK STRUT
TORSION LINKS

FWD   INBD

UP LOCK
ROLLER
SNUBBER AND LEVELING CYLINDER
BRAKE EQUALIZING RODS

TRUCK

STATIC GROUND WIRE
TIRE AND WHEEL
ASSEMBLY
BRAKE COLLAR
JACKING POINT   BRAKE ASSEMBLY
(UNDER AXLES)   TOW LUG

Figure 11.20 Main Landing-Gear Components

Wing Gear Operation

A typical wing landing gear operating sequence is illustrated in figure
11.20. The gear retracts or extends when hydraulic pressure is applied
to the up or down side of the gear actuator. The gear actuator applies
the force required to raise and lower the gear. The actuator works in
conjunction with a walking beam to apply force to the gear shock strut,
swinging it inboard and forward into the wheel well. Both the actuator
and the walking beam are connected to lugs on the gear trunnion. The
outboard ends of the actuator and walking beam pivot on a beam
hanger which is attached to the aircraft structure. A wing gear locking
mechanism located on the outboard side of the wheel well locks the gear
in the "up" position. Locking of the gear in the "down" position is
accomplished by a downlock bungee which positions an upper and
lower jury strut so that the upper and lower side struts will not fold.

Figure 11.21 Typical Landing Gear Safety Circuit

Limit Switches

A landing gear safety switch (Figure 11.21) in the landing gear safety circuit is usually mounted in a bracket on one of the main gear shock struts. This switch is actuated by a linkage through the landing gear torque links. When the weight of the aircraft is on the strut (on the ground) the torque links are closed together, causing the adjusting links to open the safety switch. During take-off, as the weight of the aircraft leaves the struts, the struts and torque links extend, causing the safety switch to close, a ground is completed when the safety switch closes. The solenoid then energizes and unlocks the selector valve so the gear handle can be positioned to raise the gear. This switch is sometimes called a squat switch or on some newer installations a 'WOW' switch (weight on wheels).

Gear Indicators

To provide a visual indication of landing gear position, indicators are installed in the cockpit or flight compartment.

Gear warning devices are incorporated on all retractable gear aircraft and usually consist of a horn or some aural device and a red warning light. The horn blows and the light comes on when one or more throttles are retarded and the landing gear is not down and locked.

Several designs of gear position indicators are available. One type displays moveable miniature landing gears which are electrically positioned by movement of the aircraft gear. Another type consists of two or three green lights which illuminate when the landing gear is down and locked. A third type (figure 11.22) consists of tab-type indicators with markings "up" to indicate that the gear is up and locked, a display of red and white diagonal stripes (barber-pole) to show when the gear is unlocked, or a silhouette of each gear to indicate when it locks in the "down" position.

(A) Landing Gear "Up and Locked"

(B) Gear unlocked and in an intermediate position

(C) Landing gear "Down and Locked"

Figure 11.22 A Typical Gear Position Indicator and Warning Light.

Safety Systems

In addition to the electrical safety mentioned previously, most aircraft with retractable landing gear provide a mechanical device to prevent collapse of the gear when the aircraft is on the ground. These devices are called ground locks. One common type is a pin installed in aligned holes drilled in two or more units of the landing gear support structure. Another type is a spring loaded clip designed to fit around and hold two or more units of the support structure together. All types of ground locks usually have red streamers permanently attached to them to readily indicate whether or not they are installed.

Most landing gear selector valves, whether they are operating a hydraulic, electric, pneumatic or mechanical retracting mechanism, shape the selector handle in the shape of a wheel. This shape aids the flight crew in easy identification in a dimly lighted cockpit. In addition to its "wheel shape" the selector handle is normally designed to throw to the position the gear will be traveling, that is, up for gear retraction, and down for gear extension. Several types are designed with neutral or mid-stroke position for cruise. The selectors are normally designed with a positive movement for selector position changes, often detented mechanically to help prevent inadvertant movement.

Maintenance of Retracting Systems

Landing gear hydraulic system maintenance is similar to the other types of hydraulic systems. It is inspected for internal and external leakage as well as proper operation during routine scheduled inspections (see Inspections, Chapter 9). While performing operational checks, the technician must inspect the complete landing gear installation for adjustments, clearances and sequence of operation. In all cases and for all inspections consult the manufacturers service manual for proper operation, clearances, sequencing of systems and for possible allowable leakage rates. A good detailed visual inspection before and after a retraction test should reveal any malfunctions. With the aircraft properly jacked and auxiliary power (hydraulic and electric) applied, operate the landing gear through several normal retraction sequences, as recommended by the manufacturer's service manual, check all normal systems and components for operation, fit, adjustment and proper operation. Operate the alternate gear extension system one time and assure proper operation. Lubricate all components as required by the service manual and repair any malfunctions before returning the aircraft to service. Use the troubleshooting procedures outlined at the end of Chapter 9 to isolate and correct all malfunctions.

12

SHOCK STRUTS
STEERING - SHIMMY DAMPERS

General

Most aircraft have some provision for absorbing the landing impact and the shocks of taxiing over rough ground. Some aircraft, however, do not actually absorb these shocks but rather accept the energy in some form of elastic medium and return it at a rate and time that the aircraft can accept. The most popular form of landing gear that does this is the spring steel gear used on most of the single-engine aircraft. These airplanes use either a flat steel leaf or a tubular spring steel strut that accepts the loads and returns it in such a way that it does not cause the aircraft to rebound.

Some of the older aircraft used rubber to cushion the shock. This may be in the form or rubber doughnuts (rings) or as a bungee cord, which is a bundle of small strands of rubber encased in a loosely woven cloth tube. (Figure 12.1).

Figure 12.1 Rubber bungee cords enclosed in the fabric housings in this landing gear accept both landing impact and taxi shocks.

213

By far the most widely used shock asorber for aircraft is the air-oil shock strut, more commonly known as the oleo strut.

Since there are many different designs of oleo shock struts, only information of a general nature is included in this section. For specific information about a particular installation, consult the applicable manufacturer's instructions.

Air-Oil Struts

A typical oleo (pneumatic/hydraulic) shock strut (figure 12.2) uses compressed air combined with hydraulic fluid to absorb and dissipate shock loads.

The shock strut is made up essentially of two telescoping cylinders or tubes with externally closed ends. The two cylinders, known as cylinder and piston, when assembled, form an upper and lower chamber for movement of the fluid. The lower chamber is always filled with fluid, while the upper chamber contains compressed air. An orifice is placed between the two chambers and provies a passage for the fluid into the upper chamber during compression and return during extension of the strut.

To be more specific as to the type of fluid and air used in an oleo strut, most installations use Mil-H-5606 petroleum based fluid. Some manufacturer's recommend servicing with the Mil-H-6083 preservative fluid and most manufacturer's prefer dry nitrogen (N^2) over compressed air due to the low moisture content of N^2 which helps reduce internal corrosion.

Most shock struts employ a metering pin similar to that shown in figure 12.3 for controlling the rate of fluid flow from the lower chamber into the upper chamber. During the compression stroke, the rate of fluid flow is not constant, but is controlled automatically by the variable shape of the metering pin as it passes through the orifice.

On some types of shock struts, a metering tube replaces the metering pin, but shock strut operation is the same (figure 12.4).

Some shock struts are equipped with a damping or snubbing device consisting of a recoil valve on the piston or recoil tube to reduce the rebound during the extension stroke and to prevent too rapid extension of the shock strut. This could result in a sharp impact at the end of the stroke and possibly damage the landing gear.

Suitable connections are provided on all shock struts to permit attachment to the aircraft. A common name for these connections is the trunnion and bracket discussed earlier. Wheel axle attachments are provided on the lower cylinder for installations of the wheels and brakes on the main struts.

A fitting consisting of a fluid filler inlet and air valve assembly is located near the upper end of each shock strut to provide a means of filling the strut with hydraulic fluid and inflating it with air. The air filler valve used is identical to those used in servicing hydraulic accumulators (see figure 8.12).

A packing gland designed to seal the sliding joint between the upper and lower telescoping cylinders is installed in the open end of the outer cylinder. A packing gland wiper ring is also installed in a groove in the lower bearing or gland nut on most shock struts to keep the sliding

Compression stroke

Extension stroke

Air

Hydraulic fluid

Figure 12.2 Shock Strut Operation

Figure 12.3 Landing Gear
Shock Strut of the Metering
Pin Type

Figure 12.4 Landing Gear
Shock Strut of the Metering
Tube Type

surface of the piston or inner cylinder free from dirt, mud, ice and snow. Entry of foreign matter into the packing seals would result in leaks. (Figure 12.5).

The majority of shock struts are equipped with torque links (arms) attached to the upper and lower cylinders to maintain correct alignment of the wheel. Some nose gear shock struts are provided with an upper locating (centering) cam attached to the upper cylinder and a mating lower locating cam attached to the lower cylinder (figure 12.6). These cams line up the wheel and axle assembly in the straight ahead position when the shock strut is fully extended. This prevents the nose wheel from being cocked to one side when it is retracted, thus preventing possible structural damage. The cams also keep the nose wheel straight ahead prior to landing.

Generally, nose gear struts are equipped with a locking (or disconnect) pin to enable quick turning of the aircraft when it is standing idle on the ground or in the hangar. Disengagement of this pin will allow the wheel fork spindle to rotate 360°, thus enabling the aircraft to be turned in a very small space, such as a hangar. On some installations this device is provided by a removable center pin in the torque arms.

Figure 12.2 shows the inner construction of a shock strut and illustrates the movement of the fluid during compression and extension.

When the compression begins the inner piston moves into the outer cylinder. The metering pin is forced through the orifice and, by its variable shape, controls the rate of fluid flow at all points of the compression stroke. In this manner the greatest possible amount of

Figure 12.5 Cutaway Drawing of Main Landing-Gear Shock Strut

heat is dissipated through the walls or the strut. At the end of the downward stroke, the compressed air is further compressed, limiting the compression stroke of the strut.

The extension stroke occurs as the aircraft weight starts moving upward in relation to the ground and wheels. At this instant, the compressed air acts as a spring to return the strut to normal (extended position). It is at this point that a snubbing or damping effect is produced by forcing the fluid to return through the restriction of the snubbing device. This action prevents rebounding and possible damage. A sleeve, spacer or bumper ring incorporated in some strut limits the extension stroke. The torque links will limit the full extension of the inner piston when the strut is fully extended.

For efficient operation of shock struts, the proper fluid level and air pressure must be maintained. If there is an insufficient amount of fluid in the strut it will "bottom out" on landing due to the lesser amount of fluid flowing thru the orifice. If the air (N^2) charge is insufficient the strut will also bottom out, but this problem will occur during taxiing as

Figure 12.6a
Cutaway View of a Nose
Figure 12.6 Nose Gear Shock Strut   Gear Internal Centering Cam

well as landing. To check the fluid level, the shock strut must be deflated and in the fully compressed position. The fluid level is normally to the bottom of the air value port when it is removed on a properly serviced strut.

CAUTION: Deflating a shock strut can be a dangerous operation, observe all necessary safety precautions. Refer to the manufacturers instructions for proper deflating techniques.

Servicing Shock Struts

The following procedures are typical of those used in deflating a shock strut, servicing with hydraulic fluid, and re-inflating:
1. Shock strut in normal ground position.
2. Remove cap from air valve.
3. Slowly release air pressure.
4. Remove valve core. (Except MS 28889-1 valve).
5. Ensure strut is compressed.
6. Remove air valve.
7. Fill with approved fluid to air valve level.
8. Reinstall air valve, torque as specified.
9. Install air valve core.

Figure 12.7 Servicing a landing gear strut

10. Inflate strut with nitrogen or compressed air. According to manufacturers instructions in the service manual or the strut servicing instruction plate attached to the strut.

11. Tighten the swivel hex nut to proper torque. (Except AN 812).

12. Replace the valve air cap.

13. Check for leaks, both hydraulic fluid and air.

Bleeding Shock Struts

If the fluid level of a shock has become extremely low, if the strut packing seals have been replaced, or if for any other reason air is

Figure 12.8 Instruction plates for a landing gear

trapped in the strut cylinder, it may be necessary to bleed the strut during servicing operations. Bleeding is usually performed with the aircraft on jacks. In this position the shock strut can be extended and compressed (exercised) during the filling operation, thus expelling all the entrapped air. The following is a typical bleeding procedure: (See figure 12.7).

1. Construct a suitable hose from the filler opening to the strut base.
2. Jack aircraft until all struts are fully extended.
3. With air valve removed, fill strut to level of air valve.
4. Install hose, put free end in container.
5. Place exerciser jack at jacking point.
6. Compress strut slowly, allow it to extend by it's own weight until all air is expelled. Repeat as often as required.
7. Remove exerciser jack, bleeder hose and install air valve.
8. Service with air in accordance with manufacturers instruction.

Air-oleo struts always have an instruction plate or decal permanently attached to the outside of the strut or nearby. This plate (decal) specifies the type of hydraulic fluid to be used in the strut and gives instructions for inflation, deflation, and filling with fluid. Typical instruction plates are shown in figure 12.8.

Wheel Alignment

It is important to keep the wheels properly aligned to minimize tire wear. The aircraft service manual normally specifies the amount of toe-in and the amount of camber the landing gear should have, and in the case of the spring steel landing gear used on light single-engine aircraft, this is specified at a particular weight.

The terms toe-in, toe-out, and camber refer to the alignment of the wheel in reference to the aircraft fuselage. Toe-in, for example, means that if a line were to be drawn following the wheel position, at a point

POSITIVE CAMBER

NEGATIVE CAMBER

INBOARD ▶

CAMBER IS A MEASURE OF THE AMOUNT THE WHEEL
IS TILTED. IF THE WHEEL TILTS OUTWARDS, IT HAS
POSITIVE CAMBER.

Figure 12.9

STRAIGHTEDGE BETWEEN
WHEELS

FORWARD

SQUARE

TOE-IN OR TOE-OUT IS THE AMOUNT THE WHEELS
DEVIATE FROM A STRAIGHT-AHEAD CONDITION.
IF THE WHEELS TRY TO MOVE TOGETHER, THEY
ARE TOED IN.

Figure 12.10
Conditions
of wheel alignment

ahead of the nose of the aircraft this line would meet. Toe-out would
cause this line to meet, or cross, aft of the fuselage.

Camber is a measure of the amount the wheel leans, as viewed from
straight ahead. If the top of the wheel leans outward, the camber is
positive, but if it leans inward, the camber is negative. Camber on a
spring-steel type landing gear is affected by the weight of the aircraft
and should be adjusted to give zero-degree camber at the normal
aircraft operating weight. (See figure 12.9).

In order to measure toe-in, toe-out, hold a carpenter's square against
a straight edge placed across the front of the main wheels-measure the
distance between the blade of this carpenter's square and the front and
rear flange of the wheel. Toe-in, toe-out is adjusted on spring steel
landing gear by placing shims between the axle and the gear leg. (See
figure 12.10). On landing gear using an oleo type strut, toe-in, toe-out is
adjusted by adding or removing washers from between the torque link
center pivot point, (figure 12.11).

A spring steel landing gear moves as the weight is placed on the gear,
this makes an alignment check difficult unless special procedures are

OLEO STRUT CYLINDER

OLEO STRUT PISTON

TORQUE
LINKS

PLACE WASHERS
HERE FOR ADJUSTING
TOE-IN OR TOE-OUT

SHIM

*Toe-in or toe-out may be adjusted by
repositioning the washers between the torque
links of a landing gear oleo strut.*

*Toe-in or toe-out on a spring steel
landing gear is adjusted by using tapered shims
between the landing gear leg and the wheel axle.*

Figure 12.11

GREASE

Figure 12.12

used. The recommended procedure is to roll each wheel onto a pair of aluminum plates with grease between them. If you rock the aircraft back and forth a bit the greased plates will allow the wheels to assume their true position of alignment. (See figure 12.12).

Nose Wheel Steering-Shimmy Dampers

Almost all airplanes with tricycle landing gear have some provisions for steering on the ground by turning the nose gear. Some of the smaller airplanes have a castering nose gear and steering is done by the independent use of differential braking. Other small airplanes use cables, push-pull tubes connected to the rudder pedals, some directly, others that are steerable up through a specified angle, after which the steering disconnects and the gear is free to caster up to the limit of it's travel.

Some steering mechanisms are engaged - disengaged as the nose gear retracts and extends on the retractable type gear. One method used is illustrated in figure 12.13. The steering bellcrank is connected to the steering rods and through the rod to the the rudder pedals. When the gear is extended, the steering bellcrank engages the steering arm which is attached to the upper part of the strut. Moving the steering arm will turn the nose wheel strut and the nose wheel for steering. As the nose gear retracts the steering bellcrank disengages from the bushing on the steering arm and steering action is disengaged. The strut roller and bracket alignment guide (item 12 and 14 figure 12.13) centers the strut for retraction.

Shimmy Dampers

The torque links hold the nose wheel in alignment and must be kept in such a condition that there is a minimum of side play or end play in the

1.	Rod, steering	24.	Tire
2.	Jam nut	25.	Housing, strut
3.	Bolt and nut assembly	26.	Shimmy dampener
4.	Steering bellcrank	27.	Bolt, washer, nut, and cotter pin
5.	Bushing, steering arm		
6.	Fork	28.	Bracket, shimmy dampener
7.	Bolt, washer, nut, and cotter pin	29.	Bolt, washer, nut, and cotter pin
8.	Cap, air valve	30.	Jam nut
9.	Body, air valve	31.	Rod end bearing
10.	Safety wire	32.	Drag link, lower
11.	Cap bolt and washer	33.	Bolt, washer, nut, and cotter pin
12.	Roller, aligner guide		
13.	Bolt, washer, nut, and cotter pin	34.	Bolt, washer, nut, and cotter pin
14.	Bracket, aligner	35.	Drag link, upper
15.	Spring, inner	36.	Bolt and nut assembly
16.	Arm, steering	37.	Bolt, washer, and nut
17.	Spring, outer	38.	Jam nut
18.	Bolt, washer, nut, and cotter pin	39.	Spring, downlock
		40.	Hook, downlock
19.	Link, upper	41.	Rod, actuator
20.	Rod, piston	42.	Cylinder, hydraulic
21.	Bolt, washer, nut, and cotter pin	43.	Arm, spring
		44.	Engine mount
22.	Link, lower	45.	Arm, spring
23.	Wheel		

Figure 12.13 Nose gear for light airplane showing the steering mechanism

connecting rods and bolts. The shimmy damper is a hydraulic snubbing unit which reduces the tendency of the wheel to oscillate from side to side.

Shimmy dampers are usually constructed in one of two general designs, piston type and vane type, both of which might be modified to provide power steering as well as shimmy damper action. A piston type shimmy damper is simply a hydraulic cylinder containing a piston rod and piston filled with hydraulic fluid. Figure 12.14 illustrates the typical piston type damper. There is an orifice in the piston which restricts the speed of the piston moving in the cylinder. The piston rod is connected to a stationery structure, any movement of the nose gear will cause the piston to move inside the cylinder. If the movement is slow there will be little resistance from the shimmy damper as the fluid can flow through

Figure 12.14 Drawing of a shimmy damper.

the orifice to transfer from one chamber to the other, however, if the movement is rapid, there is a strong resistance because of the time required for the fluid to flow through the orifice. This action dampens rapid oscillations.

Vane-Type Shimmy Dampers

Vane-type shimmy dampers (Figure 12.15) are designed with a set of moving vanes and a set of stationary vanes as shown. The moving vanes are mounted on a shaft which extends outside the housing. When the shaft is turned, the chambers between the vanes change in size, forcing the fluid through the orifices from one chamber to another, this will provide a dampening effect to any rapid movement. The body is normally mounted on a stationary part of the nose gear and the shaft to a turning point.

Figure 12.15 Principle of a vane-type shimmy damper.

Figure 12.15a Typical vane-type shimmy damper.

Shimmy dampers do not require extensive maintenance but shoud be checked regularly to check for leakage and effective operation. Some dampers have fluid reservoir attached which must be checked periodically and fluid added when required.

Piston Type Shimmy Dampers

Figure 12.16 is a typical shimmy damper with reservoir. This piston type shimmy damper consist of a spring-loaded reservoir piston to maintain the confined fluid under constant pressure. A ball-check permits the flow of fluid from the reservoir to the operating cylinder to make up for any fluid loss. A red indicator line on the reservoir piston indicates fluid level in the reservoir. When the red mark is not visible, the reservoir must be serviced.

This same feature, a pressurized reservoir and a fluid level indicator can also be provided on a vane type shimmy damper. (See figure 12.15a). Consult the manufacturers service manual for each specific installation service and maintenance requirments.

Power Steering Systems

There are many different designs and configurations to provide powered nose wheel steering. These systems range from all electric actuated systen as used on the Gates Learjet, a small business jet, to the largest hydraulic powered system using the latest electronic controls, as is the case on the Boeing 747, and 767 airliners. Since these systems are both complex and specific in their operation they will not be described

Nose wheel straight ahead   Nose wheel castering

Figure 12.16 Shimmy damper operational schematic

here, the systems described will contain many of those features but will serve to represent a typical system instead of any one particular aircraft.

Larger aircraft, business jets, twin engine airplanes, and airliners with their larger mass and a need for positive control will usually use hydraulic system pressure for their source of power. Even though these larger aircraft nose wheel steering systems units differ in their construction, basically all of these systems work in the same manner and require the same sort of units, for example, each steering system usually contains (figure 12.17):

  1. A cockpit control, wheel, handle, lever switch to start and stop the system.

  2. Mechanical, electrical or hydraulic connections for transmitting cockpit input to the steering unit.

  3. A control unit, which is usually a metering or control valve.

  4. A source of power, usually the aircraft hydraulic system.

  5. One of more steering cylinders with linkage to the nose wheel.

Figure 12.16a

Figure 12.17 Nosewheel system mechanical and hydraulic units.

6. A pressurizing assembly to keep fluid in the system for shimmy dampening.

7. A follow-up mechanism to return the control valve to neutral.

8. Safety valves to allow the wheel to swivel in case of hydraulic system failure.

Power Steering Operation

As shown in figure 12.18 pressure from the hydraulic system goes to the steering system through the safety shut-off valve to the metering

Figure 12.18 Nosewheel steering hydraulic flow diagram.

valve. The metering valve then routes pressurized fluid to steering cylinder 'A', as the piston extends it pushes on the steering spindle which pivots at point 'X', and the nose gear begins to turn. As the spindle turns right it forces fluid out cylinder 'B' back to port 'B' of the metering valve. The metering valve then sends return fluid into a compensator, which routes the fluid to the aircraft system return manifold.

Follow Up Linkage

The nose gear spindle has gear teeth which mesh with a gear on the bottom of the orifice rod (see figure 12.17). Thus, as the nose gear turns, the spindle and orifice rod turn in the opposite direction. This rotation is transmitted to the scissors follow-up links located at the top of the nose gear strut. As the follow-up links return, they rotate the connected follow-up drum, which transmits the movement causing the differential arm and link to move the metering valve back to neutral.

The compensator unit (figure 12.19), which is a part of the nose wheel steering system keeps fluid in the steering cylinders pressurized at all

Figure 12.19 Cutaway view of metering valve and compensator.

Figure 12.20 Typical steer damper.

times. The compensator is a three port valve, which encloses a spring-loaded piston and poppet. The left port is an air vent, which prevents trapped air at the rear of the piston from causing unwanted back-pressure. The second port, located at the top of the compensator, connects through a line to the metering valve return port. The third port is located at the right side of the compensator. This port, which is connected to the hydraulic return manifold, routes the steering system return fluid into the manifold when the poppet valve is open.

The compensator poppet opens when pressure acting on the piston becomes high enough to compress the spring. This requires 100 psi; therefore, fluid in the metering valve return line contains fluid trapped under that pressure. Since pressure in a confined fluid is transmitted equally in all directions (Pascals law), 100 psi also exists in metering valve passage H and in chamber E, D, and F (figure 12.19). This same pressure is also applied to the steering cylinders providing adequate dampening pressure.

The emergency bypass valve (figure 12.18) prevents sudden external forces (obstacles encountered while taxiing), from causing steering cylinder pistons creating excessive pressure in the sytem while the metering valve is closed. It can by-pass fluid from cylinder A to cylinder B through the inter-connecting lines. An external pin can be pulled to permit fluid flow through this valve to allow for towing operations.

A vane type steer damper is basically the same as a vane type shimmy damper. The rotating vane becomes a pressurized chamber similar to the piston type shimmy-steering damper. It may contain an external centering coil spring (see figure 12.20) for automatic centering of the nose wheel. The hydraulic steering system components are basically the same as the piston type.

13

BRAKES AND BRAKE SYSTEMS

Aircraft Brakes

Many of the early airplanes had no brakes at all, but relied instead on a tail skid dragging on the ground to serve as a brake. This worked well for slow landing, light aircraft but maneuvering after landing was difficult, usually a dolly was placed under the tail skid so the airplane could be moved.

As airplanes became heavier and faster and runways were hard-surfaced the tail skids gave way to wheel brakes. Early airplane brakes were adopted from the automobile and these brakes were adequate for light airplanes.

Drum Brakes

Most of the early brakes were of the drum and shoe type (figure 13.1), in which a metal shoe had a riveted lining attached. These brakes are still in wide use in automobiles but are rarely seen on airplanes.

The braking action of the drum and shoe is usually a hydraulic system consisting of a master cylinder operated by the pilot, either by hand lever action or toe pressure on the top portion of the rudder pedals. (See Figure 13.13).

The hydraulic pressure forces the wheel slave cylinder to extend bringing the shoe lining in contact with the rotating wheel drum. The rotation of the drum wedges the lining more tightly against it, increasing the friction. This increase in friction by the rotating wheel is called servo action. When the brake is released the coil springs pull the linings away from the drum.

Some brakes have their shoes mounted on a floating plate to provide a wedging action when the aircraft rolls in either direction. These are called duo-servo (dual servo).

Figure 13.1 A dual-servo type brake assembly.

Another type of drum brake, classified as non-servo brake and used on both small and large aircraft was called the expander tube brake. In this brake, a flat synthetic rubber tube around the brake body on the axle was filled with hydraulic fluid under pressure from the brake master cylinder, or from the power brake control valve. As the fluid filled the tube, it forced asbestos-compound blocks out against the rotating drum. When the brake was released, a spring in the brake body pressed the blocks against the expander tube and away from the drum (see figure 13.2).

Any drum and shoe type brake in which a great deal of heat is generated has a problem of fading. As the drum is heated, it expands in a bellmouth fashion and loses a great deal of its effectiveness. To prevent the loss of braking action, nearly all aircraft now use some form of disc brake.

Disk Brakes

The single and dual types are more commonly used on small aircraft; the multiple disk is normally used on medium-sized aircraft; and the segmented rotor are commonly found on heavier aircraft.

The most recent development in aircraft brakes in the carbon-to-carbon disk brakes. While much more expensive than the multiple disk segmented rotor brakes, which will be described in detail, the carbon brakes are advertised to produce ten times the life of steel-to-steel. (See figure 13.3).

Assembled expander tube brake.

Figure 13.2

Single Disk Brakes

With the single-disk, braking action is accomplished by applying friction to both sides of a rotating disk which is keyed to the landing gear wheel. There are several variations of the single-disk brake; however, all operate on the same principle and differ mainly in the number of cylinders and the type of brake housing. Brake housings may be either the one-piece or divided type. Figure 13.4 shows a single-disk brake installed on an aircraft, with the wheel removed. The brake housing is attached to the landing gear axle flange by mounting bolts.

Figure 13.5 shows an exploded view of a typical single-disk brake assembly. This brake has a three cylinder, one piece housing. Each cylinder in the housing contains a piston, a return spring, and an automatic adjusting pin. There are six brake linings, three inboard and three outboard of the rotating disk. These linings are called 'pucks'.

Figure 13.3 Multiple-disk brakes using thick carbon disks. These brakes can absorb tremendous amounts of kinetic energy and yet have relatively low weight.

Figure 13.4 Typical single-disk brake installation.

1. Brake disk
2. Lining puck
3. Adjusting pin nut
4. Cylinder head
5. O-ring gasket
6. O-ring packing
7. Adjusting pin grip
8. Washer
9. O-ring packing
10. Piston
11. Internal retainer ring
12. Spring guide

13. Brake return spring
14. Adjusting pin
15. Bleeder screw
16. Washer
17. Bleeder valve
18. Bleeder adapter
19. Gasket
20. Fluid inlet bushing
21. Gasket
22. Screw
23. Washer
24. Brake housing

Figure 13.5 Exploded view of single-disk brake assembly.

Hydraulic pressure from the brake control unit forces the pistons and pucks against the rotating disk. The disk is keyed to the wheel and free to move laterally within the cavity of the wheel. This lateral movement ensures equal pressure on both sides of the disk.

When the pressure is released, the return springs force the piston back to provide a set running clearance. The self adjusting feature will maintain the desired running clearance, regardless of the lining wear.

Dual-disk brakes are used on aircraft when more braking friction is desired. The dual-disk brake is very similar to the single-disk type, except that two rotating disks are used instead of one, with additional pucks between them.

There are single-disk brakes used on light aircraft that are called spot disk type. This type normally is similar in construction to the single-disk just discussed, but they do not contain a return spring in the piston cavity. They do not have self adjusting features and usually no running clearance. The rotation of the disk, which is sometimes chromed to help resist corrosion, will provide the running clearance. (See figure 13.6).

Figure 13.6 Single-disk brake used on a small general aviation aircraft

The advantages of the disk type brakes over the shoe and drum are that the disk tends to resist fading, the brake linings (pucks) are easier to inspect than the shoe lining and maintenance of disk brakes is much easier.

Multiple-Disk Brakes

Multiple-disk brakes are heavy duty brakes, designed for use with power brake control valves or power boost master cylinders. Figure 13.7 is an exploded view of the complete multiple-disk brake assembly. The brake consist of a bearing carrier, four rotating disks called rotors, three stationary disks called stators, a circular actuating cylinder, and various other components.

Hydraulic pressure is applied to the housing which contains the annular actuating piston. Pressure forces the piston to move outward, compressing the rotating disks, which are keyed to the wheel, and compressing the stationary disks, which are keyed to the carrier. The carrier is bolted to the shock strut. The resulting friction causes the braking action.

When pressure is relieved, the retractor springs force the piston back into the carrier. The automatic adjuster traps a predetermined amount of fluid to give a correct clearance between the rotors and stators. (Figure 13.8).

Bleeder valve (typical)
Automatic adjuster
O-ring
Bearing carrier and sleeve

Retractor spring
assembly (typical 10 places)

Felt wiper ring
Felt wiper ring
O-ring
Backup ring
Annular piston
Retractor plate
Nut (typical 10 places)

Flinger ring
Bearing retaining nut

Snap ring
Pressure plate and
insulator
Rotor
Stator
Rotor
Stator
Rotor
Backup plate
Backup plate retainer
Locking piece

Figure 13.7 Multiple-disk brake.

Figure 13.8 Cross-sectional view of multiple disc brake.

Segmented Rotor Brakes

Segmented Botor brakes are heavy-duty brakes, especially adapted for use with high-pressure hydraulic systems. These brakes may be used with either power brake control valves or power boost master cylinders, (both will be discussed in this chapter). Braking is accomplished by means of several sets of stators, containing high friction type linings, contacting the rotor segments. A cut away view of the brake is shown in figure 13.9.

The segmented rotor brake is very similar to the multiple disk type described previously. The units are shown in Figure 13.9a.

1. Carrier assembly.
2. Piston cup (outer).
3. Piston cup (inner).
4. Piston (outer).
5. Piston (inner).
6. Piston end (outer).
7. Piston end (inner).
8. Pressure plate.
9. Stator drive sleeve.
10. Auxiliary stator and lining assembly.
11. Rotor segment.
12. Rotor link.
13. Stator plate.
14. Backing plate.
15. Torque pin.
16. Adjuster pin.
17. Adjuster clamp.
18. Adjuster screw.
19. Adjuster washer.
20. Adjuster return spring.
21. Adjuster sleeve.
22. Adjuster nut.
23. Clamp holddown assembly.
24. Shim.
25. Bleeder screw.
26. Drive sleeve bolt.
27. Dust cover (inner).
28. Dust cover (outer).

Figure 13.9 Segmented rotor brake - cutaway view.

Figure 13.9a Segmented rotor brake assembly units.

The housing may contain an annular piston or multiple pistons as shown in figure 13.10. The housing is cast of aluminum or magnesium alloy and attaches to the strut by bolts through the torque tube (carrier), cavities in the housing hold the pistons which provide the clamping action as they force the pressure plate against the stack of disks. Drilled passages within the housing connect the cylinders to allow for the flow of hydraulic fluid.

Some housings have each alternate cylinder connected to one hydraulic system and a backup system connected to the other cylinders. A brake with this arrangement supplies adequete pressure from either the main or back-up system.

When the brake pressure is applied, the pistons force the pressure plate over and clamp the disk stack against the backing plate.

Each piston is fitted with an o-ring packing, backed up with a teflon back-up ring. A composition insulator is attached to each piston, bearing against the pressure plate. This insulator minimizes heat transfer from the disk stack onto the piston, where it could over heat the seals. (Figure 13.11).

Most multiple-disk brakes have return springs to pull the pressure plate back when the brake pressure is released. These springs also serve an automatic adjusters to maintain brake clearance. The grip and tube

Figure 13.10 Brake housing of a multiple-disk

PRESSURE
PLATE

INSULATOR

GRIP AND
TUBE
ASSEMBLY

STATIONARY
DISK

RETAINER
RING

ADJUSTING PIN

SPRING HOUSING

SPRING HOLDER

Figure 13.11 Automatic adjusters such as this are used
in each of the cylinders of a multiple-disk brake.

inside the spring holder forces the spring holder to compress the return
spring until the holder bottoms out against the spring housing. As the
disks wear, the pressure plate moves further away from the bottom of
the spring housing, and the tube is forced to slip through the grip.

Figure 13.11a Special tool used to install the rivets in the lining of a Cleveland brake

Brake Assembly Maintenance

Brake inspection and service is performed both on the aircraft and, when extensive repair are required, the brake is removed for shop repair.

Typical repairs and inspections are:

On the aircraft:

1. Check for lining wear, measuring the automatic adjuster pins, linings.

2. Check for air in system, spongy action.

3. Check entire system-brake assembly for leaks.

4. Check for security of attachment, bolt torque.

Off the aircraft:

1. Check all threaded connections, bolts self locking nuts, housing threads for hydraulic fitting attachment.

2. Check the condition of the disk for wear, cracks, disk slots for elongation, glazing of linings, warping.

3. Check pressure plate, back up plate for wear. Replace worn wear pads.

4. Check the automatic adjuster, threads grip and tube.

Figure 13.12 Typical independent type brake system.

5. Check the torque tube condition.

6. Check the housing and pistons for wear.

7. Replace all o-ring seals, back-up rings.

8. Replace all worn linings, using special rivet tools on riveted linings. (See figure 13.11a).

9. Check entire brake for condition, reinstall component parts and properly torque and safety according to manufacturers specifications. When the linings have been replaced, they should be conditioned, or burned in, by taxiing the aircraft straight ahead at a fair speed and stopping in a smooth, even application of the brake. Allow the brake to cool for about a minute and repeat the procedure, this will cure the new linings and help condition them for longer life, less fading problems.

Brake Systems

Brakes are installed in each main wheel, and on rare occasion in the nose wheels, such as the Boeing 727 airliner. In order to permit steering the aircraft in differential braking the brake systems are independent of each other. The right-hand landing gear brake is controlled by the right rudder toe pedal and the left hand wheel is controlled by the left hand rudder toe pedal (figure 13.12).

For the brakes to function efficiently, each component in the brake system must function properly, and each brake assembly must operate with equal effectiveness. It is important that the entire brake system be inspected frequently and an ample supply of hydraulic fluid be maintained in the system. Each brake assembly must be adjusted properly and friction surfaces kept free of grease and oil.

Three types of brake systems are in general use: (1) Independent systems, (2) Power control systems, and (3) Power boost systems.

Independent Brake Systems

In general, the independent brake systems is used on light, small aircraft. It is termed 'independent' because it has it's own reservoir and is entirely independent of the aircraft's main hydraulic system.

Independent brake systems are powered by master cylinders similar to those used in the conventional automobile brake system. The system is composed of a reservoir, one or two master cylinders, mechanical linkage connecting the brake pedal to the master cylinder, fluid lines, and a brake assembly in each main gear wheel.

The master cylinder is actuated by toe pressure on its related pedal. The master cylinder builds up pressure by the movement of the piston inside the sealed, fluid filled cylinder. The resulting pressure is transmitted to the brake assembly in the wheel. This results in the friction necessary to stop the wheel.

When the brake pedal is released the master cylinder piston is returned to the 'off' position by a return spring. Fluid that was moved into the brake assembly is then pushed back to the master cylinder by the brake piston. (Figure 13.13).

Some light aircraft are equipped with a single master cylinder which is hand-lever operated and applied brake action to both main wheels simultaneously. Steering on this system is accomplished by nose wheel steering linkage.

The typical master cylinder has a compensating port or valve that permits fluid to flow from the brake chamber back to the reservoir when excessive pressure is developed in the brake line due to temperature changes. This ensures that the master cylinder will not lock or cause the brakes to drag.

Various manufacturers have designed master cylinders for use on aircraft. All are similar in operation, differing only in minor details and construction. Two well known master cylinders, the Goodyear and Warner, are described and illustrated in this section.

Figure 13.13 A shoe-type brake system

In the Goodyear master cylinder (figure 13.14) fluid is fed from an external reservoir by gravity to the master cylinder. The fluid enters through the cylinder inlet port and compensating port fills the master cylinder casting ahead of the piston and the line leading to the brake cylinder.

Application of the brake pedal causes the piston rod to push the piston forward inside the master cylinder casting. A slight forward movement blocks the compensating port and pressure build up begins. This pressure is transmitted to the brake cylinder.

When the brake pedal is released and returns to 'off', the piston return spring pushes the front piston seal and the piston back to full 'off'. This again clears the compensating port. Any excess volume of fluid is relieved through the compensator port, back to the reservoir.

If any fluid is lost back of the front piston seal due to leakage, it is automatically replaced from the fluid reservoir by gravity.

Any fluid lost in front of the piston from leaks, is replaced through the piston head ports, and around the lip of the front seal when the piston makes the return stroke to the full 'off' position. The front piston seal functions as a seal only during the forward stroke.

Figure   13.14 Goodyear   master   brake   cylinder.

The rear piston seal seals the rear end of the cylinder at all times and the flexible rubber boot serves only as a dust cover.

The brakes may be applied for parking by a ratchet-type lock built into the mechanical linkage between the master cylinder and the foot pedal.

The Warner master cylinder (figure 13.15) incorporates a reservoir, pressure chamber, and compensating device in a single housing. The reservoir is vented to atmosphere through the filler plug, which also contains a check valve. A fluid level tube is located in the side of reservoir housing.

Toe pressure on the brakes pedal is transferred to the cylinder piston by mechanical linkage. As the piston moves downward, the compensating valve closes and pressure is trapped in the pressure chamber. Further movement of the piston forces fluid into the brake assembly, creating the braking action.

When toe pressure is removed from the brake pedal, the piston return spring returns the piston to the 'off' position. The compensating

Figure 13.15 Warner master brake cylinder.

THE MASTER CYLINDERS MOUNT ON THE RUDDER
PEDALS, AND PRESSURE ON THE TOP OF THE PEDALS
DEPRESSES THE PISTONS IN THE MASTER CYLINDERS.

(A)

INTERNAL VIEW OF THE
BRAKE MASTER CYLINDER.

(B)

DETAIL OF THE
COMPENSATOR PORT
IN THE BRAKE
MASTER CYLINDER.

(C)

Figure 13.16

Figure 13.17 A diaphragm-type master cylinder used with some of the smallest, least complicated hydraulic brakes.

device allows fluid to flow to and from the reservoir and pressure chamber when the brakes are in the 'off' position and the entire system is under atmospheric pressure (See figure 13.16).

Certain models of the Warner master cylinder have parking feature which consists of a ratchet and spring arrangement. The rachet locks the unit in the 'on' position, and the spring compensates for expansion and contraction of fluid.

One type master cylinder seldom used on modern airplanes, was used on light airplanes either as an independent brake system or with both brakes connected to one master cylinder. Such a master cylinder made by Scott Aviation was called a diaphragm-type as shown in figure 13.17. The sealing device and pressure creating device inside the master cylinder is a flexible rubber diaphragm actuated by foot pedal pressure. The diaphragm forces the fluid under pressure to the wheel slave cylinder and brake return springs returned it to the relaxed diaphragm when foot pedal pressure was released, a diaphragm return spring aids in the fluid return.

Power Brake Control Systems

Power brake systems are used on aircraft requiring a large volume of fluid to operate the brakes. Large aircraft, because of their weight and size, require this type system. Larger brakes mean greater fluid displacement and higher pressures, and for this reason independent master cylinder systems are not practical. A typical power brake control system is shown in figure 13.18.

Figure 13.18 Typical power brake control valve system.

In this system a line is tapped off from the main hydraulic system pressure line. The first unit in this system is a check valve which prevents loss of brake system pressure in case of main hydraulic system failure. The next unit is accumulator, as described in chapter eight, the accumulator traps fluid under pressure and acts as a surge chamber to dampen excessive loads imposed upon the brake system.

Following the accumulator are the pilots' and co-pilots' control valves. The control valves regulate and control the volume and pressure of the fluid which actuates the brakes.

Four check valves and two orifice check valves are installed in the pilots' and co-pilots' brake actuating lines. The orifice check valves allow unrestricted flow of fluid in one direction, flow in opposite direction is restricted by the orifice in the poppet. Orifice check valves help prevent chatter. The check valves allow the fluid to flow in one direction only.

The next unit in the brake actuating lines is the pressure relief valve. In this particular system, the pressure relief is preset to open at 850 psi to discharge fluid into the return line, and closes at 760 psi minimum

Each brake actuating line incorporates a shuttle valve for the purpose of isolating the emergency brake system from the normal brake system. When brake actuating pressure enters the shuttle valve, the shuttle is

Figure 13.19 Sliding spool power brake control valve.

automatically moved to the opposite end of the valve. This closes off the hydraulic brake system actuating line that is inoperative. Fluid returning from the brakes travel back into its system to which the shuttle was last open (normal or emergency).

Power Brake Control Valve (Sliding Spool Type)

A sliding spool power brake control valve (figure 13.19) basically consists of a sleeve and spool installed in a housing. The spool moves inside the sleeve, opening or closing either the pressure or return port of the brake line. Two springs are provided. The large spring, referred to in figure 13.19 as the plunger spring, provides "feel" to the brake pedal. The small spring returns the spool to the "off" position.

When the plunger is depressed the large spring moves the spool closing the return port and opening the pressure port to the brake line. When the pressure enters the valve, fluid flows to the opposite end of the spool through a hole, when the pressure pushes the spool back far enough toward the large spring to close the pressure port, but does not open the return port. The valve is then in the static condition. This movement partially compresses the large spring, giving 'feel' to the brake pedal. When the brake pedal is released the small spring moves the spool back and opens the return port. This allows fluid pressure in the brake line to flow out through the return port.

Brake Debooster Cylinders

In some power brake control valve (PBCV) systems, debooster cylinders are used in conjunction with the PBCV. Debooster units are generally used on aircraft equipped with a high pressure hydraulic system and low pressure brakes. Brake debooster cylinders reduce the pressure to the brake and increase the volume of fluid flow.

Figure 13.20 shows a typical debooster cylinder installation, mounted on the landing gear shock strut in the line between the PBCV and the brake.

As shown in the schematic diagrams of the unit, the cylinder housing contains a small piston chamber, a large piston chamber, a ball check valve, and a piston return spring. (Figure 13.20a).

In the 'off' position the piston is held in the small end of the debooster by the spring. The ball check is held on seat by a spring. Fluid displacement by thermal expansion can open the ball check and escape through the PBCV.

When the brakes are applied, pressurized fluid enters the small end piston. The ball check prevents fluid from passing through downward. Force is transmitted to the large piston, as the piston moves downward a new flow is created below the large piston to the brake. A greater volume of fluid is displaced due to the larger diameter of the large piston. Pressure is reduced also due to the large piston area (F=A x P).

Normally the brakes will be fully applied before the piston reaches the lower end of its travel. However, if the piston fails to meet sufficient resistance to stop it (due to a loss of fluid from the brake unit or connecting lines), the piston will continue to move downward until the riser unseats the ball-check valve in the hollow shaft. With the ball-check unseated, fluid from the PBCV will pass through the piston shaft acts on the large piston area, the piston will move up, allowing the ball-

Debooster
cylinder

1. Emergency system pressure line	10. Lower support clamp	18. Shock strut
2. Main brake pressure line	11. Riser tube	19. Torque link
3. Upper support clamp	12. Packing	20. Brake shuttle valve
4. Packing	13. Tee fitting	21. Upper end cap
5. Packing	14. Brake line (to pressure relief valve)	22. Snapring
6. Debooster cylinder assembly	15. Brake pressure relief valve	23. Spring retainer
7. Piston	16. Overflow line	24. Valve spring
8. Piston spring	17. Brake line (debooster to shuttle valve)	25. Ball
9. Packing		26. Ball pedestal
		27. Barrel
		28. Lower end cap

Figure 13.20 Brake debooster cylinder.

Figure 13.20a Brake debooster valve. The 1,500 psi system pressure is reduced to 300 psi before it is directed into the brakes.

check valve to seat when pressure in the brake assembly becomes normal.

When the brake pedals are released pressure is removed from the inlet port, and the piston return spring moves the piston rapidily back to the top of the debooster. The rapid movement causes a suction in the line to the brake assembly, resulting in faster release of the brakes.

Lockout deboosters such as the one shown in figure 13.21 allow the piston to go all the way to the bottom. The pin pushes the ball off it's seat, but the spring-loaded valve prevents fluid entering the lower

Figure 13.21 Lockout debooster for a power brake sytstem

chamber until the reset handle is lifted. This device serves as hydraulic fuse in a system using a brake debooster.

Boosted Brakes

There is a size of airplane which requires more braking force than can be applied with an independent master cylinder, yet it does not require the complex power brake systems just described. This need is met with a boosted brake system.

A typical boosted brake master cylinder is shown in figure 13.22. This cylinder is mounted on the rudder pedal and attached to the toe brake in such a way that depressing the pedal pulls on the rod and forces fluid out to the brake. If the pilot needs more pressure on the brakes than he can apply with the pedal, he continues to push, and as the toggle mechanism straightens out, the spool valve is moved over so it will direct hydraulic system pressure behind the piston where it assists the pilot in forcing fluid out to the brake. When the pedal is released, the spool moves back to its original position and vents the area on top of the piston back to the system reservoir. At the same time the compensator poppet unseats and vents the brakes to the reservoir.

Figure 13.22 Brake valve for a hydraulic system pressure boosted brake.

Inspection and Maintenance of Brakes and Brake Systems

Proper Functioning of the brake system is of the utmost importance. Hence, conduct inspections at frequent intervals, and perform needed maintenance promptly and carefully.

When checking for leaks, make sure the system is under operating pressure. However, tighten any loose fittings with the pressure off. Check all flexible hoses carefully for swelling, cracking, or soft spots, and replace if evidence of deterioration is noted.

Maintain the proper fluid level at all times to prevent brake failure or the introduction of air into the system. Air in the system is indicated by a spongy action of the brake pedals. If air is present in the system, remove it by bleeding the system.

There are two general methods of bleeding brake systems, bleeding from the top downward (gravity method) and bleeding from the bottom upward (pressure method). The method used generally depends on the type and design of the brake system to be bled.

Gravity Method Of Bleeding Brakes

In the gravity method, the air is expelled from the brake system through one of its bleeder valves provided on the brake. (See figure 13.23).

BLEEDER VALVE

LOWER
INBOARD SCREW

BLEEDER
TUBE

WHEEL
JACK

CONTAINER

Figure 13.23 Bleeding brake system top-down method.

External reservoir

Brake
pressure
applied

Wheel brake
cylinder

Master brake cylinder

Bleed hose

Air bubbles

Fluid can

Brake shoe

Figure 13.23a Gravity method of bleeding brakes.

Figure 13.24 Pressure method of bleeding brakes.

A bleeder hose is attached to the brake bleeder valve, the free end is put in a container of hydraulic fluid.   Operate the brake master cylinder, or if a power system, use hydraulic system pressure. Each time the pedal is depressed, open the bleed valve, allow air-laden fluid to be forced out of the system. When the pedal pressure is released, close the bleed valve to prevent drawing in more air. Bleeding should continue until no more air bubbles come into the container. (Figure 13.23a).

Pressure Bleeding Method

In this method the air is expelled through the brake sytem reservoir. Pressure is applied using a bleed tank (figure 13.24). A bleed tank is a portable tank containing hydraulic fluid under pressure. The connector hose attaches to the brake bleeder valve and is provided with a shut-off valve.

Perform both bleeding procedures strictly in accordance with the manufacturer's instructions for aircraft concerned.

Although the bleeding of systems presents individual problems, observe the following precautions in all bleeding operations:

1. Be certain all bleeding equipment is absolutely clean and the proper type of hydraulc fluid used.

2. Maintain an adequete supply of fluid in the reservoir or pressure tank. Low fluid level will allow air to enter the system.

3. Continue bleeding until no more air bubbles are present, and brake pedal is firm.

4. When bleeding is complete, check for leaks, check for proper reservoir level.

Brake Inspections, Problems

Brakes which have become over heated from excessive braking are dangerous and should be treated accordingly. Excessive brake heating weakens the tire and wheel structure and increases tire pressure.

Check for lining wear, discussed previously. Check manufacturers service manual for proper brake lining limitations. Check the linings or automatic adjuster pins.

Check the disk condition for excessive wear of the wear pads, disk slots for wear, lining wear on the stators, and cracking of rotors or stators. Check torque tube for wear of cracking.

Check for brake operation, if brakes drag or fail to completely release after the pressure is removed, this will cause excessive wear and overheating.

Warped or glazed disks will cause chattering. Grabbing brakes are usually the result of oil or grease on the linings. In all brake malfunctions consult the specific aircraft or brake manufacturer's service manual for proper, timely, corrective action.

Brake Anti-Skid Systems

The purpose of a wheel brake is to bring a rapidly moving aircraft to a stop during ground roll. It does this by changing the energy of movement into heat energy through the friction developed in the brakes. A feature found in high performance aircraft braking systems is skid control or anti-skid protection. This is an important system because if a wheel goes into a skid, it's braking value is greatly reduced.

The skid control system perfoms four functions: (1) normal skid control, (2) locked wheel skid control, (3) touchdown protection, and (4) fail safe protection. The main components of the sytem consist of two skid control generators, a skid control box, two skid control valves, a skid control switch, a warning, and an electrical control harness with a connection to the squat switch. (See figure 13.25.)

Normal Skid Control

Normal skid control comes into play when wheel rotation slows down but has not come to a stop. When this slowing down happens the wheel sliding action has just begun but has not yet reached a full scale slide. In this situation the skid control valve removes some of the hydraulic pressure to the wheel. This permits the wheel to rotate a little faster and stop it's sliding. The more intense the skid is, the more braking pressure is removed.

The skid detection and control of each wheel is completely independent of the others. The wheel skid intensity is measured by the amount of wheel slow-down.

Figure 13.25 Brake System Schematic.

Skid Control Generators

The skid control generator is the unit that measures the wheel rotational speed. (See figure 13.26 and 13.26a). These generators are designed on some installations as a DC (Direct Current) unit where the voltage output is measured, some installations use an AC (alternating current) unit in which case the frequency is the variable. Both are small electrical devices, one for each wheel, mounted in the wheel axle. The generator armature is coupled to, and driven by, the main wheel

Figure 13.26 DC wheel speed sensor, used in an antiskid brake system

through the drive cap in the wheel. As it rotates, the generator develops a voltage and current signal. The signal strength indicates the wheel rotational speed. This signal is fed to the control box through the harness.

Figure 13.26a AC wheel speed sensor, used in an antiskid brake system

Figure 13.27 The basic components of an antiskid brake system, the wheel speed sensor, the control box and the control valve.

Skid Control Box

The skid control box (figure 13.27) reads the signal from the generator and senses change in signal strength. It can interpet these as developing skids, locked wheels, brake applications and brake releases. It analyzes all it reads, then sends appropiate signals to solenoids in the skid control valves.

Skid Control Valves

The two skid control valves mounted on the brake control valve are solenoid operated. (See figure 13.28a). Electric signals from the skid control box actuate the solenoids. If there is no signal (because there is no wheel skidding), the skid control valve will have no effect on the brake operation. But, if a skid develops, either slight or serious, a signal is sent to the skid control valve solenoid (servo in figure 13.25). This solenoids action lowers the metered pressure in the line between the metering valve and the brake cylinders. It does so by dumping fluid into the reservoir return line whenever the solenoid is energized. Naturally, this immediately relaxes the brake application. The pressure flow into the brake lines from the metering valves continues as long as the pilot depresses the brake pedal. But the flow and pressure is re-routed to the reservoir instead of the wheel brakes.

Power Brake Control Valve

The nose gear down line pressure enters the brake control valve where it is metered to the wheel brakes in proportion to the force applied on the pilots (co-pilots) foot pedal. However, before it can go to the brakes, it must pass through a skid control valve. There, if the solenoid is actuated, a port is opened in the line between the brake control valve and the brake. This port vents the brake application pressure to the

Figure 13.28 Antiskid brake control valve.

hydraulic system return line. This reduces the brake application. and
the wheel rotates faster again. The system is designed to apply enough
force to operate just below the skid point. This gives the most effective
braking.

Figure 13.28a

Pilot Control

The pilot can turn off the operation of the anti-skid system by a switch in the cockpit. A warning lamp lights when the system is turned off or if there is a system failure, (not shown in figure 13.25).

Locked Wheel Skid Control

The locked wheel skid control causes the brake to be fully released when its wheels lock. A locked wheel easily occurs on a patch of ice due to lack of tire friction with the surface. It will occur if the normal skid control does not prevent the wheel from reaching a full skid. To relieve a locked wheel skid, the pressure is bleed off longer than in normal skid function. This is to give the wheel time to regain speed. The locked wheel skid control is out of action during aircraft speeds of less than 15-20 MPH.

Touchdown Protection

The touchdown protection circuit prevents the brakes from being applied during the landing approach even if the pedals are depressed. This prevents the wheels from being locked when they contact the runway. The wheels have a chance to begin rotating before they carry the full weight of the aircraft. Two conditions must exist before the skid control valves permit brake application. Without them the skid control box will not send the proper signal to the valve solenoids. The first is that the squat switch must signal that the weight of the aircraft is on the wheels. The second is that the wheel generators sense a wheel speed of over 15-20 MPH.

Fail Safe Protection

The fail safe protection circuit monitors operation of the skid control system. It automatically returns the brake system to full manual in case of system failure. It also turns on a warning light.

Parking Brakes In An Anti-Skid System

Due to the construction of the brake control valves and the function of the anti-skid valves, parking brake fluid is trapped in the lines to the brakes, through the anti-skid valves. This is accomplished with the anti-skid system turned off, see figure 13.25.

14

AIRCRAFT
WHEELS AND TIRES

General

Aircraft wheels provide the mounting for tires which absorb shock on landing, support the aircraft on the ground and assist in ground control during taxi, takeoff and landing. Wheels are usually made from either aluminum or magnesium. Either of these materials provide a strong, light weight wheel requiring very little maintenance.

1. Split wheel - the most popular type is shown in figure 14.1 for a heavy aircraft wheel. Figure 14.2 for a light aircraft wheel.

2. Removable flange type figure 14.3.

3. Drop center fixed flange figure 14.4.

The split wheel is used on most aircrafts today. Illustrations of wheels used on light civilian type and heavy transport type aircraft are shown to illustrate the similarities and differences.

Split Wheels

Figure 14.1 and the description that follows was extracted from B.F. Goodrich maintenance manual on wheels. The wheel illustrated in figure 14.1 is used on the Boeing 727 transport aircraft.

Description - the numbers in parenthesis refer to figure 14.1.

A. The main landing gear wheel is a tubeless, split-type assembly made of forged aluminum.

B. The inner and outer wheel half assemblies are fastened together by 18 equally spaced tie bolts (11), secured with nuts (9). A tubeless tire valve assembly installed in the web of the inner wheel half (48), with the valve stem (7) protruding through a vent hole in the outer wheel half (30), is used to inflate the tubeless tire used with this wheel. Leakage of air from the tubeless tire through the wheel half mating surfaces prevented by a rubber packing (14) mounted on the register surface of the half. Another packing (13) mounted on the inner register surface of the inner wheel half seals the hub area of the wheel against dirt and moisture.

265

Figure 14.1 Parts list-split wheel, heavy aircraft.

Index No.	Description		
	WHEEL, LANDING GEAR, 49 x 17, TUBELESS, MAIN		
1	CONE BEARING		
2	RING, RETAINING	25	IDENTIFICATION PLATE
3	SEAL	26	INSTRUCTION PLATE
4	CONE, BEARING	27	PLATE, IDENTIFICATION
	VALVE ASSY, TUBELESS TIRE	28	INSERT, HELI-COIL
5	CAP, VALVE	29	CUP, BEARING
6	VALVE, INSIDE	30	WHEEL HALF, OUTER
7	STEM, VALVE		WHEEL HALF, ASSY, INNER
8	GROMMET, RUBBER (TIRE AND RIM ASSOC.)	31	NUT
9	NUT	32	WEIGHT, WHEEL BALANCE, 1/4 c
10	WASHER	33	BOLT, MACHINE
11	BOLT	34	NUT
12	WASHER	35	WASHER, FLAT
13	PACKING, PREFORMED	36	IDENTIFICATION PLATE
14	PACKING, PREFORMED	37	INSTRUCTION PLATE
15	PLUG, MACHINE THD, THERMAL PRESSURE	38	BOLT, MACHINE
	RELIEF, ASSY OF	39	NUT
16	PACKING, PREFORMED	40	WASHER, FLAT
	WHEEL HALF ASSY, OUTER	41	BOLT, MACHINE
17	NUT	42	BRACKET
18	WEIGHT, WHEEL BALANCE, 1/4 oz.	43	SHIELD, HEAT
19	BOLT, MACHINE	44	SCREW
20	WASHER	45	INSERT
21	NUT	46	INSERT, HELI-COIL
22	WASHER, FLAT	47	CUP, BEARING
23	BOLT, MACHINE	48	WHEEL HALF, INNER
24	WASHER, FLAT		

C.A. retaining ring (2) installed in the hub of the inner wheel half holds the seal (3) and bearing cone (4) in place when the wheel is removed from the axle. The seal retains the bearing lubricant and keeps out dirt and moisture. Tapered roller bearings (1, 4, 29, 47) in the wheel half hubs support the wheel and axle.

D. Inserts (45) installed over bosses in the inner wheel half (48) engage the drive slots in the brake disks, rotating the disks as the wheel turns. A heat shield (43), mounted underneath and between the inserts, keeps excessive heat, generated by the brake, from the wheel and the tire. Two alignment brackets (42), 160°; apart, are attached with the heat shield to the wheel half. The brackets prevent brakes disk misalignment during wheel installation.

Figure 14.2 Parts list-split wheel, light aircraft.

Index No.	Description		
1	WHEEL ASSEMBLY (With Valve Assy)	13	WHEEL-HALF ASSY, Outer
2	SEAL ASSY	14	PLATE, Identification
	CONE, Bearing	15	PLATE, Instruction
	VALVE ASSY, Tubeless tire	16	CUP, Bearing
3	CAP, Valve		WHEEL-HALF ASSY, Inner
4	CODE, Valve	17	WIRE, Lock
5	NUT	18	SCREW
6	SPACER	19	KEY, Torque
7	GROMMET	20	INSERT, Heli-coil
8	STEM, Valve	21	PLATE, Identification
9	NUT	22	PLATE, Instruction
10	WASHER	23	CUP, Bearing
11	BOLT	24	WHEEL-HALF, Inner
12	PACKING		

E. Three thermal plugs (15), equally spaced and mounted in the web of the inner wheel half directly under the mating surfaces, protect against excessive brake heat expanding the air pressure in the tire and causing a blowout. The inner core of the thermal relief plug is made of fusible metal that melts as a predetermined temperature, releasing the air in the tire. A packing (16) is installed underneath the head of each thermal relief plug to prevent leakage of air from the tires.

Figures 14.2 was extracted from the B.F. Goodrich maintenance manual on wheels. The wheel illustrated is typical of split wheels used on light aircraft.

Description - numbers in paretheses refer to figures 14.2.

A. This main wheel is a tubeless split-type assembly made of forged aluminum.

B. The inner (24) and outer (16) wheel half assemblies are fastened together by 8 equally spaced tie bolts (11), secured with nuts (9). A tubeless tire valve assembly installed in the outer wheel half (16) is used to inflate the 6.50-8 tubeless tire used with this wheel. Leakage of air

A. Drop center.   B. Flat base.

Figure 14.3 Removable Flange Wheels.

from the tubeless tire through the wheel half mating surfaces is prevented by a rubber packing (12) mounted in the mating surface of the outer wheel half.

C. A seal (1) retains grease in the bearing (2) which is installed into the bearing cup (23) inner wheel half, and (15) outer wheel half. Tapered bearings (2) installed in the bearing cups in the wheel valves support the wheel on the axle.

D. Torque keys (19) installed in cutouts in the inner rim of the wheel engage the drive tabs in the brake disks, rotating the disk as the wheel turns.

Figure 14.4 Fixed flange, drop center wheel.

Figure 14.5 Main Landing Gear Wheel Assembly

Removable Flange Wheels

The drop center and flat base removable flange wheels (figure 14.3) have a one-piece flange held in place by a retainer snap ring. Wheels of the removable-flange type are used with low pressure casings and may have either the drop center or a flat base. A flat base rim may be removed quickly from the tire by removing the retaining lock ring that holds the one-piece removable flange in place, and lifting the flange from the seat. When a brake drum of the conventional type is installed on each side of the wheel, this provides a dual brake assembly.

A brake drum liner may be held in place by means of steel bolts projecting through the casting with lock nuts on the inner side. These can be tightened easily through spokes in the wheel.

The bearing races are usually shrink-fitted into the hub of the wheel casting and provide the surfaces on which the bearings ride. The bearing are the tapered roller type. Each bearing is made up of a cone and rollers. Bearings should be cleaned and repacked with grease periodically in accordance with the manufacturer's instructions.

Fixed Flange Wheels

Drop center fixed flange aircraft wheels (figure 14.4) are special use wheels such as military for high pressure tires. Some may be found installed on older type aircraft.

Outboard radial ribs are provided generally to give added support to the rim at the outboard bead seat. The principal difference between wheels used for streamline tires and those used of smooth contour tires is that the latter are wider between the flanges.

Wheel Bearings

The bearing of an airplane wheel are of the tapered roller type and consist of a bearing cone, rollers with a retaining cage, and a bearing cup, or outer race. Each wheel has the bearing cup, or race, pressed into place and is often supplied with a hub cap to keep dirt out of the outside bearing.

Suitable retainers are supplied inboard of the inner bearing to prevent grease from reaching the brake lining. Felt seals are provided to prevent dirt from fouling multiple-disk brakes. Seals are also supplied on amphibian airplane to keep out water. See figure 14.5.

Wheel Inspections

With tire/tube removed, clean wheel in approved cleaning solvent and the bead seat with denatured alcohol. Inspect wheel for cracks, corrosion, and elongated bolt holes.

Inspect bearings before repacking with the approved wheel bearing grease. Check for damage to bearings and cups such as, pitting, nicks, overheating, (which is indicated by a blue-yellow discoloration) corrosion, brinnelling caused by overloading, over torque or hard landings.

Aircraft Tires

Aircraft tires, tubeless or tube type, provide a cushion of air that helps absorb the shocks and roughness of landing and takeoff; they support the weight of the aircraft on the ground and provide the necessary traction for braking and stopping aircraft on landing.

Aircraft Tire Construction

Aircraft tires are one of the strongest pneumatic tires made. They withstand landing speeds up to 250 MPH and support static and dynamic loads as high as 22 and 33 tons. Typical construction is shown in figure 14.6.

Figure 14.6 Construction of an aircraft tire.

Tread

Widely used pattern is the ribbed, which will provide good traction. Made of tough and durable rubber compounds.

Tread Reinforcement

One or more layers of reinforced nylon cord fabric strengthens the tread for high speed operations, used mainly for high speed tires.

Breakers

Not always used, extra layers of nylon to protect casing plies and strengthen tread area.

Casing Plies/Cord Body

Diagonal layers of rubber coated nylon cord fabric, (running at opposite angles to one another) provide the tire strength. Completely encompassing the tire body, folded up around the wire beads and back against the tire sidewalls (the "ply turn-ups").

Beads

Made of steel wires embedded in rubber and wrapped in fabric, the beads anchor the carcass plies and provide firm mounting surfaces on the wheel.

Figure 14.7 Deflector, or chine, tire for the nose wheel of a jet aircraft, having its engines mounted on the aft fuselage.

Flippers

These layers of fabric and rubber insulate the carcass from the bead wires and improve the durability of the tire.

Chafers

Layers of fabric and rubber that protect the carcass from damage during mounting and demounting. They insulate the carcass from the brake heat and provide a good seal against movement during dynamic operations.

Bead Toe

The inner edge closest to the tire center line.

Bead Heel

The outer bead edge which fits against the wheel flange.

Innerlinner

On tubeless tires, this inner layer of less permeable rubber acts as a built-in tube, it prevents air from seeping through casing plies. For tube type tires, a thinner liner is used to prevent tube chafing against the inside ply.

Tread Reinforcing Ply

Rubber compound cushion between tread and casing plies, provides toughness and durability. Adds protection against cutting and bruising

Sidewall

Covers over the sides of the cord body to protect the cords from the injury and exposure. Does not add to the strength of the cord body.

Special Sidewall

A construction called a "chine tire" is a nose tire designed with built-in deflector to divert runway water to the side, thus reducing water spray in the area of rear mounted jet engines. (Figure 14.7).

Apex Strip

The appex strip is additional rubber formed around the beads to give a contour for anchoring the ply turnups.

Tire markings

All commercial aircraft tires approved under FAA test requirements TSO C62C are marked clearly with the following minimum information: (1) manufacturers name, (2) size, (3) load rating, (4) speed rating, (5) skid depth, (6) manufacturers part number, (7) serial number, (8) manufacturers plant identification along with, (9) the TSO marking.

Retread tires carry the same information as new tires, plus "R level" indicating the number of times the casing has been retreaded. The retread plant or country is marked as well. (See figure 14.8).

A red dot on the outside of the sidewall, the same side as the serial number, indicates the light spot on the tire. When a tube is installed, the balance mark on the tube is aligned with the red spot. When tubeless tires are used, the red spot is aligned with the wheel valve, unless otherwise specified by the manufacturer.

Tire Types

Type III is the most popular low-pressure tire used today on piston powered airplanes. The section width is relatively wide in relation to the bead diameter. This allows lower inflation pressure for improved cushioning and flotation. (Figure 14.9).

The section width and rim diameter are used to designate the size of a

MANUFACTURER

GOODYEAR

FLIGHT EAGLE

DESIGN TYPE

MADE IN U.S.A.

COUNTRY OF MANUFACTURE

SERIAL NUMBER

LOAD RATING G17.800 LB
TUBELESS ISO C&C

LOAD RATING
TUBELESS
APPLICABLE SPEC.

PART NUMBER

PART NO. 348F83-2

34 x 9.25-16

TIRE SIZE

18 PLY RATING
33 SKID 210 MPH

PLY RATING
SKID DEPTH
SPEED RATING

Figure 14.8

Figure 14.9 Rib-tread tire.   Type III tire.

tire. For example, a tire having a section width of nine and a half inches and which fits on a 16 inch wheel would be indentified as a 9.50-16 tire.

Type VII extra high pressure tires are the standard for jet aircraft. They have exceptionally high load-carrying ability and are available in ply rating from 4 to 38. The tire sizes are designated by their outside diameter and section width, with a designation such as 38 x 13. (Figure 14.10).

New Design

An all new design, a combination of both the type III and type VII is a low profile designed which is being used to replace all other type tires.

They are sized by the tire outside diameter, section width and bead seat. An example 52 x 20.5 - 23 or 15 x 6.0 - 6.

Ply Ratings

In the past, tires were rated for strength by the actual number of cotton plies. Today, the improved materials used in tire construction have fewer layers (plies), but will provide the same strength. So, today, tires are given a ply rating, rather than specifying the actual number of layers of fabric material used. For example, a 10 ply rating is equal to

Figure 14.10 Type VII tire.

the strength of 10 actual layers of cotton material, it may be far fewer than 10 layers of modern material.

The ply rating of a tire relates to its maximum static load and its inflation pressure.

Tube Or Tubeless

Aircraft tires are manufactured as both tube and tubeless, with the basic differnce between the two being the inner liner.

Tubeless tires are identified by the word "tubeless" on their sidewall, and a lack of identification signifies that a tube should be used in the tire.

Aircraft Tubes

All aircraft tubes are made of a specially compounded natural or synthetic rubber that holds air with a minimum of leakage. Some tubes use a reinforced nylon fabric molded to the inner circumference to protect against chafting the rim and for heat protection.

Tire Inspection On The Aircraft-Inflation

The inflation pressure of an aircraft tire is critical. Due to the excessive flexing of the sidewalls (more that twice as much as automobile tires) and heat of braking.

Over inflation of aircraft tires causes accelerated centerline wear. When a tire is worn in this way, it has less resistance to skidding.

Underinflation causes excess heat to be generated within the tire. It wears away the shoulders of the tire.

The proper inflation must be maintained in close adherence to the manufacturers service manual.

Inflation pressure should be checked when the tire is cold, and for this reason you should allow two to three hours to elapse after a flight before you measure the pressure.

Inflation pressure also varies with the ambient temperature. If extreme temperature changes are anticipated the service manual should be checked for recommended pressure adjustments.

Tubeless tires have a maximum allowable diffusion loss, usually about 5 percent for a 24 hour period. The pressure drop is due to normal nylon cord body expansion.

All aircraft tires are now made with nylon cord, and the intial 24 hour stretch of a newly mounted tire may result in a 5 to 10 percent drop in air pressure. Allow a 12 hour waiting period before installing a tire to compensate for this low pressure

Figure 14.11 The tires on a dual installation must be matched for pressure, diameter, and tread condition and should be from the same manufacturer.

Dual Installations

Differences of air pressure in tires mounted as duals, whether main or nose, should be cause for concern, as it means that one tire is carrying more load than the other. If there is a difference of more than 5 psi. it should be noted in the log book. Check this reading again after subsequent periods of time, if necessary, check for leaks, and repair as necessary (see figure 14.11). Use a chart, Figure 14.12 is an example.

Nylon Flat-Spotting

Nylon tires develop temporary flat spots under static load. Under normal conditions a flat spot will disappear by the end of the taxi run. If it dosen't, follow manufacturers recommended corrective action.

Tire Balance

To prolong the tire life and to reduce unnecessary vibrations which may affect the aircraft operations, tire balance in very important. Tire

MATCHING DUAL TIRES		
Matching tires on dual wheels, or dual wheels on a multi-wheel gear configuration, is necessary so that each tire will have the same contact area with the ground and thereby carry an equal share of the load. Only those tires having inflated diameters within the tolerances listed below should be paired together on dual wheels. Tires should not be measured until they have been mounted and kept fully inflated for at least 12 hours, at normal room temperatures.	O. D. Range of Tires	Maximum Tolerance Permissable
	Up to 24″	1/4″
	25″ to 32″	5/16″
	33″ to 40″	3/8″
	41″ to 48″	7/16″
	49″ to 55″	1/2″
	56″ to 65″	9/16″
	66″ and up	5/8″

Figure 14.12 Matching tires on dual wheel installations.

out of balance conditions can be indicated by a cupping wear pattern on the tire shoulder. Uneven wear pattern, not cupping, on only one shoulder of a tire installed on a spring type landing gear should not be misdiagnosed as tire balance problems. This is a normal wear pattern on this type aircraft. Usually, the shoulder farthest from the fuselage will wear first. The tire may be reversed on the wheel to extend its life.

Leaks At Valve

Check valve core leaks with small amount of water at the end of the stem. Replace valve core when bubbles appear. Always keep a valve cap on the stem to keep out dirt.

Tread Injuries

Remove any forgein objects imbedded in tread with a blunt awl or medium size screwdriver. When cord bodies are exposed or cuts penetrate cord body the tire should be removed and repaired, recapped or scrapped. If the cut does not expose the carcass cord body, taking the tire out of service is not required.

Remove any tire that shows signs of a bulge in the tread or sidewall.

Sidewall Injuries

Inspect both sidewalls for evidence of weather or ozone checking and cracking, radial cracks, cuts, snags, gouges, etc. If cords are exposed or damaged, the tires should be removed from service.

See figure 14.13 for preventive maintenance summary.

PREVENTIVE MAINTENANCE SUMMARY

- Check tire pressures with an accurate gage at least once a week, and before each flight. Tires should be at ambient temperature.
- Check newly mounted tires or tubes daily for several days.
- Newly mounted tires should not be placed in service until cord body stretch has been compensated with re-inflation.
- Check for abnormal diffusion loss.
- Follow inflation recommendations carefully — guard against underinflation.
- Observe load recommendations.
- Move aircraft regularly or block up when out of service for long periods.

Figure 14.13 Preventive maintenance summary.

Wheel Damage

Wheels which are cracked or injured should be taken out of service, repaired or replaced.

Thermal Fuse

If a tire has been subjected to a temperature high enough to melt one of these fuse plugs, the tire should be carefully inspected and the wheel replaced.

When checking for allowable limits of tire and wheel damage, consult manufacturers service manual. Replacement of wheel attaching parts, fuse plugs, brake keys, bearing cups, and painting should also be done in accordance with the service manual to be sure specific steps are followed.

Mounting And Demounting

These instructions are intended to be simple so that they can be carried out with tools which are commonly available. Specialized equipment is usually available at larger airports.

Before mounting any tire, examine wheel for cracks or injured parts. Inspect tire for damage, inspect tube for damage, check inside tire for forgeign material.

Dust inside tire and out side tube with tire talc or soap stone to prevent tube sticking to the tire. Mount tube in tire with valve stem projecting on the serial number side of the tire.

Lubricate tubeless tire toe of beads with soap solution to facilitate proper bead seating to prevent air loss.

Balance marks appear on some tubes to indicate the heavy portion of the tube. The tube balance mark should align with the tire balance (red dot) mark.

Balance of tires on tubeless installations is putting the red dot on the tire at the wheel valve.

Inflation

CAUTION: When torquing wheel half bolts and nuts, great care must be exercised to follow the wheel manufacturer's torquing requirements exactly. Do not attempt to inflate a tire-wheel assembly until proper torque is completed. Use a cross pattern for torquing.

Inflate tires in a proper safety cage to guard against the effect of an explosion of either the tire, tube or wheel (figure 14.14).

Seating Tube Type Tires

To seat the tire beads properly, first inflate the tire to the reccomended pressure, then completely deflate and finally reinflate to the correct pressure. This helps to remove tube wrinkles, prevents pinching the tube, eliminates possibly stretching one section of the tube, and it assists in the removal of air that might be trapped between the tube and tire. NOTE: This procedure is not necessary for tubeless tires. Let assembly stand for 12 to 24 hours to check for structural weakness in either the tire or tube, Recheck pressure to check for leaks.

Paint a small (1 inch long) slippage mark, using red or white paint, across the tire (1 inch long) onto the rim, 1 inch also, to indicate slippage after the assembly has been in service.

Figure 14.14 For the initial inflation, the tire and wheel should be placed in a safety cage and the air hose attached to the valve with a clip-on-type chuck.

Demounting

CAUTION: Use caution when unscrewing valve cores, the air pressure can cause the core to be ejected like a bullet.

Always deflate tires completely before demounting. Deflate before wheels are removed from the aircraft.

Figure 14.15 Break the bead of a tire away from the wheel rim with a steady push as near the rim as possible.

Break beads loose from wheel flange and bead seat. Be very careful not to injure the beads or relatively soft metal of the wheel. Use approved tools (see figure 14.15).

Remove wheel half bolts, 'O' ring seal (on tubeless wheels) remove tire, tube and clean the wheel halves, inspect as required, and repaint if necessary.

Tire Storage

All tires and tubes should be stored in a cool, dry area, out of direct sunlight and away from any electrical machinery. The temperature should be maintained between 32° and 80° (0° and 27°C).

Tires should be stored in vertical racks. If horizontally stored tire racks must be used, do not stack them more than five tires high for small tires, four for medium size tires and three high for large tires.

Keep tubes in their original cartons whenever possible. If cartons are not available dust the tubes with tire talc and wrap in heavy paper.

Tubes may be stored with just enough air in them to round them out. Do not hang tubes over nails or pegs.

15

HYDRAULIC FLIGHT CONTROL SYSTEMS

General

Many modern aircraft use fully powered flight control system to aid the pilot in the movement of directional control devices. Large aircraft, airliners for example, use various devices to control the roll, pitch, and yaw of the airplane in flight. The speed of this type aircraft, plus the force necessary to move these devices, makes it impossible for the pilot to accomplish this task by his own power.

Hydraulically assisted flight controls have been in use for many years, starting with simple aileron boost systems, very similar in theory to the boosted brake system illustrated in Chapter 13, to the fully powered systems of today. An increasing number of aircraft, both large and small, use electronically controlled hydraulic systems. This is accomplished through the aircraft auto pilot system or, on newer designs, such as the Boeing 767, through computer directed controls. The hydraulic units are very similar in design to the rudder servo mechanism illustrated in Chapter 8, Figure 8.28.

The complete systems, both electronic and hydraulic, are very complex and no attempt will be made to describe them here. However, some of the relatively simple hydraulic components and their controls will serve to familiarize the student/technician with these systems.

To illustrate a powered flight control system's primary controls the CANADAIR Canadian CHALLENGER 601 will be used as an example of a smaller business jet. The Boeing 727 system will be used to illustrate the leading edge and training edge flap devices, the secondary controls.

283

Canadian Challenger 601

The Canadian 601 uses three independent hydraulic systems to operate the ailerons, elevators, rudder, flight and ground spoilers. Refer to figure 9.9 for the basic hydraulic systems. The roll (ailerons), pitch (elevators), and yaw (rudder) controls are of the dual type, that is, the pilot's and co-pilot's handwheels, control columns and rudder pedals are interconnected and working in unison.

No. 1,2 and 3 hydraulic systems are used to supply hydraulic power to the components operating the flight control surfaces. (See figur 9.9).

The hydraulically actuated control surfaces are each powered by at least two hydraulic systems. The systems are fully independent from each other, and one alone is sufficient for operation. System logic ensures that loss of one hydraulic system will not affect or prevent the operation of any other control surface. Hydraulic power distribution is shown in figure 15.1.

Each flight control surface power control unit (PCU) is monitored for failure by the servo monitor system. Failure detection is either internal to the PCU (aileron and rudder PCU's) or external as part of the input linkage (elevators). A proximity switch is used to detect failures which are displayed on the servo monitor panel on the cockpit center pedestal.

Figure 15.1 Hydraulic Distribution

Introduction

The Challenger flight controls are divided into five main systems incorporating the following controls:

1 - Roll Control
   - ailerons
2 - Pitch Control
   - elevators
3 - Yaw Control
   - rudder
4 - Flight Control Monitoring
5 - Lift Modulation
   - flight spoilers
   - ground spoilers

Roll, pitch and yaw controls are called primary controls while lift controls are called secondary controls (Figure 15.2).

Roll Control

General

Roll control is provided by two hydraulically operated ailerons hinged on the rear spar of the wings between station 282 and 353 (Figure 15.2).

Figure 15.2

Figure 15.2 a

Aileron control is achieved through a cable and pulley system operated from two interconnected hand wheels mounted on the control columns.

The two handwheels are linked by a cable system and an interconnecting shaft that incorporates a disconnect mechanism (roll disconnect), which allows the pilot to isolate to L/H or R/H aileron control circuit should either circuit become jammed. A spring loaded artificial feel unit is incorporated in each circuit aft quadrant.

A power control unit (PCU) is associated with each aileron. Each PCU is a dual unit consisting of two equal and parallel power components with a common interconnecting input linkage. The outboard power components are connected to hydraulic system 3 while the inboard ones are supplied by system 1 on L/H and system 2 R/H. (See figure 15.2a).

Power control Unit (PCU) (Figure 15.3)

The hydraulic actuation of the ailerons is accomplished by identical aileron PCU's. Each PCU consists of two identical, parallel working actuators. The actuators contain double acting, equal area cylinders and are attached to a common mounting plate.

Each of the dual power controls contain a manifold which is in turn houses a combination control and anti-jam valve, a failure monitoring sensor, a damping valve, a compensator, two anti-cavitation values, a relief valve and a presure differential indicator.

A summing and feedback feature is incorporated as part of the input linkage to null the system when the aileron position corresponds to pilot's input demands.

The dual actuators are mounted on a common base and are powered from independent hydraulic systems. The L/H and R/H outboard actuators are powered by the No. 3 hydraulic system whereas the L/H and R/H inboard actuators are powered by the No. 1 and No. 2 system respectively.

The pressure differential indicator indicates the presence or absence of adequete pressure drop across the fluid compensator. Indication is by means of a pin in the manifold which will extend, revealing its green painted end if the required pressure drop is present (10-25 psid). Exposure of the green pin indicates that the PCU is charged with fluids and that some hydraulic pressure is available. If the green pin is not visible, this will indicate that either there is insufficient fluid in the PCU or insufficient pressure.

The releif valve located in the manifold retract line provides pressure relief should the cylinder retract pressure exceed 3400 psi.

The anti-cavitation valves prevent cavitation in the extend or retract

Figure 15.3 Aileron PCU Schematic

chambers of the main cylinder, and open if the pressure in the chambers drops below return pressure.

Two filters installed in the inlet ports prevent foreign material from being introduced into the main cylinder and/or the aircraft system.

Pitch Control

General (Figure 15.4)

Pitch control is provided by a set of hydraulically operated elevators hinged to the rear spar of the horizontal stabilizer with no mechanical interconnection.

AFT
LINKAGE

BALANCE
SPRING

LOAD
LIMITERS

ELEVATOR
PCU₁

JAM-TOLERANT
INPUT RODS

AUXILIARY (DOWN)
CENTERING MECHANISM

GAIN CHANGE
MECHANISM

AFT QUADRANT

Figure 15.4

Their displacement is controlled by fore and aft movement of the control columns which through mechanical cables and linkages is transmitted to the power control units (PCU's) installed in the horizontal stabilizer.

The two control columns are linked by an interconnecting shaft that incorporates a disconnect mechanism (pitch disconnect), which allows the pilot to isolate the L/H or R/H control circuit should either circuit become jammed.

A pitch feel simulator (artificial feel) unit provides the control column with the required "stick" force, which is varied relative to the horizontal stabilizer position.

Each elevator is driven by two identical power control units (PCU's) (figure 15.5) powered as follows:

Hydraulic system No.1 operates the L/H elevator outboard PCU.

Hydraulic system No.2 operates the R/H elevator outboard PCU.

Hydraulic system No.3 operates the inboard PCU's of each elevator.

Each PCU contains a servo valve distributing hydraulic pressure on either side of a cylinder operating the elevator.

Figure 15.5 Elevator P.C.U.

Yaw Control

General

Yaw control is provided by a hydraulically actuated rudder hinged on the rear spar of the vertical stabilizer.

Two anti-jam breakout mechanism (L/H and R/H) ensure that jamming of a system does not affect normal rudder control through the remaining system. (Figure 15.6).

Figure 15.6 Rudder Control

The rudder surface is driven by three identical power units (PCUs) and each PCU is powered by one the three hydraulic systems.

Each PCU contains a control valve distributing hydraulic pressure on either side of a cylinder operating the rudder.

Power Control Units (Figure 15.7)

The operation of the PCU's is identical to that of the elevator PCU's. With the exception of some internal dimensional differnces the units are the same. Failure detection is by means of a proximity sensor installed in each PCU, which feeds a signal to the servo monitor.

Lift Modulation

General

Lift modulation is accomplished by the development of any one or a combination of the spoilers and flaps.

The flight spoilers consist of a single panel hinged to the upper surface of each wing. They are hydraulically powered from systems No. 1 and No. 2, but mechanically controlled by a lever on the center console. The flight spoilers can be deployed by the flight crew up to a maximum of 40°.

Figure 15.7 Rudder PCU Control

The ground spoilers consist of a panel hinged forward of each inboard flap on the upper trailing edge. They are electrically controlled and powered from hydraulic system No.1.

Flight Spoilers (Figures 15.8-15.9)

The command input is from a lever located on the center console. Movement of the spoilers control lever is transmitted via a push/pull rod to a torque shaft, which in turn transmits the command to a forward cable quadrant.

The PCU control valves are spring loaded down, but the spring loaded detent mechanism, connected to the input linkage, applies force to position it in the mid-position.

A micro switch on each mechanism provides a signal to the corresponding left or right flight spoiler light on the center pedestal

**FLIGHT SPOILER LH
(SPOILER RH IDENTICAL)**

CONTR
VALVE

CONTR.
VALVE

PILOT INPUT

NO. 1 SYSTEM

NO. 2 SYSTEM

LEGEND

———————— SUPPLY LINE
■■■■■■ RETURN LINE
———————— SUPPLY & RETURN LINE

Figure 15.8 Flight Spoiler Hydraulic Schematic

beside the spoiler lever. These lights illuminate green whenever the
spoilers are deployed more than 20°, and indicate that the detent
mechanism is operating.

Each flight spoiler surface is actuated by two identical PCU's. The
PCUs are independent and powered by the No.1 and No.2 hydraulic
system as follows: Inboard-system No.1 and Outboard-system No.2.

Figure 15.9 Flight Spoilers - Components

Spoiler position is reflected on an indicator in the center instrument panel. The position for each spoiler is detected by a surface position transmitter mounted on the rear wing spar. Proximity switches - one per spoiler, located between the center hinges, provides position signals to corresponding left and right caution lights on the glareshield.

These lights, marked LH FLT SPLR and RH FLT SPLR, illuminate amber whenever the flight spoilers are not down. These proximity sensors also supply inputs to the take-off configuration warning.

Operation

Flight spoiler development is intiated by pulling the spoiler control lever aft through a series of eight detents, with position markings for 1, ¼, ½, ¾, and full.

The control linkage moves the control valves on the PCU's, which move the spoilers proportionally as the handle is moved.

When the spoilers start moving, their proximity switches illuminate the amber LH and RH FLT SPLR lights on the glareshield, and the position transmitters feed signals to the spoiler pointers on the control surface position indicatore on the center instrument panel.

When the spoilers move past the ½(20°) position, the micro switches on the spring loaded detents on the PCU's are activated, and illuminate the green LEFT and RIGHT flight spoilers lights on the center pedestal.

To retract the flight spoilers, the handle is moved forward. The green lights extinguish as the spoilers retract below the mid-position, and the amber lights extinguish when the spoilers are fully stowed.

Ground Spoilers

Description

The ground spoilers consist of a single panel hinged to the upper wing surface just forward of the inboard flaps. The ground spoilers have only two operating positions: 0° and 45°. The "not down" position is indicated with amber lights located on the glareshield. The spoilers are operated each by a single actuator powered from the No.1 hydraulic system.

The main components of the system are: (Figure 15.10).
- The Spoiler Control Lever, which actuates two switches in the fully aft position (an aft position beyond full flight spoiler selection).
- The Spolier Control Unit, located in the avionics bay.
- The Dual Hydraulic Selector Valve, located in the MLG bay.
- Two Hydraulic Spoiler actuators with internal locks.
- The Proximity Switches that send a deployed signal to the glareshield indicator lights.

The ground spoiler actuator (Figure 15.11) has an internal mechanical locking device that locks the spoiler in the down position. Hydraulic pressure is required to release this lock before the actuator can extend.

Operation

Ground spoiler operation is controlled by the spoiler control lever in the cockpit, which must be placed in the fully aft EXTEND position by pushing a button on the handle and simultaneously lifting the handle aft. Thus, the ground spoilers can only be extended when the flight spoilers are already fully extended.

The spoiler control lever activates two switches, which direct an extend command from the spoiler control unit to the valve solenoids. The spoiler control unit receives inputs from power lever position

Figure 15.10 Ground Spoiler Control

switches, weight-on-wheels information from the landing gear control unit, wheel spin-up information from the anti-skid control unit, and power from the Ground Spoiler Panel ON/OFF TEST switch.

The two parts of the valve are hydraulically interconnected to ensure simultaneous operation of the spoilers. Neither spoiler actuator can be pressurized to extend unless both valves are energized.

With both solenoid valves de-energized hydraulic pressure is supplied to the 'retract' port of both actuators powering the spoilers to retract.

With both solenoid valves energized hydraulic pressure is routed through the No. 1 valve to the No. 2 valve and the "extend" port of both actuators causing both spoilers to deploy.

CYLINDER

PISTON

EXTEND PORT

RETRACT PORT

RETAINER

LOCK SEGMENT

SPRING

RETRACT ◄──► EXTEND

LOCKING PISTON

CYLINDER

ACTUATOR PISTON

NOTE
ACTUATOR PISTON SHOWN
FULLY RETRACTED AND
LOCKED

Figure 15.11 Ground Spoiler Actuator

Introduction

The wing flap system which will be described here will be the Boeing 727 Airliner. The wing flap system includes both trailing edge flaps as well as the leading edge devices. Refer to Figure 9.11 for the basic hydraulic system schematic.

Wing Flaps (Figure 15.12-15.13)

The trailing edge flaps are driven by torque tubes and jackscrews which are powered by separate hydraulic motors for the inboard and outboard set of flaps. The flap handle positions flap selector valves which direct system A hydraulic pressure to the flap motors. A cable operated followup system closes the selector valves when the flaps reach the selected position.

Full span leading edge devices include three inboard flaps and four outboard slats on each wing. The outboard trailing edge flaps operate a

Figure 15.12

followup system which positions the leading edge device control valve. As the outboard edge flaps extend to 2°, slats number 2, 3, 6, and 7 are extended. At 5° of outboard trailing edge flap extension, all of the remaining leading edge devices are extended.

All leading edge devices are mechanically locked down to prevent them from blowing back in the event that hydraulic pressure is lost after flap extension.

Flap position Indicators

Both trailing edge flap position indicators contain left and right needles which indicate the position of the respective flaps. White bands on the face of the instrument indicate the maximum needle deviation at each flap extension.

Two leading edge flap lights, one amber and the other green, indicate leading edge position. The amber light is on when any leading edge

Figure 15.13 Leading Edge Flaps

device is in transit. When the selected leading edge devices are down and locked, the green light comes on and the amber light goes out. If the green light fails to come on, the leading edge annunciator on the engineer's aux panel can be used to determine the position of each flap and slat.

When the switch on the leading edge flap annunciator panel is held to position test, a green light indicates in-transit and no light indicates up and locked. All of the lights should illuminate when the switch is held to light test. When the switch is released, all lights should be out.

After all flaps are extended, the alternate flap master switch can be turned off. The leading edge devices remain locked down by mechanical locks. It requires system A pressure to unlock and retract the leading edge devices. The trailing edge flaps are locked down by friction brake incorporated in each flap drive system.

The trailing edge flaps can be retracted by turning on the alternate flap master switch and placing the control switches up. The leading edge devices cannot be retracted by the alternate flap system.

— CONTENTS —

ABBREVIATIONS

A	Amperes
A/C	Aircraft
AC	Alternating Current
ACU	Air Conditioning Unit
ADC	Air Data Computer
ADCU	Auto Deploy Control Unit
ADF	Automatic Direction Finding
ADG	Air Driven Generator
ADI	Attitude Director Indicator
ADS	Air Data Sensor
ADV	Advisory
AFCS	Automatic Flight Control System
A/I	Anti-Ice
ALT	Altitude
ALTN	Alternate
AOA	Angle-of Attack
AP	Autopilot
AP	Auxiliary Power (APU Generator)
APC	Autopilot Computer
APC	Auxiliary Power Contactor
AP/EPC	Auxiliary Power/External Power Contactor
APP	Approach
APU	Auxiliary Power Unit
ASI	Airspeed Indicator
ATC	Air Traffic Control
ATT	Attitude
AUTO	Automatic
AUTO PERF RES	Automatic Performance Reserve
AUX	Auxiliary
AWS	Aural Warning System
AV	Arming Valve
BARO	Barometer
BC	Back Course
BFO	Beat Frequency Oscillator
BITE	Built In Test Equipment
BRT	Bright
BTBR	Bus Tie Breaker Relay
BUTE	Bent-Up-Trailing-Edge
CAP	Capture
CB	Circuit Breaker
CH (CHAN)	Channel
CL	Closed
CM	Comparator Monitor
CONT	Control
CSD	Constant Speed Drive
CTA	Current Transformer Assembly

ABBREVIATIONS

DC	Direct Current
DG	Directional Gyro
DH	Decision Height
DIFF	Differential
DME	Distance Measuring Equipment
DNLK	DownLock
DRC	Dual Remote Compensator
EAS	Equivalent Air Speed
ECM	Electronic Control Module
ECS	Environmental Control System
ECU	Electronic Control Unit (APU)
EDP	Electrical Distribution Panel
EDP	Engine Driven Pump
EGT	Exhaust Gas Temperature
ELEC (ELECT)	Electric
EMER	Emergency
EP	External Power
EPC	External Power Contactor
EPM	External Power Monitor
ESS	Essential
ETC	Essential Transfer Contactor
FCU	Fuel Control Unit
FD	Flight Director
FDC	Flight Director Computer
FDMS	Flight Director Mode Selector
FF	Fuel Flow
FLT CONT MON	Flight Control Monitoring
FOD	Foreign Object Damage
FR	From
GA	Go Around
GEN	Generator
GCR	Generator Control Relay
GCU	Generator Control Unit
GLC	Generator Line Contactor
GLCR	Generator Line Contactor Relay
GND	Ground
GPWR	Ground Power
GS	Glide Slope
GTC	Generator Transfer Contactor
GCTA	Generator Current Transformer Assembly
H	Altitude
HDG	Heading
HF	High Frequency
HOT	High Oil Temperature
HSI	Horizontal Situation Indicator
HSTCS	Horizontal Stabilizer Trim Control System

01-04   ABBREVIATIONS

HSTCU	Horizontal Stabilizer Trim Control Unit
HYD	Hydraulic
IAS	Indicated Air Speed
ICTA	Instrument Current Transformer
IDG	Integrated Drive Generator
ILS	Instrument Landing System
IN (INBD)	Inboard
INPH	Interphone
INST	Instrument
INSTL	Installation
I/P	Input
IRC	Instrument Remote Controller
ISOL	Isolation
ITT	Inter-Turbine Temperature
IVSI	Inertial Lead Vertical Speed Indicator
JB	Junction Box
KTS	Knots
KVA	Kilo Volt Amperes
LCTA	Line Current Transformer Assembly
LCV	Level Control Valve
LCV	Load Control Valve (APU)
LGCU	Landing Gear Control Unit
LH(L)	Left Hand
LK	Lock
LKD	Locked
LOC	Localiser
LOP	Low Oil Pressure
LRU	Line Replacement Unit
LTS	Lights
LWD	Left Wing Down
LVDT	Linear Variable Differential Transformer
M	Mach
M/C	Master Caution
MLG	Main Landing Gear
MIC	Microphone
MKR	Marker
MMO	Maximum Mach Operating
N_1	Low Pressure Compressor Speed (Fan Speed)
N_2	High Pressure Compressor Speed (Core Speed)
NAV	Navigation
NL	Nose Left
NLG(NG)	Nose Landing Gear
NM	Nautical Miles
NORM	Normal

ABBREVIATIONS

NR	Nose Right
N/W	Nose Wheel
O/P	Output
OUT(OUTBD)	Outboard
OVHT	Overheat
OVLD	Overload
OVSP	Overspeed
OXY	Oxygen
PASS	Passenger
PBA	Push Button Annunciator
PCU	Power Control Unit
PLA	Power Lever Angle
PMG	Permanent Magnet Generator
PMP	Power Management Panel
P_s	Static Pressure
PSI	Pounds per Square Inch
PSID	Pounds per Square Inch Differential
P_t	Total Pressure
PTT	Press to Transmit (to talk)
PTT	Press to Test
QTY	Quantity
RAT	Ram Air Turbine
RCCB	Remote Control Circuit Breaker
RH(R)	Right Hand
RLY	Relay
RMI	Radio Magnetic Indicator
RPM	Revolutions Per Minute
RTO	Rejected Take-Off
RUD	Rudder
RWD	Right Wing Down
RX	Receiver
RVDT	Rotary Variable Differential Transformer
S/A	System Annunciator
SAC	Stability Augmentation Computer
SAS	Stability Augmentation System
STAB AUG	Stability Augmentation
SAT	Static Air Temperature
SBY(STBY)	Standby
SBW	Steer-By-Wire
SCV	Steering Control Valve
S/O	Shut-Off
SPLR	Spoiler
SPKR	Speaker
SSV	Steering Selector Valve
STAB	Stabilizer

ABBREVIATIONS

306

STA EL	Station Elevation
SUBS	Subsequent
SYNC	Synchronize
SYS	System
TAS	True Air Speed
TAT	Total Air Temperature
TBD	To be Decided (Determined)
TBO	Time Between Overhaul
TCS	Touch Control Steering
TCTA	Tie Current Transformer Assembly
TD	Time Delay
T/O	Take-off
TOC	Take-Off Configuration
T/R	Thrust Reverse(r)
TRU	Transformer Rectifier Unit
T_t	Total Temperature
T_x	Transmitter
UBC	Utility Bus Contactor
UNLKD	Unlocked
UHF	Ultra High Frequency
UTIL	Utility
VANG	Vertical Angle
VFE	Maximum Airspeed with Flaps Extended
VG	Variable Geometry
VG	Vertical Gyro
VHF	Very High Frequency
VIB	Vibration
VMO	Maximum Operating Airspeed (Velocity)
VN or VNAV	Vertical Navigation
VNCC	Vertical Navigation Computer Controller
VOL	Volume
VOR	VHF Omni Directional Radio
VS	Vertical Speed
V_s	Stall Speed
VSI	Vertical Speed Indicator
WOW	Weight-On-Wheels
XFMR	Transformer
XFR	Transfer
YD	Yaw Damper
$\triangle$ P	(DELTA P) Differential Pressure

ABBREVIATIONS

AND GATE	$A \cdot B = C$		
	A	B	C
	0	0	0
	0	1	0
	1	0	0
	1	1	1

OR GATE	$A + B = C$		
	A	B	C
	0	0	0
	0	1	1
	1	0	1
	1	1	1

NOT GATE	$\overline{A} = C$	
	A	C
	0	1
	1	0

NAND GATE	$\overline{A \cdot B} = C$		
	A	B	C
	0	0	1
	0	1	1
	1	0	1
	1	1	0

NOR GATE	$\overline{A + B} = C$		
	A	B	C
	0	0	1
	0	1	0
	1	0	0
	1	1	0

'AND' GATE WITH ONE NEGATED INPUT	$\overline{A} \cdot B = C$		
	A	B	C
	0	0	0
	0	1	1
	1	0	0
	1	1	0

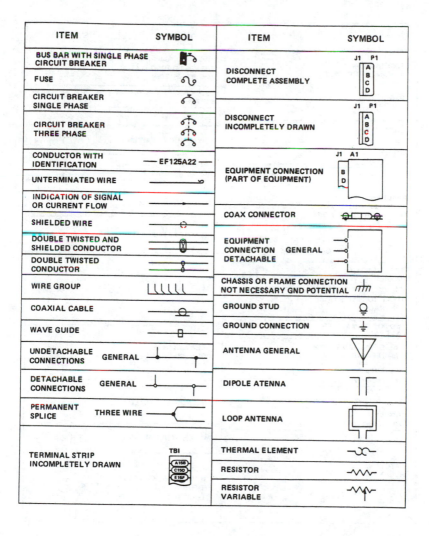

ITEM	SYMBOL	ITEM	SYMBOL
BUS BAR WITH SINGLE PHASE CIRCUIT BREAKER		DISCONNECT COMPLETE ASSEMBLY	J1 P1 A B C D
FUSE			
CIRCUIT BREAKER SINGLE PHASE		DISCONNECT INCOMPLETELY DRAWN	J1 P1 A B C D
CIRCUIT BREAKER THREE PHASE			
CONDUCTOR WITH IDENTIFICATION	EF125A22	EQUIPMENT CONNECTION (PART OF EQUIPMENT)	J1 A1 B D
UNTERMINATED WIRE			
INDICATION OF SIGNAL OR CURRENT FLOW		COAX CONNECTOR	
SHIELDED WIRE			
DOUBLE TWISTED AND SHIELDED CONDUCTOR		EQUIPMENT CONNECTION GENERAL DETACHABLE	
DOUBLE TWISTED CONDUCTOR			
WIRE GROUP		CHASSIS OR FRAME CONNECTION NOT NECESSARY GND POTENTIAL	
COAXIAL CABLE		GROUND STUD	
WAVE GUIDE		GROUND CONNECTION	
UNDETACHABLE CONNECTIONS GENERAL		ANTENNA GENERAL	
DETACHABLE CONNECTIONS GENERAL		DIPOLE ATENNA	
PERMANENT SPLICE THREE WIRE		LOOP ANTENNA	
TERMINAL STRIP INCOMPLETELY DRAWN	TBI A168 C150 E15F	THERMAL ELEMENT	
		RESISTOR	
		RESISTOR VARIABLE	

ELECTRICAL SYMBOLS

01-09
May 83

ITEM	SYMBOL	ITEM	SYMBOL
PUSH BUTTON ANNUNCIATOR (PBA) (PUSH TYPE) TYPICAL		MECHANICALLY ACTUATED SPRING LOADED SWITCH (MICRO SWITCH)	
		TEMPERATURE ACTUATED SWITCH	
		INTERIA SWITCH	
LIMIT SWITCH		CENTRIFUGAL SWITCH	
VOLTMETER			
AMMETER		PRESSURE OR VACUUM ACTUATED SWITCH	
FREQUENCY METER		LIQUID–LEVEL ACTUATED SWITCH	
INDICATOR INSTRUMENT GENERAL			
SWITCH GENERAL LOCKING MOMENTARY		ROTARY SWITCH	
2 POLE SWITCH (MOMENTARY)		RELAY	
4 POLE TOGGLE SWITCH GENERAL			
TWO POSITION SWITCH GENERAL			
THREE POSITION SWITCH (ON–OFF–ON) GENERAL		RELAY WITH DELAYED DROP OFF	
PUSH TYPE SWITCH (OFF–MOMENTARY–ON)			
PUSH TYPE SWITCH (ON–MOMENTARY–OFF)		SOLENOID OPERATED VALVE	
TOGGLE SWITCH (ON–OFF–MOMENTARY ON)			
LATCHING RELAY		MOTOR GENERAL	
		THREE PHASE CURRENT MOTOR WITH TAPPED STARPOINT	

01-10
May 83   **ELECTRICAL SYMBOLS**

ITEM	SYMBOL	ITEM	SYMBOL
RESISTOR WITH OFF POSITION VARIABLE		ENERGIZING COIL FOR VALVE/RELAY ETC	
RESISTOR VARIABLE (POTENTIOMETER)	OR	CRYSTAL	
SHUNT		SCR TYPICAL	
TEMPERATURE SENSING RESISTOR GENERAL		TRANSISTOR TYPICAL	
LIGHTSENSING RESISTOR		THERMOCOUPLE GENERAL	
HEATER ELEMENT		BATTERY	
PITOT HEATER		PHOTO CELL	
SQUIB		BELL	
CAPACITOR		BUZZER	
CAPACITOR VARIABLE		MICROPHONE	
TEMPERATURE SENSING ELEMENT/FIRE WIRE		SPEAKER	
INDUCTANCE GENERAL		PHONE	
INDUCTION COIL WITH CORE		HANDSET	
TRANSFORMER WITH AIR CORE / METAL CORE		HEADPHONE DOUBLE / SINGLE	
CURRENT TRANSFORMER		LAMP	
DIODE		INCANDESCENT LAMP	
ZENER DIODE		INDICATOR LIGHT	A= AMBER W= WHITE G= GREEN R= RED B= BLUE
ZENER DIODE SYMMETRIC			

ELECTRICAL SYMBOLS

1. Introduction

1.1 General

Fluid power systems are those that transmit and control power through use of a pressurized fluid (liquid or gas) within an enclosed circuit.

Types of symbols commonly used in drawing circuit diagrams for fluid power systems are Pictorial, Cutaway, and Graphic. These symbols are fully explained in the USA Standard Drafting Manual (Ref. 2).

1.1.1 *Pictorial symbols* are very useful for showing the interconnection of components. They are difficult to standardize from a functional basis.

1.1.2 *Cutaway symbols* emphasize construction. These symbols are complex to draw and the functions are not readily apparent.

1.1.3 *Graphic symbols* emphasize the function and methods of operation of components. These symbols are simple to draw. Component functions and methods of operation are obvious. Graphic symbols are capable of crossing language barriers, and can promote a universal understanding of fluid power systems.

Graphic symbols for fluid power systems should be used in conjunction with the graphic symbols for other systems published by the USA Standards Institute (Ref. 3-7 inclusive).

1.1.3.1 Complete graphic symbols are those which give symbolic representation of the component and all of its features pertinent to the circuit diagram.

1.1.3.2 Simplified graphic symbols are stylized versions of the complete symbols.

1.1.3.3 Composite graphic symbols are an organization of simplified or complete symbols. Composite symbols usually represent a complex component.

1.2 Scope and Purpose

1.2.1 *Scope* — This standard presents a system of graphic symbols for fluid power diagrams.

1.2.1.1 Elementary forms of symbols are:
Circles　　Rectangles　　Arcs　　Dots
Squares　　Triangles　　Arrows　　Crosses

1.2.1.2 Symbols using words or their abbreviations are avoided. Symbols capable of crossing language barriers are presented herein.

1.2.1.3 Component function rather than construction is emphasized by the symbol.

1.2.1.4 The means of operating fluid power components are shown as part of the symbol (where applicable).

1.2.1.5 This standard shows the basic symbols, describes the principles on which the symbols are based, and illustrates some representative composite symbols. Composite symbols can be devised for any fluid power component by combining basic symbols.

Simplified symbols are shown for commonly used components.

1.2 1.6 This standard provides basic symbols which differentiate between hydraulic and pneumatic fluid power media.

1.2.2 *Purpose*

1.2.2.1 The purpose of this standard is to provide a system of fluid power graphic symbols for industrial and educational purposes.

1.2.2.2 The purpose of this standard is to simplify design, fabrication, analysis, and service of fluid power circuits.

1.2.2.3 The purpose of this standard is to provide fluid power graphic symbols which are internationally recognized.

1.2.2.4 The purpose of this standard is to promote universal understanding of fluid power systems.

2. Symbol Rules

2.1 Symbols show connections, flow paths, and functions of components represented. They can indicate conditions occurring during transition from one flow path arrangement to another. Symbols do not indicate construction, nor do they indicate values, such as pressure, flow rate, and other component settings.

2.2 Symbols do not indicate locations of ports, direction of shifting of spools, or positions of actuators on actual component.

2.3 Symbols may be rotated or reversed without altering their meaning except in the cases of: a.) Lines to Reservoir, 4.1.1;b.) Vented Manifold, 4.1.2.3; c.) Accumulator, 4.2.

2.4 Line Technique

Keep line widths approximately equal. Line width does not alter meaning of symbols.

2.4.1 Solid Line — Main

(Main line conductor, outline, and shaft)

HYDRAULIC SYMBOLS

2.4.2 Dash Line — Pilot

(Pilot line for control)

2.4.3 Dotted Line

(Exhaust or Drain line)

2.4.4 Center Line

(Enclosure outline)

2.4.5 Sensing Line — Same as line to which it connects.

2.4.6 Lines Crossing (The intersection is not necessarily at a 90° angle.)

2.4.7 Lines Joining

2.5 Basic symbols may be shown any suitable size. Size may be varied for emphasis or clarity. Relative sizes should be maintained. (As in the following example.)

2.5.1 Circle and Semi-Circle

2.5.1.1 Large and small circles may be used to signify that one component is the "main" and the other the auxiliary.

2.5.2 Triangle △ ▲

2.5.3 Arrow

2.5.4 Square

Rectangle

2.6 Letter combinations used as parts of graphic symbols are not necessarily abbreviations.

2.7 In multiple envelope symbols, the flow condition shown nearest an actuator symbol takes place when that control is caused or permitted to actuate

2.8 Each symbol is drawn to show normal, at-rest, or neutral conditon of component unless multiple diagrams are furnished showing various phases of circuit operation. Show an actuator symbol for each flow path conditon possessed by the component.

2.9 An arrow through a symbol at approximately 45 degrees indicates that the component can be adjusted or varied.

2.10 An arrow parallel to the short side of a symbol, within the symbol, indicates that the component is pressure compensated.

2.11 A line terminating in a dot to represent a thermometer is the symbol for temperature cause or effect.

See Temperature Controls 7.9, Temperature Indicators and Recorders 9.1.2, and Temperature Compensation 10.16.3 and 4.

2.12 External ports are located where flow lines connect to basic symbol, except where component enclosure symbol is used.

External ports are located at intersections of flow lines and component enclosure symbol when enclosure is used, see Section 11.

2.13 Rotating shafts are symbolized by an arrow which indicates direction of rotation (assume arrow on near side of shaft).

3. Conductor, Fluid

3.1 Line, Working (main)

3.2 Line, Pilot (for control)

3.3 Line, Exhaust and Liquid Drain

HYDRAULIC SYMBOLS

shall be drawn the same as the line to which it connects.

3.5 Flow, Direction of

3.5.1 Pneumatic

3.5.2 Hydraulic

3.6 Line, Pneumatic (Outlet to Atmosphere)

3.6.1 Plain orifice, unconnectable

3.6.2 Connectable orifice (e.g. Thread)

3.7 Line with Fixed Restriction

3.8 Line, Flexible

3.9 Station, Testing, measurement, or power take-off

3.9.1 Plugged port

3.10 Quick Disconnect

3.10.1 Without Checks
Connected   Disconnected

3.10.2 With Two Checks
Connected   Disconnected

3.10.3 With One Check
Connected   Disconnected

3.11 Rotating Coupling

4. Energy Storage and Fluid Storage

4.1 Reservoir
   Vented   Pressurized

NOTE: *Reservoirs are conventionally drawn in the horizontal plane. All lines enter and leave from above.*

4.1.1 Reservoir with Connecting Lines Above Fluid Level

Below Fluid Level

* Show line entering or leaving below reservoir only when such bottom connection is essential to circuit function.

4.1.2 Simplified symbol

The symbols are used as part of a complete circuit. They are analogous to the ground symbol of electrical diagrams. IEC . Several such symbols may be used in one diagram to represent the same reservoir.

4.1.2.1 Below Fluid Level

4.1.2.2 Above Fluid Level

(The return line is drawn to terminate at the upright legs of the tank symbol.)

4.1.2.3 Vented Manifold

4.2 Accumulator

4.2.1 Accumulator, Spring Loaded

HYDRAULIC SYMBOLS

4.2.2 Accumulator, Gas Charged

4.2.3 Accumulator, Weighted

4.3 Receiver, for Air or Other Gases

4.4 Energy Source (Pump, Compressor, Accumulator, etc.)

This symbol may be used to represent a fluid power source which may be a pump, compressor, or another associated system.

Hydraulic ———   Pneumatic ——▷——

Simplified Symbol

Example:

5. Fluid Conditioners

Devices which control the physical characteristics of the fluid.

5.1 Heat Exchanger

5.1.1 Heater

Inside triangles indicate the introduction of heat.   Outside triangles show the heating medium is liquid.   Outside triangles show the heating medium is gaseous.

5.1.2 Cooler

or

(Corners may be filled in to represent triangles.)

5.1.3 Temperature Controller (The temperature is to be maintained between two predetermined limits.)

or

5.2 Filter — Strainer

5.3 Separator

5.3.1 With Manual Drain

5.3.2 With Automatic Drain

5.4 Filter — Separator

5.4.1 With Manual Drain

5.4.2 With Automatic Drain

5.5 Dessicator (Chemical Dryer)

HYDRAULIC SYMBOLS

315

5.6 Lubricator

5.6.1 Less Drain

5.6.2 With Manual Drain

6. Linear Devices

6.1 Cylinders. Hydraulic and Pneumatic

6.1.1 Single Acting

6.1.2 Double Acting

6.1.2.1 Single End Rod

6.1.2.2 Double End Rod

6.1.2.3 Fixed Cushion, Advance and Retract

6.1.2.4 Adjustable Cushion, Advance Only

6.1.2.5 Use these symbols when diameter of rod compared to diameter of bore is significant to circuit function.

Non Cushion   Cushion, Advance and Retract

6.2 Pressure Intensifier

6.3 Servo Positioner (Simplified)

Hydraulic   Pneumatic

6.4 Discrete Positioner

Combine two or more basic cylinder symbols.

7. Actuators and Controls

7.1 Spring

7.2 Manual

(Use as general symbol without indication of specific type; i.e., foot, hand, leg arm.)

7.2.1 Push Button

7.2.2 Lever

7.2.3 Pedal or Treadle

7.3 Mechanical

7.4 Detent

(Show a notch for each detent in the actual component being symbolized. A short line indicates which detent is in use.) Detent may,

HYDRAULIC SYMBOLS

for convenience, be positioned on either end of symbol.

7.5 Pressure Compensated

7.6 Electrical

7.6.1 Solenoid (Single Winding)

7.6.2 Reversing Motor

7.7 Pilot Pressure

7.7.1

Remote Supply

7.7.2

Internal Supply

7.7.3 Actuation by Released Pressure

by Remote Exhaust   by Internal Return

7.7.4 Pilot Controlled, Spring Centered

Simplified Symbol

Complete Symbol

7.7.5 Pilot Differential

Simplified Symbol   Complete Symbol

7.8.1 Solenoid or Pilot

External Pilot Supply

Internal Pilot Supply and Exhaust

7.8.2 Solenoid and Pilot

7.9 Thermal — A mechanical device responding to thermal change.

7.9.1 Local Sensing

7.9.2 With Bulb for Remote Sensing

7.10 Servo

(This symbol contains representation for energy input, command input, and resultant output.)

7.11 Composite Actuators (and, or, and/or)

Basic . . One signal only causes the device to operate.

And . . One signal and a second signal both cause the device to operate.

Or . . One signal or the other signal causes the device to operate.

And/Or . . The solenoid and the pilot or the man-

HYDRAULIC SYMBOLS

317

The solenoid and the pilot or the manual override and the pilot.

The solenoid and the pilot or a manual override and the pilot or a manual override alone.

8. Rotary Devices

8.1 Basic Symbol

8.1.1 With Ports

8.1.2 With Rotating Shaft, with control and with Drain.

8.2 Hydraulic Pump

8.2.1 Fixed Displacement

8.2.1.1 Unidirectional

8.2.1.2 Bidirectional

8.2.2 Variable Displacement, Non-compensated

8.2.2.1 Unidirectional

Simplified   Complete

8.2.2.2 Bidirectional

Simplified   Complete

8.2.3 Variable Displacement, Pressure Compensated

8.2.3.1 Unidirectional

Simplified   Complete

8.2.3.2 Bidirectional

Simplified   Complete

8.3 Hydraulic Motor

8.3.1 Fixed Displacement

8.3.1.2 Bidirectional

8.3.2 Variable Displacement

8.3.2.1 Unidirectional

8.3.2.2 Bidirectional

HYDRAULIC SYMBOLS

318

8.4 Pump-Motor, Hydraulic

8.4.1 Operating in one direction as a pump. Operating in the other direction as a motor.

8.4.1.1 Complete Symbol

8.4.1.2 Simplified Symbol

8.4.2 Operating one direction of flow as either a pump or as a motor.

8.4.2.1 Complete Symbol

8.4.2.2 Simplified Symbol

8.4.3 Operating in both directions of flow either as a pump or as a motor. (Variable displacement, pressure compensated shown.)

8.4.3.1 Complete Symbol

8.4.3.2 Simplified Symbol

8.5 Pump, Pneumatic

8.5.1 Compressor, Fixed Displacement

8.5.2 Vacuum Pump, Fixed Displacement

8.6 Motor, Pneumatic

8.6.1 Unidirectional

8.6.2 Bidirectional

8.7 Oscillator

8.7.1 Hydraulic

8.7.2 Pneumatic

8.8 Motors, Engines

8.8.1 Electric Motor

          IEC

8.8.2 Heat Engine (E.G. internal combustion engine.)

9. Instruments and Accessories

9.1 Indicating and Recording

9.1.1 Pressure

HYDRAULIC SYMBOLS

9.1.2 Temperature

9.1.3 Flow Meter
9.1.3.1 Flow Rate

9.1.3.2 Totalizing

9.2 Sensing
9.2.1 Venturi

9.2.2 Orifice Plate

9.2.3 Pitot Tube

9.2.4 Nozzle

Hydraulic   Pneumatic

9.3 Accessories
9.3.1 Pressure Switch

9.3.2 Muffler

10. Valves

A basic valve symbol is composed of one or more envelopes with lines inside the envelope to represent flow paths and flow conditioners between ports. Three symbol systems are used to represent valve types: single envelope, both finite and infinite position; multiple envelope, finite position; and multiple envelope, infinite position.

10.1 In infinite position single envelope valves, the envelope is imagined to move to illustrate how pressure or flow conditions are controlled as the valve is actuated.

10.2 Multiple envelopes symbolize valves providing more than one finite flow path option for the fluid. The multiple envelope moves to represent how flow paths change when the the valving element within the component is shifted to its finite positions.

10.3 Multiple envelope valves capable of infinite positioning between certain limits are symbolized as in 10.2 above with the addition of horizontal bars which are drawn parallel to the envelope. The horizontal bars are the clues to the infinite positioning function possessed by the valve re-represented.

10.4 Envelopes

10.5 Ports

10.6 Ports, Internally Blocked

Symbol System 10.1   Symbol System 10.2

10.7 Flow Paths, Internally Open (Symbol System 10.1 and 10.2)

Symbol System 10.1   Symbol System 10.2

10.8 Flow Paths, Internally Open (Symbol System 10.3)

HYDRAULIC SYMBOLS

10.9 Two-Way Valves (2 Ported Valves)

10.9.1 On-Off (Manual Shut Off)

Simplified

Off

On

10.9.2 Check

Simplified Symbol

Flow to the right is blocked. Flow to the left is permitted.

(Composite Symbol)

10.9.3 Check, Pilot-Operated to Open

10.9.4 Check, Pilot-Operated to Close

10.9.5 Two-Way Valves

10.9.5.1 Two-Position

Normally Closed   Normally Open

10.9.5.2 Infinite Position

Normally Closed   Normally Open

10.10 Three-Way Valves

10.10.1 Two-Position

10.10.1.1 Normally Open

10.10.1.2 Normally Closed

10.10.1.3 (Distributor Pressure is distributed first to one port, then the other).

10.10.1.4 Two-Pressure

10.10.2 Double Check Valve — Double check valves can be built with and without "cross bleed". Such valves with two poppets do not usually allow pressure to momentarily "cross bleed" to return during transition. Valves with one poppet may allow "cross bleed" as these symbols illustrate.

10.10.2.1 Without Cross Bleed (One way flow).

10.10.2.2 With Cross Bleed (Reverse flow permitted).

10.11 Four-Way Valves

10.11.1 Two-Position

Normal

HYDRAULIC SYMBOLS

Actuated

10.11.2 Three-Position

(a) Normal

(b) Actuated Left

(c) Actuated Right

10.11.3 Typical Flow Paths for Center Condition of Three-Position Valves

10.11.4 Two-Position, Snap Action with Transition.

As the valve element shifts from one position to the other, it passes through an intermediate position. If it is essential to circuit function to symbolize this "in transit" conditon, it can be shown in the center position, enclosed by dashed lines.

Typical Transition Symbol

10.12 Infinite Positioning (between open and closed)

10.12.1 Normally Closed

10.12.2 Normally Open

10.13 Pressure Control Valves

10.13.1 Pressure Relief

Simplified Symbol Denotes

Normal   Actuated (Relieving)

10.13.2 Sequence

10.13.3 Pressure Reducing

ISO

HYDRAULIC SYMBOLS

322

10.13.4 Pressure Reducing and Relieving

10.13.5 Airline Pressure Regulator (Adjustable, Relieving)

10.14 Infinite Positioning Three-Way Valves

10.15 Infinite Positioning Four-Way Valves

10.16 Flow Control Valves (See 3.7)

10.16.1 Adjustable, Non-Compensated (Flow control in each direction).

10.16.2 Adjustable with Bypass

Flow is controlled to the right. Flow to the left bypasses control.

10.16.3 Adjustable and Pressure Compensated with Bypass

10.16.4 Adjustable, Temperature and Pressure Compensated.

11. Representative Composite Symbols

11.1 Component Enclosure

Component enclosure may surround a complete symbol or a group of symbols to represent an assembly. It is used to convey more information about component connections and functions. Enclosure indicates extremity of component or assembly. External ports are assumed to be on enclosure line and indicate connections to component.

Flow lines shall cross enclosure line without loops or dots.

11.2 Airline Accessories (Filter, Regulator and Lubricator).

Composite

Simplified

HYDRAULIC SYMBOLS

11.3 Pumps and Motors

11.3.1 Pumps

11.3.1.1 Double, Fixed Displacement, One Inlet and Two Outlets.

11.3.1.2 Double, with Integral Check Unloading and Two Outlets.

11.3.1.3 Integral Variable Flow Rate Control with Overload Relief.

11.3.1.4 Variable Displacement with Integral Replenishing Pump and Control Valves.

HYDRAULIC SYMBOLS

11.4 Valves

11.4.1 Relief, Balanced Type

11.4.2 Remote Operated Sequency with Integral Check.

11.4.3 Remote and Direct Operated Sequence with Differential areas and Integral Check.

11.4.4 Pressure Reducing with Integral Check.

11.4.5 Pilot Operated Check

11.4.5.1 Differential Pilot Opened.

11.4.5.2

HYDRAULIC SYMBOLS

11.4.6 Two-Positions, Four Connection Solenoid and Pilot Actuated, with Manual Pilot Override.

Simplified Symbol

Complete Symbol

HYDRAULIC SYMBOLS

11.4.7 Two-Position, Five Connection. Solenoid Control Pilot Actuated with Detents and Throttle Exhaust.

Simplified Symbol

Complete Symbol

11.4.8 Variable Pressure Compensated Flow Control and Overload Relief.

HYDRAULIC SYMBOLS

CONTENTS

INTRODUCTION

Three independent systems provide hydraulic power to operate the ailerons, elevators, rudder, flight and ground spoilers, wheel brakes, nose wheel steering and landing gear extension and retraction.

All systems operate at a working pressure of 3000 psi, and use synthetic hydraulic fluid SKYDROL 500 B.

The three systems—designated as No. 1, No. 2 and No. 3—are continuously operating and supply power to their respective sub-systems as shown in figures 1 and 2.

System management is controlled from the hydraulic systems control panel in the flight deck which contains pump on/off switches, low pressure caution lights, high temperature caution lights, pressure gauges and reservoir quantity gauges. (figure 3)

No. 1 system derives primary power from an engine driven pump (1A PUMP) mounted on the left engine. Additional power is provided by an electric pump (1B PUMP).

No. 2 system is similar, except that the EDP 2A PUMP is mounted on the right engine, and the electric pump is designated as 2B PUMP.

No. 3 system derives power from a continuously operating electric pump (3A PUMP), with a second electric pump available for additional power (3B PUMP).

The 3B PUMP is also automatically powered from the air driven generator in cases of an extreme emergency.

Each system consists of the following major components:

- Hydraulic Reservoir
- Two Hydraulic Pumps
- Hydro-Pneumatic Accumulator
- Pressure Manifold
- Return Manifold
- A section of the Hydraulic Systems Control panel

Figure 1   Hydraulic System Distribution

- Ground Service Panel
- Heat Exchanger (1 and 2 systems only)

All system components are connected by rigid lines and flexible hoses. Deutsch Permaswage couplings are used at permanent joints, and Harrison Flareless couplings are used at removable pipe connections.

Figure 2 Hydraulic Power Distribution

Figure 3   Hydraulic Control Panel

NO. 1 HYDRAULIC SYSTEM

General (Figure 4)

Hydraulic power is supplied by the engine driven 1A PUMP installed on the No.1 engine accessory gear box. An alternate power supply is also provided by an electric pump (1B PUMP). This pump is powered from AC Bus 2.

The main components of the No. 1 hydraulic system are located on the left hand side of the aft equipment bay (Figure 5).

Description

The No. 1 hydraulic system consists of:

- Engine Driven Pump
- Electric Pump
- Firewall Shut-Off Valve
- Hydraulic Fluid Reservoir
- Two Pump Case Drain Filters
- Pressure Manifold
- Return Manifold
- Accumulator
- Heat Exchanger (shared with No.2 system)
- Overflow Reservoir
- Ground Service Panel
- Part of the Hydraulic Systems Control Panel in cockpit.

Figure 4　No. 1 Hydraulic System—Schematic

Figure 5   No. 1 System—Major Components

Engine Driven Pump (Figure 6)

The engine driven pump (EDP) 1A is installed on the gear box of the engine No.1.

It is a demand flow, variable delivery, pressure compensated piston type pump.

Figure 6   Engine Driven Pump

The pump specifications are as follows:

- Rated delivery   10.65 GPM (U.S.)
- Rated discharge pressure   3000 PSI
- Minimum full flow pressure   2850 PSI
- Max. case drain flow at 0 output flow   0.6 GPM (U.S.)
- Rated temperature   180°F (82.2°C)
- Rated speed   5000 RPM

A drain line, connected from the front of the pump casing to a drain gallery, dumps the fluid overboard in case of pump seal leakage.

NOTE: EDP's from systems No.1 and No.2 are identical and inter- changeable.

Electric Pump

The electric pump (1B PUMP) of No.1 system is mounted on the left hand side of the aft equipment bay.

It is a demand flow, variable delivery, pressure compensated piston type pump.

The pump specifications are as follows:

- Rated delivery   3.7 GPM (U.S.)
- Rated discharge pressure   3000 PSI
- Minimum full flow pressure   2700 PSI
- Max. case drain flow at 0 output flow   0.7 GPM

Electric motor specifications are:

- Input   115/200 VAC, 3 0, 400 Hz
- Rating   7.5 H. P. Max. continuous
- Rated current   24 amps. max.
- Starting current   125 amps.

Electric pump 1B is supplied from AC Bus 2.

The pump is selected with the ELECT PUMP switch on the hydraulic control panel (Figure 3)

NOTE: Electric pumps from system No. 1, 2 and No. 3 are identical and interchangeable.

Firewall Shut-off Valve (Figure 7)

The firewall shut-off valve mounted in the aft equipment bay is an electrically operated gate valve.

The valve is located on the EDP suction line and incorporates a thermal relief valve as well as a gate position indicator. Electrical power to the valve is provided from DC bus 1 via a relay that is energized when the L. H. ENG FIRE PUSH PBA on the glareshield is latched in.

Figure 7   Shut-Off Valve

Hydraulic Fluid Reservoir (Figure 8)

The hydraulic reservoir is self-pressurizing to ensure positive pump feed at altitude and has a capacity of 150 cu. in.

Two separate chambers in the reservoir contain a large and a small piston, which are rigidly connected together (bootstrapped). With system pressure of 3000 psi acting on the small piston, a pressure of 55 psi is obtained in the large piston chamber, which forms the fluid reservoir and feeds the pumps.

Figure 8 Hydraulic Fluid Reservoir

The reservoir also contains a fluid level indicator which gives a direct reading for ground checks or filling. A transmitter also transmits the fluid level to an indicator located on the cockpit hydraulic control panel (Figure 3).

Temperature sensing is accomplished with two temperature switches mounted in the base. One of the temperature switches activates a cooling fan in the air/oil heat exchanger when the fluid attains a temperature of 160°F (71°C). The second provides an overheat warning in the cockpit should the fluid temperature reach 205°F (96°C).

The reservoir is protected against overpressure by a relief/drain valve. This valve can be manually opened for system bleeding after ground servicing. In addition it acts as a relief valve should reservoir internal pressure become excessive (approximately 69 PSI).

The reservoir has 6 ports:

- one Pressure Port
- two Suction Ports (one for each pump)
- two Return Ports (one from system return and one from the filters and heat exchanger line)
- one Bleed/Overspill Port (relief/drain valve).

Case Drain Filters (Figure 5)

Each pump has its own case drain filter, which filters the pump case drain fluid before it is returned to the reservoir.

The filter elements are rated for 15 microns absolute and contain a differential pressure indicator actuating at 18.5 PSID.

Should the filter element become excessively clogged, there is no bypass capability.

An automatic shut-off is included to prevent fluid drainage on removal of the bowl and filter element.

Pressure Manifold

No. 1 system incorporates a pressure manifold which accepts fluid from both system pumps and a ground pressure port. The fluid is filtered within the manifold and ported to the system pressure lines. The pressure manifold also contains a pressure transducer which drives the pressure gauge on the control panel.

The system relief valve installed in the manifold is designed to limit system pressure to 3500 PSI.

The removable filter has an absolute rating of 15 micron and incorporates a differential pressure indicator which will activate should 55 PSID be felt across the filter element. There is no bypass of the filter should it become excessively restricted. An automatic shut-off is incorporated to prevent fluid drainage during the removal of bowl and filter element.

Return Manifold

The return manifold consists of a return filter with a bypass relief valve. The filter rating is 5 microns and the differential pressure indicator will actuate at 70 PSID. The relief valve will allow full flow at 160 PSI. An automatic shut-off valve is incorporated to prevent spillage during filter removal.

Accumulator

No. 1 system incorporates one accumulator for shock damping and temporary emergency power.

It is a hydro-pneumatic piston type accumulator using nitrogen as pre-charge gas. The hydraulic fluid capacity of the accumulator when charged is 50 cubic inches. Pre-charge pressure is 1500 PSI.

The accumulator pressure gauge and charging valve are located on the No. 1 system service panel.

Heat Exchanger

Fluid cooling of No. 1 and No. 2 systems is accomplished with a common air/oil heat exchanger. Located in the center of the aft equipment bay, the heat exchanger is designed to limit system fluid temperature to approximately 180°F (82°C).

Cooling air is obtained from the ram air duct, supplemented by a fan located within the heat exchanger housing. Although utilizing a common heat exchanger unit, system fluid from No. 1 and No. 2 hydraulic pump case drain lines follow independent paths within the heat exchanger to ensure that no fluid mixing occurs.

Cooling fan operation is automatically actuated, by a thermal switch located in the reservoir, when a rising fluid temperature of 160°F (71°C) is sensed. De-activation of the fan occurs when the fluid temperature is lowered to 140°F (60°C).

Ground testing of the fan is accomplished by a push-button switch which is located on junction box No. 5 in the aft equipment bay. (figure 11)

Overflow Tank

The overflow tank is a plastic bottle connected to the reservoir relief/drain valve port.

Its purpose is to collect fluid from the reservoir during bleeding or in case of relief valve actuation. It has a capacity of approximately 1 QT.

Ground Service Panel

The No. 1 system service panel is located just within the aft equipment bay door on the left side. The panel incorporates the following items:

- an Accumulator Gauge including a nitrogen charging valve.
- one Disconnect for system filling.
- one Pressure and one Return Disconnect for ground power.

All disconnects are of the quick-disconnect type and include dust caps.

Hydraulic Systems Control Panel (Figure 3)

Located on the overhead panel, the hydraulic systems control panel includes the following No. 1 system indicators and controls:

Pressure Gauge:

Graduated from 0 to 4 × 1000 PSI. The gauge is driven electrically from a pressure transducer installed on the pressure manifold.

Fluid Level Gauge:

Marked at 0, 50, 100 percent with green band from 45–85%.
The gauge is driven electrically by the transmitter located on the reservoir.

High Temperature Caution Lights:

The HI-TEMP caution light is operated by a temperature switch mounted on the reservoir, if the fluid temperature in the reservoir reaches 205°F (96°C) (Figure 11).

Low Pressure Caution Lights:

Two low pressure caution lights identified L. ENG. PUMP and ELECT PUMP are connected to two pressure switches on the pressure manifold.

These switches sense pump delivery pressure. Should output pressure of the pump decrease below 1800 PSI the corresponding switch will operate the low pressure caution light.

Electric Pump Switch:

When required the No. 1 hydraulic system can be powered by the electric 1B Pump. This pump is activated from the ELECT PUMP switch on the control panel.

NO. 2 HYDRAULIC SYSTEM

General

Hydraulic power is supplied by the engine driven pump (EDP) 2A installed on the No. 2 engine accessory gear box.

An alternate power supply is also provided by an electric pump (2B PUMP). This pump is powered from the AC Bus 1.

The main components of the No. 2 hydraulic system are located on the right hand side of the aft equipment bay (Figure 5).

Description

Since hydraulic system No. 2 is essentially identical to No. 1 system, only the components differing from system No. 1 will be described in this section.

Hydraulic Fluid Reservoir

No. 2 reservoir, although identical in operation, differs in capacity. Capacity of No. 2 reservoir is 240 cubic inches.

This difference is due to the fact that the No. 2 system also powers the outboard braking system.

No. 2 reservoir also incorporates an additional return connection for the outboard braking system.

Heat Exchanger

Common with No. 1 system, but both systems are isolated from each other.

NO. 3 HYDRAULIC SYSTEM

General

The No.3 Hydraulic system is similar to the No. 1 and No. 2 systems except that hydraulic pressure is supplied by two electric pumps, 3A PUMP and 3B PUMP. Electrical power supply to the pumps is provided by:

- 115/200 volt, 3 phase from AC Bus 1 to the 3B pump.
- 115/200 volt, 3 phase from AC Bus 2 to the 3A pump.

Each pump is manually controlled by an ELECT PUMP ON/OFF switch on the hydraulic systems control panel.

A heat exchanger is not required for this system since it is cooled by the hydraulic lines running through the fuel in the wing tanks.

All components are located near the main landing gear wheel wells.

Description (Figures 9 & 10)

The No. 3 hydraulic system consists of:

- two Electric Pumps
- Hydraulic Fluid Reservoir
- two Pump Case Drain Filters
- Pressure Manifold
- Return Manifold
- Accumulator
- Overflow Reservoir
- Ground Service Panel
- Section of the Hydraulic Systems Control Panel

Since many components of system No. 3 are identical to No. 1 system, only those components that differ will be described here.

**AILERONS
RUDDER
ELEVATORS**

**LANDING GEAR
NOSE WHEEL STEERING
INBOARD BRAKES**

LEGEND

▬▬▬▬ SUPPLY LINE
∎∎∎∎∎ SUCTION LINE
—·—·— FILTER LINE
·············· RETURN LINE
▬▬▬▬ BLEED & INSTR. LINE
════════ NITROGEN PRESSURE LINE

Figure 9   No. 3 Hydraulic System—Schematic

Electric Pumps

The two electric pumps are located in the left and right side fillets of the aft belly fairing.

The 3A PUMP is mounted on the left hand side and the 3B PUMP on

ACCUMULATOR
CHARGING POINT
AND PRESSURE
GAUGE

PRESS RET

NO. 3
HYDRAULIC
SYSTEM
SERVICE PANEL

GROUND
SERVICING
PANEL

AC PUMP 3B

NITROGEN
CHARGING
POINT

PRESSURE
MANIFOLD

RETURN MANIFOLD

OVERSPILL
RESERVOIR

CASE DRAIN
FILTER

ACCUMULATOR

AC
PUMP
3A

FILL

RESERVOIR

FWD

ACOUSTIC
FILTER

Figure 10   No. 3 System Components

the right hand side. They are of the same type and specification as those of No. 1 and No. 2 systems.

The 3A PUMP is the primary pump and the 3B PUMP is the secondary pump.

The pressure lines incorporate an acoustic filter to reduce the noise produced by the pumps.

Hydraulic Fluid Reservoir

The reservoir of the No. 3 systems operates on the same principle as those of No. 1 and No. 2 systems.

The capacity of the reservoir is 690 cubic inches. The larger capacity is required since system No.3 also supplies hydraulic fluid to the landing gear.

The inlet and outlet ports are identical to those in No. 2 system.

Accumulator

The No. 3 system accumulator is of the same type and function as those of No. 1 and No. 2 systems but differs in capacity (100 cubic inches). Also, the pressure gauge and the charging valve are located adjacent to the accumulator instead of the ground service panel.

Ground Service Panel

Located in the aft R/H wing root, the service panel provides one pressure and one return quick disconnect for ground power. The system filling point is located in the R/H wheel well.

Hydraulic Systems Control Panel

With the exception of two "ON/OFF" switches for electrical pumps 3A and 3B (instead of one), the system No. 3 section of the control panel is identical to those of Systems No. 1 and No. 2.

OPERATION

General

During normal take-off and landing conditions, all six hydraulic pumps are operating. During cruise, only the 1A PUMP (EDP), 2A PUMP (EDP) and the 3A PUMP are in operation. The three other pumps (1B, 2B and 3B) are manually switched off once the aircraft has reached a safe altitude.

Ground Operation

NOTE: AC power from the APU generator or external AC is required to operate the hydraulic systems with engines stopped.

Selection of the No. 1 ELECT PUMP switch to ON will activate the pump. Once hydraulic pressure has reached 2300 PSI in the pressure manifold, the LOW PRESS light below the pump switch will be extinguished. The above events are repeated on the selection of the remaining electrical pumps.

With the electrical pumps selected ON the pressure gauges for each system should read 3000 PSI.

Should the temperature in either the No. 1 or No. 2 reservoir reaches 160°F the heat exchanger fan motor is activated.

If, in any of the three reservoirs, the temperature exceeds 205°F the applicable Hi Temp caution light will illuminate amber on the hydraulic control panel, as well as master caution and HYD system annunciator (Figure 11).

Engine Starting

Starting No. 1 engine will automatically result in the activation of the 1A PUMP and subsequent de-activation of the L ENG PUMP low pressure light.

Figure 11   Hi-Temp. Schematic

Figure 12 Control and Indication

353

Similarly, starting of No. 2 engine will activate the 2A PUMP and de-activate the R ENG PUMP low pressure light.

Flight Operation

Normal Conditions

During take-off and landing all hydraulic pumps will normally be operating. Once a safe altitude has been achieved and the flaps have been

AIRCRAFT CONFIGURATION	PUMP AVAILABILITY					
	1 EDP	1 B	3 A	3 B	2 B	2 EDP
WOW + EXTL AC OR APU	X	✓	✓	✓	✓	X
WOW + LEFT ENGINE + LEFT IDG	✓	✓	✓	✓	✓	X
WOW + RIGHT ENG. + RIGHT IDG	X	✓	✓	✓	✓	✓
WOW + BOTH ENGINES LEFT IDG + RIGHT IDG	✓	✓	✓	✓	✓	✓
W OFF W + BOTH ENGINES + LEFT IDG + RIGHT IDG	✓	✓	✓	✓	✓	✓
W OFF W + BOTH ENGINES + LEFT IDG	✓	X	✓	✓	✓	✓
W OFF W + BOTH ENGINES + RIGHT IDG	✓	✓	✓	✓	X	✓
W OFF W + LEFT ENGINE + LEFT IDG	✓	X	✓	✓	✓	X
W OFF W + RIGHT ENGINE + RIGHT IDG	X	✓	✓	✓	X	✓
W OFF W + APU + NO IDG'S	*	X	✓	✓	X	*
W OFF W + NO IDG'S FOR 2 SECS	*	X	X	✓ **	X	*

* WITH ENGINES WINDMILLING, EDP'S WILL OPERATE

** WILL OPERATE REGARDLESS OF PUMP SWITCH POSITION

NOTE: WITH A/C ON JACKS, WOW SWITCHES MUST BE CHEATED TO OBTAIN 1B & 2B PUMP OPERATION

Figure 13   Hydraulic Pump Availability

NOTES

1. 1B PUMP IS OFFLOADED WHEN GEN. 2 IS NOT ON LINE
   -EXCEPT WHEN WEIGHT ON WHEELS.

2. 2B PUMP IS OFFLOADED WHEN GEN. 1 IS NOT ON LINE
   -EXCEPT WHEN WEIGHT ON WHEELS.

3. IF ADG DEPLOYS, 3B PUMP IS POWERED AUTOMATIC-
   ALLY FROM ADG BUS, REGARDLESS OF PUMP SWITCH
   POSITION.

Figure 14 Hydraulic System Schematic

selected UP, the alternate pumps in each system may be selected OFF (i.e. 1B, 2B and 3B pumps) without a low pressure caution being activated.

In the preparation for landing the secondary pumps should be re-selected ON. Failure to do so will result in a low pressure caution light activation along with a master caution annunciation once the flaps have been selected DOWN (Figure 12).

Abnormal Conditions

If during flight, a generator (IDG) or engine should fail, the corresponding generator line contactor will be de-energized. This action will result in the inability of the associated electric AC pump to operate; i.e. should No. 1 engine or IDG fail, the electric 2B PUMP would be inhibited. Conversely, should No. 2 IDG or engine fail the electric 1B PUMP would be inoperative. This load shedding reduces the loading of the remaining IDG.

NOTE: The 3A and 3B pumps are unaffected by a failure of an engine or IDG.

Emergency Conditions

Should a complete power failure be experienced without the auxiliary power unit (APU) operative, the air driven generator (ADG) will automatically deploy and activate the 3B PUMP independent of pump selection, thus providing sufficient hydraulic power for landing gear, brakes and flight controls.

A detailed listing of pump availability according to aircraft configuration is shown in figure 13.

Figure 14 shows an overall hydraulic system schematic.

CONTENTS

MAIN GEAR

General

A main gear assembly is mounted to each wing and a door allows for partial enclosure of the gear when retracted (figure 3). Each main gear assembly consists of a main beam, an oleo-pneumatic shock strut, a main gear actuator, a trailing link, hydraulic brake lines, a wheel axle and two main wheels. To uplock the gear, a latch pin provided on the main gear is engaged into an uplock unit attached to the airframe. The downlock is an integral part of the main gear actuator. Provision is also made on the actuator for the insertion of a ground lock pin. Fitted on either side of the axle are a main wheel, a brake assembly and a wheel speed sensor.

Description

Main Beam (Figure 4)

The main beam is swung from the wing at the ends of its trunnion and forms the primary structural part of the main gear. The front end of the trunnion seats in the wing rear spar and the rear end in an auxiliary spar. The following components are attached either wholly or partly to the main beam: the oleo strut, the trailing link, the main gear actuator, the downlock assist actuator, a set of proximity switches and the uplock pin.

Main Gear Actuator (Figure 5)

The main gear actuator retracts and extends the main landing gear and incorporates an internal lock mechanism that locks it in the extended position. A fluid port near one end of the cylinder admits fluid for the extension of the piston rod and a second port, connected to an external pipe, transfers fluid to the opposite end of the cylinder. Incorporated in

PINTLE PIN

MAIN BEAM

ACTUATOR
ATTACHMENT
POINT

UPLOCK PIN

DOOR MECHANISM
ATTACHMENT POINT

LOWER SWIVEL JOINT

Figure 4   Main Landing Gear Main Beam

Figure 5 Main Landing Gear Actuator

this second port is a restrictor to control the retraction rate of the piston rod. Within the end of the cylinder opposite the fluid ports is a gland housing and a claw that forms the static portion of the lock mechanism.

Passing through the piston rod is a ground locking rod, which together with the piston rod carries the moving portion of the lock mechanism which consists of a lock sleeve and a lock piston head.

The lock piston head is formed with an inclined shoulder that acts as an engagement surface for the claw during the locking process. Positive engagement of the lock mechanism is assured by hydraulic pressure which is assisted by a locking spring fitted in a spring carrier on the ground locking rod.

An indicator assembly is attached to the cylinder. The assembly houses a pivoting toggle which protrudes into the cylinder and is actuated by movement of the lock sleeve. This movement is transmitted to a spring-loaded indicator rod which carries a target for the downlock proximity switches. This indicator rod is also used as a visual indication of actuator locking.

With the actuator retracted and uplocked (Figure 6), pressurized fluid enters the actuator to act on the lock sleeve and lock piston head to extend the piston rod. As the lock piston head enters the claw, the tongues of the claw spread outward to contact the end face of the lock sleeve; this momentarily retards the progress of the lock sleeve until the lock piston head has entered the claw. The tongues then spring inwards to engage on the shoulder of the lock piston head. The lock sleeve is now permitted to continue its movement due to the fluid pressure and the force of the spring to enclose the tongues. This final movement of the lock sleeve moves the toggle to operate the lock sleeve indicator and align the target with the proximity switch.

To unlock and retract the piston rod, pressurized fluid enters the actuator and moves the lock sleeve against the locking spring force. The tongues of the claw are uncovered and expand to release the lock. Initial movement of the lock sleeve allows the toggle to return to its original position and the target no longer aligns with its proximity switch. Continued fluid pressure moves the complete piston to start the retraction stroke.

Brake Line Assemblies (Figure 7)

The hydraulic lines for the brake system run parallel down the main beam and then on to either side of the trailing link. The line assembly consists of an upper swivel coupling and pipes, and a lower left and right swivel coupling with its associate center and lower pipes.

Shock Strut (Figure 8)

The oleo-pneumatic shock-strut consists of an inner cylinder, an outer cylinder, a center-tube (fixed to the latter at the top) and a clack valve

Figure 6 Main Landing Gear Actuator—Functional Schematic

carried at the lower end of the center tube. A charging valve at the top of the strut enables servicing of the strut. An annular space formed between the inner and outer cylinders forms a "recoil-chamber".

Fixed to the inside of the outer cylinder is a piston ring capable of floating between two flanges of the inner cylinder.

Figure 7 Main Landing Gear Brake Lines

Fluid flow to and from the recoil chamber at any time is determined by the relative positions of the two cylinders and the piston ring.

Upon landing, shock is absorbed by the restriction to the fluid flow through the clack valve and the passages around it (Figure 9). As the inner cylinder travels into the outer one, the recoil chamber gets filled first, and

Figure 8   Main Landing Gear Shock Strut

further travel causes progressively greater compression of the nitrogen, creating a greater cushioning effect. When the shock is fully absorbed, the compressed nitrogen tends to force the inner cylinder to reverse its travel. However, part way through this operation, both the piston ring and the clack valve assume a more restrictive position thereby slowing inner cylinder travel and preventing an abrupt recoil.

Trailing Link and Axle

The trailing link is a structural member with a hollow axle passing through its base. It is attached to the inner cylinder of the shock strut at one end and to the main beam at the other. The latter is by a hinge pin

METERING PIN

PISTON HEAD

PISTON RING
SEAL

SEAL RETAINER

SEAL CARRIER

BEARING

SPARE SEAL

OUTER CYLINDER

FLOATING PISTON

GLAND NUT

INNER CYLINDER

COMPRESSION

EXTENSION

LEGEND
NITROGEN
FLUID

Figure 9   Main Landing Gear Shock Strut—Functional Schematic with a raised boss that forms the target for the main gear proximity switches. The axle is retained on the trailing link by a pin fitted with a jacking dome.

Main Gear Doors

Each main gear is partially enclosed by a door when retracted. The door is attached by a piano wire hinge to the wing and is mechanically linked to the gear. The door is held open by the gear when it is extended. Brush seals on the door provide the sealing between the gear and the wing.

Main Gear Selector Valve (Figure 12)

The main gear selector valve is used to control the supply of hydraulic fluid for the extension and retraction of the main gear. The valve is bolted to the equipment support beam located on the top of the main wheel well. The control of the valve is through solenoids fitted to the valve. These in turn, are controlled by signals from the landing gear circuitry. At any given time the valve will be in down, up or null positions. Down or up positions will cause the valve to direct No. 3 hydraulic pressure to the respective side of the main gear actuator. In the null position the valve will connect both sides of the actuator to No. 3 Hydraulic system return.

Main Gear Downlock Assist Actuator (Figure 13)

The actuator is a single-acting unit, trunnion-mounted in the airframe and attached to the top of the main landing gear. A piston rod, fitted with a seal assembly and two bearings operates in a cylinder, closed at one end.

During normal operation, No. 2 hydraulic system return fluid is drawn into and expelled from the cylinder by the extension and retraction of the main landing gear as the piston rod moves under no load. When the emergency release system is used, pressurized fluid from the assist actuator selector valve passes to the actuator to assist the extension of the main landing gear. A pressure relief valve in the actuator line prevents damage should pressure exist simultaneously in the assist actuator and the main gear actuator "UP" line.

Main Gear Uplock (Figure 14)

This assembly is a locking device which retains the main landing gear in the retracted position. The lock is made mechanically and released

Figure 12   Main Landing Gear Selector Valve

Figure 13   Main Landing Gear Downlock Assist Actuator

hydraulically by the uplock actuator. Provision is also made for manual release of the uplock in an emergency or for ground servicing. A target for a proximity switch is secured to an extension of the uplock lever cross shaft.

When the unit is in the locked condition, the latch is secured by the roller and the springs are in tension. The uplock actuator plunger is withdrawn (Figure 15).

During a main gear extension cycle, the uplock actuator plunger is hydraulically extended to move the uplock lever, which pivots and lifts the roller out of engagement with the latch. The latch rotates by spring force and gear weight, and allows the gear to extend.

Figure 14   Main Landing Gear Uplock

Figure 15 Main Landing Gear Uplock—Functional Schematic

When the main landing gear is selected up, the uplock actuator plunger is withdrawn. As the landing gear retracts the uplock pin strikes the inclined face of the latch, which rotates. This movement allows the roller to ride over and engage the latch to keep it in the locked positon.

The locking mechanism can be manually released in an emergency or for ground servicing, independent of the uplock actuator. The manual release lever lifts the roller out of engagement with the latch, allowing the latch to release the gear.

NOSE GEAR

General (Figure 16)

The nose landing gear is a twin-wheel, forward retracting unit, positioned on the fuselage centerline beneath the flight deck. The gear retracts into a well which is fully enclosed by doors.

The nose gear consists of a shock strut assembly, dual nose wheels, drag brace with downlock, a nose gear actuator and a rack and pinion type steering system. An uplock pin on the shock strut engages an uplock unit attached to the airframe. Overcentering springs acting in conjunction with the drag brace ensure engagement of the downlock. A cam device in the shock-strut centralizes the nose wheels before stowage in the nose wheel well.

Hydraulic pressure is supplied by No. 3 system to operate the nose gear and nose gear forward doors. The aft door is mechanically connected to the gear. A door operating system ensures the sequencing of the forward doors.

Description

Nose Gear Actuator (Figure 17)

The nose gear actuator extends and retracts the nose gear using hydraulic pressure from system No. 3 through the nose gear selector valve. A fluid port at one end of the actuator allows fluid to extend the piston rod, and located in this port is a restrictor to control the rate of travel of the actuator. A second port nearby is connected to an external pipe which transfers the fluid to the opposite end of the actuator. Unlike the main gear actuator, this actuator has no internal locking provisions.

ACTUATOR

FEEDBACK
ASSEMBLY

DRAG BRACE

FEEDBACK
LINKAGE

DOWNLOCK ASSIST
SPRINGS

AFT DOOR
ATTACHMENT
ROD

TORQUE
LINKS
(SCISSORS)

STEERING
ACTUATOR

TOW BAR
ATTACHMENT
LUGS

SHOCK STRUT

UPLOCK PIN

Figure 16   Nose Landing Gear

Figure 17   Nose Gear Actuator

Shock Strut Assembly (Figures 18 and 19)

The nose gear shock strut is oleo-pneumatic and consists of an inner cylinder telescoping into an outer cylinder forming a recoil chamber. An inner tube, fixed to the top of the outer cylinder carries a spring-loaded taxi-recoil valve.

Fixed to the inside of the outer cylinder is a piston ring capable of floating between two flanges of the inner cylinder. Fluid flow to and from the recoil chamber is controlled by the relative positions of the two cylinders and the piston ring (Figure 20).

Landing shocks are absorbed by the restriction to the fluid flow through

Figure 18 Nose Landing Gear Shock Strut

the orifices and passages in the taxi-recoil valve (Figure 21). As the inner cylinder enters farther into the outer, nitrogen gets progressively compressed causing further snubbing. When the inner cylinder stops the nitrogen pressure tends to reverse the travel. However, the piston ring position between the flanges as well as the seating of the taxi-recoil valve due to spring tension prevents too fast a rate of recoil.

Fitted inside the shock-strut is a pair of self-centering cams, held on to

Figure 19   Nose Gear Steering Cuff and Taxi Recoil Valve

their respective cylinders by a set of dowels. As the nose gear strut extends, the cams contact and center the nose wheels aligning them so the gear can be retracted into the wheel well.

A steering cuff and a baulk ring are mounted on the outer cylinder and

Figure 20 Nose Landing Gear Shock Strut—Functional Schematic

can be moved around it by the steering system. The baulk ring holds the steering actuator rack out of engagement with the pinion of the steering system during castoring action. Bolted to the steering cuff is a proximity switch bracket and a pair of lugs for a towing bar.

An axle is fitted to the lower end of the inner cylinder (Figure 21). The nose gear uplock pin is installed on the forward end of the axle. An end fitting at the base of the inner cylinder carries the jacking dome.

Figure 21   Nose Landing Gear Shock Strut Inner Cylinder and Axle

Torque Links

A pair of torque links serve to transfer steering action from the cuff to the nose wheels. The upper torque link is attached to the cuff at one end. The two free ends of the torque links are fastened together by a knuckle bolt. A bracket bolted to the upper torque link carries a target for a proximity switch.

Note: A disconnect of the torque links has not been provided.

Nose Gear Drag Brace (Figure 22)

The drag brace consists of an upper and lower link hinged at the center joint. The upper link is attached to the airframe and the lower to the nose gear. The nose gear downlock mechanism is contained within the upper link and consists of a sealed, spring-loaded plunger, which engages with the lock face of a cam fitted to the lower link. It also acts as a piston when hydraulically actuated.

The plunger is housed and projects through a bearing in which it is free to move. Movement within the bearing is limited by a lock pin that passes through a slot in the plunger.

Stops on the upper link prevent the cam from rotating overcenter. The upper and lower links are connected by a hinge pin. A fitting on the hinge pin is formed with a target for a proximity switch. Another proximity switch is secured to the cam, the target for this switch being the leading face of the plunger.

On selection of landing gear UP, fluid pressure is admitted to the upper link to act on the plunger piston to move it against the spring and withdraw the plunger.

The cam, now free, allows the lower link to pivot about its hinge pins and fold as its geometry follows the retraction movement of the landing gear.

On completion of the cycle, fluid pressure is off-loaded and the spring-loaded plunger returns to its original position in preparation for the next operation.

On selection of landing gear DOWN, the lower link unfolds as it follows the movement of the landing gear. The cam rotates, contacts the leading face of the plunger and forces it against its spring. This action continues until the landing gear is fully extended. In this position the cam is against its stops, the plunger is released by the action of the spring and shoots forward over the lock face of the cam to lock the landing gear in the extended position.

Nose Gear Uplock (Figure 23)

This device retains the nose landing gear in the retracted position. The lock is made mechanically and released hydraulically by the uplock actuator.

Figure 22   Nose Landing Gear Drag Brace

The mechanism is housed between two halves of a body bolted together to form a shell. The latch lever is formed with a fork in which is located a roller that engages with a shoulder of the latch to retain it in the locked position. An integral button forms a striker face for the actuator plunger. Fitted to the latch lever pivot pin are the emergency and manual release levers.

A sleeve fitted to the latch lever provides an anchor point for two tension

MANUAL RELEASE LEVER

EMERGENCY RELEASE LEVER

PROXIMITY SWITCH PLATE

UPLOCK ACTUATOR

LATCH LEVER

ROLLER

BODY

ACTUATOR PLUNGER

BUTTON

DOWN-STOP PIN

UP-STOP PIN

LATCH

Figure 23 Nose Landing Gear Uplock

springs, the other ends of which are similarly anchored to the heel of the latch. Two pins fitted to the body act as up and down stops for the latch. Attached to the body are the lock actuator and a proximity switch mounting plate.

The operation of the nose gear uplock is similar to that of the main gear uplock except when the gear is retracting. At this time, the latch moves until it abuts the upstop pin and the roller on the latch lever engages with the latch to maintain it locked. The manual release of the mechanism in an emergency or for servicing is similar.

Nose Gear Door Operating System

This system includes two forward doors, an aft door, a door selector valve, a door actuator and the associated circuitry.

The forward doors are outward opening and are normally closed except during nose gear transit. They are hydraulically operated and electrically controlled to act in sequence with the nose gear. The aft door is closed only when the nose gear is retracted. It is hinged at the rear and mechanically linked to the nose gear. All three doors are of honeycomb construction and are made of Kevlar composite material.

A nose gear door selector valve is mounted at the top left side of the nose wheel well and is controlled by solenoids. The selector valve assumes various positions depending on the signals received from the landing gear control unit. The valve routes hydraulic system No. 3 pressure to the open or close side of the door actuator which is mounted on the right side of the wheel well.

The actuator operates the door through mechanical linkages which include a cam and roller-type lock mechanism to keep the doors in the fully closed position. In the "null" or de-energized mode of the selector valve, both sides of the actuator cylinder are connected to return line and the pressure port is shut off from the actuator.

When a gear UP selection is made, the door selector valve solenoid (open) is energized (Figure 26) and hydraulic fluid is routed to open the nose doors. As soon as both the doors are opened, the left and right door open microswitches, initiate nose gear retraction. During retraction, hydraulic pressure holds the doors open. When the nose gear is fully retracted, an uplock signal (generated by the nose gear uplock proximity switch) energizes the door selector valve in the opposite direction (close) and causes the doors to close fully. The cam and roller mechanism engages now to maintain the doors (closed) uplocked. When the doors are fully closed, the nose door uplock proximity switch sends a door uplock signal to the landing gear control unit which now de-energizes the door selector

Figure 26 Nose Gear Door Control—Schematic

valve to the null mode by de-energizing the retract relay, relieving all hydraulic pressure from the door.

The door operating sequence during nose gear extension is similar. The doors are opened, gear extends (the doors are hydraulically maintained open) and the doors close after nose gear downlock is sensed by the drag brace switches.

Figure 27 Nose Landing Gear Selector Valve

Two door proximity switches connected in series illuminate a NOSE DOOR OPEN light on the center instrument panel when either or both doors are not fully closed.

Nose Gear Selector Valve (Figure 27)

This valve routes hydraulic system No. 3 pressure to the nose gear actuator and is mounted on the forward face of the Sta. 202 bulkhead and is accessible from inside the nose wheel well. It is controlled by two solenoids which can move the valve to down, up or null positions. In the null position, the valve connects both sides of the nose gear actuator to the return line of hydraulic system No. 3. In the up or down positions, the valve connects pressure to the respective line on the actuator. The solenoids are controlled by inputs from the landing gear control unit and nose door micro switches.

CONTROL AND INDICATION

General

Landing gear control and indication is provided by the landing gear control panel, the landing gear control unit, the weight on wheels fail annunciators and various proximity switches. For location see figures 28 and 29.

Each gear (left main, right main and nose) has an uplock switch, two downlock switches (1 & 2) and two weight on wheels switches (1 & 2). Additionally the nose gear has a fully extended (or centered) switch.

Gear control and indication circuitry performs two distinct, independent functions (Figure 30)

- Weight on Wheels
- Gear Control

The weight-on-wheels circuit processes information from the W. O. W. proximity switches (squat switches) and informs various other systems of "air/ground" status.

Indication of weight on wheels malfunction is given by the WOW input/output fail annunciators.

The gear control circuit processes commands from the gear control lever along with signals from the various uplock and downlock switches in order to control gear sequencing and to provide gear safe and unsafe visual warnings. In addition, this circuit receives inputs from cabin altitude, flaps, throttle levers and the weight on wheels circuit and provides outputs to enable nose wheel steering, cabin ordinance signs and gear configuration aural warning.

Proximity Switch

These devices have largely replaced the micro-switch in areas where switch rigging is difficult and damage or contamination is likely. Their

WOW
O/P FAIL
WOW
I/P FAIL

LANDING GEAR
CONTROL PANEL

PROXIMITY SWITCH

LANDING GEAR
CONTROL UNIT

Figure 28   Landing Gear Control and Indication Components

advantage lies in their inherent reliability due to solid state, rugged (completely sealed) construction plus the fact that they are not in mechanical contact with the operating mechanism. Disadvantages preventing their use everywhere include; size, cost and susceptibility to electromagnetic interference. With the exception of the nose gear No. 2 downlock micro

Figure 29   Landing Gear Proximity Switch Locations

switch, all proximity switches associated with landing gear control and indication are identical and interchangeable.

The proximity switch contains an oscillator, a detector and an electronic switch (see figure 31). When powered, the oscillator produces a magnetic field around the sensitive surface. By sensing the strength of this field, the detector can determine if the target is in proximity to the sensitive

Figure 30 Landing Gear Control and Indication Block Diagram

surface or not. Field strength decreases as the target moves into the field due to eddy currents induced in the metal target. The detector operates an electronic switch to supply a ground to the landing gear control unit when the target is in proximity.

NOTE: Some proximity switches on the Challenger supply a ground when target is out of proximity e.g. Passenger Door circuit.

Figure 31   Proximity Switch—Operation

Landing Gear Control Panel (Figure 32)

Mounted on the center instrument panel this panel provide the pilot with selection of gear position and a number of indications.

The gear handle may be selected up or down as required but a lever lock (or downlock) solenoid prevents gear up selection until the aircraft is airborne. The lever lock may be manually released by depressing the DNLCK REL button, located to the left of the gear handle.

When the gear is in transit, (i.e. extending or retracting) the gear handle flashes RED to indicate a gear unsafe condition.

Three green lights above the handle illuminate NOSE, LEFT and RIGHT when the respective gears are in the down and locked (safe for landing) condition.

A MUTE HORN button enables the pilot to silence a certain type of gear configuration aural warning. Once activated the button illuminates amber and remains illuminated until the condition is corrected.

At the lower right of the panel, is a test switch. When depressed, this switch illuminates the gear handle flashing red, the three green SAFE lights, the MUTE horn lamp, the ordinance signs (NO SMOKING FASTEN SEAT BELTS) if selected to AUTO (see LIGHTING) and the NOSE DOOR OPEN red light, thus testing the lamps and the output circuitry. The WOW output fail amber light also illuminates during a test but only if the aircraft has weight off wheels and the test button is held for more than 15 seconds.

Landing Gear Control Unit

This unit contains all the circuitry to process weight on wheels and gear control information.

The landing gear control unit is organized in three channels, weight on wheels 1, weight on wheels 2 and gear control, each with its own dual power supply (see figure 32).

Figure 33 shows a logical presentation of the landing gear control unit organized by outputs (for actual circuit configuration refer to figure 32).

Weight on Wheels Circuit (Figure 33 a)

This circuit informs various systems (as shown) that the aircraft is on the ground by detecting that either of the left gear WOW switches and any right gear WOW switch are in proximity. Conversely the circuit in-

Figure 32-Sht.1 Landing Gear Control Unit—Weight on Wheels

394

Figure 32-Sht.2   Landing Gear Control Unit—Indications

dicates an airborne condition if both WOW switches on either gear (left or right) are out of proximity.

The proximity switches and the circuitry require electrical power, as shown, to operate. Any WOW switch not receiving power indicates an airborne condition.

Weight on Wheels Input Fail Circuit (Figure 33 b)

This circuit is a comparator which produces an output to illuminate the amber WOW INPUT FAIL light if a disagreement exists between the

Figure 32-Sht.3 Landing Gear Control Unit

WOW switches. There is a 10 to 15 second delay before illumination to prevent warnings during a normal landing or take off.

Weight on Wheels Output Fail Circuit (Figure 33 c)

This circuit is a comparator which produces an output to illuminate the amber WOW OUTPUT FAIL light if a disagreement exists between the various WOW outputs. As before, a 10 to 15 second delay prevents spurious warnings. The WOW OUTPUT FAIL light will also illuminate if power is lost to either WOW channel.

This circuit may be tested, when airborne, by depressing the TEST button on the landing gear control panel.

When pressed and held for 15 seconds the WOW output fail light will illuminate along with the other lights that are illuminated during the test.

Lever Lock Solenoid (Figure 33 d)

This circuit automatically releases the lever lock, thus enabling gear UP selection provided all four main gears WOW switches indicate an airborne condition. Should one or more WOW switches be in disagreement the latch must be manually released.

a) WEIGHT ON WHEELS (WOW)

b) WEIGHT ON WHEELS — INPUT FAIL

Figure 33 Landing Gear Control Unit

C) WEIGHT ON WHEELS – OUTPUT FAIL COMPARATOR

Figure 33   Continued

d) LEVER LOCK SOLENOID

e) LANDING GEAR EXTEND

f) LANDING GEAR RETRACT

g) NO SMOKING & FASTEN SEAT BELTS CIRCUIT

Figure 33 Continued

h) LANDING GEAR CONFIGURATION WARNING

i) GEAR UNSAFE (IN TRANSIT) RED WARNING

j) GEAR SAFE (3 GREENS) INDICATION

Figure 33   Continued

Landing Gear Extend Circuit (Figure 33 e)

Requires only a gear down selection on the landing gear control panel to generate an extend command.

Landing Gear Retract Circuit (Figure 33 f)

This circuit commands:-

- main gear retraction if gear UP is selected and both WOW switches on either gear are out of proximity. Main gear retraction command is removed when both (left and right) uplock switches sense up and locked.
- nose gear retraction if gear UP is selected, both nose WOW switches are out of proximity and the nose gear is fully extended. Nose gear retraction command is removed when the nose uplock switch senses up and locked.

No Smoking and Fasten Seat Belts Signs (Figure 33 g)

The customer fitted NO SMOKING signs will illuminate, if selected to AUTO, when gear DOWN is selected, cabin altitude exceeds 10,400 ft, landing gear TEST is selected or the flaps are selected beyond the 0° position.

The customer fitted FASTEN SEAT BELTS lights will illuminate if selected to AUTO; when gear DOWN is selected, cabin altitude exceeds 10,400 ft, flaps are extended or landing gear TEST is depressed.

Landing Gear Configuration Warning (Figure 33 h)

An aural warning will sound if any No. 2 downlock switch does not sense down and locked and:-

- flaps are extended beyond 30°

          or

- either throttle is set to idle

A warning due to the second condition may be silenced by pressing the MUTE HORN button on the landing gear control panel. This action sets a latch (depicted by a relay). The MUTE HORN button illuminates amber whenever the latch is set. Latch is reset if both throttles are moved away from idle or all three No. 2 downlock switches sense down and locked.

The mute horn button also illuminates when landing gear TEST is depressed.

Gear Unsafe (In Transit) Warning (Figure 33 i)

The landing gear handle flashes red if:

- the gear handle is UP and any uplock switch (left gear, right gear, nose gear, nose door) does not sense up and locked.
- the gear handle is DOWN and any No. 1 downlock switch (left gear, right gear, nose gear) does not sense down and locked.

  This indication may be tested by depressing landing gear TEST.

Gear Safe (3 greens) Indication (Figure 33 j)

Each of these three lights illuminates when the respective No. 1 downlock switch senses down and locked.

These indications may be tested by the landing gear TEST switch.

OPERATION

Retraction and Normal Extension

Main Gear Retraction (Figure 34)

Upon a landing gear UP selection, the retract sequence of the main gear is as follows:

Landing gear control lever sends a gear up command to the landing gear control unit and, providing certain conditions are satisfied, the MLG selector valve is energized, directing hydraulic pressure to the landing gear up line.

Hydraulic pressure is routed to both main gear actuators and uplocks via the check valve and restrictor in the runaround and dump valve.

The actuator internal downlock is released and hydraulic pressure retracts the actuator. This causes the main gear to retract and the door follows by its mechanical linkage.

Gear unsafe red flashing lights come on in the landing gear control handle and LEFT and RIGHT green lights go out.

Uplock roller on gear leg, contacts the main gear uplock where it is mechanically latched. Once latched, the uplock maintains the gear uplocked (This enables the selector valve to be moved to null subsequently).

The proximity switch on the uplock assembly is actuated and causes the MLG selector valve to de-energize.

The selector valve takes up a null position blocking hydraulic pressure to the main gear actuator. At the same time, both sides of the actuator are connnected to hydraulic return lines, (providing thermal relief if necessary).

Landing gear control handle red flashing lights go out on receiving main, nose gear, and nose gear door uplock signals via the landing gear control unit.

Rotation of the main wheels is automatically stopped by hydraulic pres-

Figure 34   Landing Gear—Hydraulic Schematic

sure, tapped from the nose landing gear up line, through the brake metering valves.

Main Gear Extension

Main gear extension is electrically controlled and hydraulically operated. On landing gear DOWN selection the extension sequence is as follows:

Landing gear control lever sends a gear down command to the landing gear control unit and this energizes the main gear selector valve, directing hydraulic pressure to the landing gear down line.

Down line pressure is routed to uplocks via the one-way restrictor valve and run-around and dump valve.

The uplock actuator extends and unlatches the main gear.

Gear unsafe red flashing lights come on in the landing gear control handle.

Down line pressure extends the gear actuators and mechanically linked doors to the fully extended position; the extension rate being controlled by a restrictor in the actuator up line. The fluid forced out of the up side of the actuator is re-circulated into the gear down line via the runaround and dump valve.

The actuator internal downlock is automatically made, and the downlock proximity switches, via the landing gear control unit, cause the landing gear control handle red flashing lights to go out and the main gear LEFT and RIGHT green lights to come on.

For added security, the main gear selector valve remains energized at all times maintaining hydraulic pressure to the down line.

Nose Gear Retraction

Nose gear retraction is electrically controlled to occur at the same time as the main gear retraction. Selecting the landing gear UP, the retract sequence of the nose gear is as follows:

Landing gear control lever sends a gear up command to the landing gear control unit which energizes the NLG door selector valve to direct pressure to the door open line. Once both doors are fully open, the retract command is redirected to energize the NLG selector valve, directing hydraulic pressure to the landing gear up line.

Pressure is routed through a restrictor and the NLG dump valve to the downlock actuator.

The single acting downlock piston is retracted to unlock the drag brace.

Gear unsafe red flashing lights come on in the landing gear control handle, NOSE gear green light goes out, and the NOSE DOOR OPEN red light illuminates.

Pressure is also routed through a restrictor to the nose gear actuator.

The nose gear actuator extends, forcing the drag brace to fold and draw the nose gear forward and up into the wheel well. The rear nose gear door is mechanically linked to the gear and so follows its movement into the closed position.

The uplock roller on the gear, contacts the uplock and is mechanically latched. The uplock proximity switch energizes the leg locked relay which energizes the NLG door selector valve to the door close position. Hydraulic pressure is then directed to the nose gear door actuator via a restrictor and a dump valve.

The door uplock proximity switch sends a command to the landing gear control unit to de-energize the NLG and NLG door selector valves and extinguish the red flashing lights in the landing gear control handle.

Nose landing gear and nose gear door selector valves take up a null position.

Two nose door closed proximity switches turn off the NOSE DOOR OPEN light.

Nose Gear Extension

Nose gear extension is electrically controlled to occur at the same time as the main gear extension. On landing gear DOWN selection, the extension sequence of the nose gear is as follows:

The landing gear control lever sends a gear down command to the landing gear control unit which energizes the NLG door selector valve to the door open position. Hydraulic pressure is then directed to the door actuator via the NLG door dump valve.

Gear unsafe red flashing lights come on in the landing gear control handle.

NOSE DOOR OPEN light on the center instrument panel comes on.

When the right nose door open micro switch is made the NLG selector valve is energized to direct hydraulic pressure to the nose gear down line.

Down line pressure is routed through a one way restrictor to the uplock actuator, unlatching the nose gear.

Nose gear actuator retracts, unfolding the drag brace and extending the nose gear, with its mechanically linked rear door.

In the fully extended position the drag brace downlock engages. The No. 1 downlock sensors, via the landing gear control unit, cause the red flashing lights to go out. Downlock sensor No. 2 causes the NOSE green light to illuminate. It also energizes the downlock relay which causes the NLG door selector valve to be energized to close the doors. When the doors are closed the two door closed proximity switches turn off the NOSE DOOR OPEN light.

For added security, the NLG selector valve and the NLG door selector valve remain energized maintaining hydraulic pressure to the door closed and gear down lines at all times.

Emergency Extension

General

The landing gear manual release system (Figure 35) provides an alternative means of lowering the gear. This system would be used in the event of a malfunction in the landing gear control system or no hydraulic power being available from the No. 3 hydraulic system.

By means of a single handle in the flight compartment it is possible to release the NLG door closed lock and both main and nose landing gear uplocks, operate the main landing gear assist actuator selector valve and dump hydraulic pressure. The gear extends due to its weight. The nose landing gear and nose landing gear forward doors are assisted in this mode by spring pressure. The main landing gears are each assisted by a single acting actuator operating off No. 2 hydraulic system.

The system comprises a single cable layout running from the nose gear uplock release mechanism, aft to the main gear dump valve operating lever. Cables attached to the dump valve lever operate the left and right main gear uplock release mechanisms and a rod from the lever operates the selector valve for the main gear assist actuators. A cable from the nose gear uplock mechanism releases the nose door closed lock and a rod from the mechanism rotates a cross shaft to operate the nose gear and nose gear door dump valves. The manual release handle is connected to an operating lever which, through a pulley, transmits the load to the single cable, to operate the system.

Manual Release Handle

The release handle is mounted on the rear of the center pedestal control panel. The handle is T-shaped and incorporates a ratchet release button.

Operating Lever

The operating lever is mounted in a bracket attached to the aft face of the nose wheel well. A pair of plates, pivoted on the lever, support a pulley on the centerline of the lever. The plates are spring-loaded to approximately 3 pounds to pretension the cable that runs in the pulley. The spring-loaded pulley also acts as a compensating device for different thermal expansion of the fuselage structure and cable system.

Figure 35 Landing Gear Manual Release System

408

Nose Gear Release Mechanism

The nose gear release mechanism is mounted in the uplock support bracket. A link connects the mechanism to the uplock manual release.

A rod from the mechanism rotates a cross shaft which, in turn, operates the nose gear and nose gear door dump valves. A cable from the mechanism unlatches the lock that retains the nose gear forward doors in the closed position. The dump valve cross shaft abuts a stop to limit the travel of the release mechanism, and a spring unit holds the mechanism in the reset position.

NOSE WHEEL STEERING

General

Nosewheel steering is achieved by a "Steer-By-Wire" (SBW) system (Figure 37). Steering is controlled by an Electronic Control Module (ECM) which operates a hydraulic Steering Control Valve (SCV) in response to the commands of either the handwheel and/or the rudder pedals. The SCV controls an actuator which, through a rack and pinion arrangement, rotates a steering cuff. The steering cuff in turn, rotates the nose wheels through torque links (or scissors).

The steering system has basically two modes of operation. A "steering mode" controls steering in the method described briefly above. The "steering mode" is designed to provide precise, backlash-free, control of steering at all aircraft speeds from max. take-off/landing speed to low speed ground maneuvering. The steering system is normally switched on continuously during flight and is enabled only when the aircraft is on the ground (WOW).

In the "free castoring" mode, hydraulic pressure to the steering system is shut off and the nosewheels are allowed to free castor. In this mode, restrictors in the hydraulic actuator creates a shimmy dampening effect as long as the rack and pinion are engaged. During towing or while making tight turns, the rack and pinion are allowed to separate. During this period, however, there is no shimmy dampening.

Hydraulic pressure for the steering system is from the number 3 hydraulic system. Hydraulic pressure is available from the NLG selector valve which provides pressure to the steering system when it is energized to the down (or extend) position.

Description

The components of the steering system consist of a handwheel, rudder potentiometer assembly, arming valve (AV), steering selector valve (SSV),

410

Figure 37 Nose Wheel Steering System

a steering control manifold which contains the steering control valve (SCV), feedback assembly, compensator, steering actuator, associated linkages and the Electronic Control Module (ECM).

Pilot's Handwheel (Figure 38)

The pilot's handwheel, located on the pilot's console panel, contains two independent potentiometers designated as HW_1 (Handwheel) and HW_2. HW_1 provides the steering command signal to the ECM. HW_2 feeds the second channel of the ECM and is used by the ECM for comparison with HW1 signal. If a discrepancy exists the steering system is automatically disabled.

The handwheel is spring-loaded to neutral position and movement of the wheel is slowed by a rotary damper.

Full handwheel movement ($\pm$ 90°) corresponds linearly to $\pm$ 55° of nosewheel steering angle.

Rudder Potentiometer Assembly

The rudder potentiometer assembly consists of dual independent potentiometers which are attached to the rudder primary feel unit. The 2 potentiometers are designated R1 and R2 and are used in a similar manner to the handwheel potentiometers. Full rudder pedal travel corresponds linearly to $\pm$ 7° on nosewheel steering angle. The smaller steering command inputs are required for steering control at higher speeds.

Arming Valve (Figure 39)

The arming valve (AV) is a solenoid operated shut-off valve which is controlled by the nosewheel steering arming switch on the pilot's facia panel. When set to ARM the arming valve is opened to allow hydraulic pressure to the steering selector valve.

With the solenoid de-energized, hydraulic pressure pushes the piston to one side causing the sliding valve to stop flow through the valve. The service (or outlet) port is connected to return.

When the solenoid is energized, the pressure on the piston is dumped to the return line. Pressure on the actuating piston moves the sliding valve to open up the service port to hydraulic pressure.

Figure 38 Handwheel and Rudder Controls

Steering Selector Valve

The steering selector valve (SSV) is identical to the arming valve but is operated by the ECM. Providing no faults are in the system, the ECM automatically opens the SSV upon receiving the WOW signal. When opened, the SSV routes hydraulic pressure to the steering control valve (SCV) making nose wheel steering operational.

Figure 39 Arming Valve and Steering Selector Valve

Steering Control Manifold (Figure 37)

The steering control manifold contains the steering control valve (SCV), a linear variable differential transformer (LVDT) and a transfer valve.

Steering Control Valve (Figure 40)

Upon the command signal from the ECM, the SCV routes hydraulic pressure to either side of the steering actuator to turn the nose wheels (Figure 47).

Figure 40   Steering Control Valve

The SCV is a two-stage servo valve. The first stage is an electro-hydraulic pre-amplifier which consists of a torque motor, a jet pipe and a receiver. The torque motor deflects left or right in proportion to the current it receives from the ECM.

Hydraulic pressure flows through the center of the torque motor shaft and is directed by the jet pipe onto 2 small holes on the receiver. These small holes are connected to opposite ends of the second stage spool. With the jet pipe centered, equal pressure is applied to both holes and the spool remains centered. As the torque motor deflects, increased pressure is applied to one side of the spool and decreased pressure to the other.

The spool movement directs pressure to one side of the steering actuator and turns the wheels (either left or right). The other side of the actuator is connected to return.

As the spool is displaced, it deflects a feedback spring, which re-centers the jet pipe in order to prevent excessive movement of the spool. The spool is now held in this new position. (However, hydraulic pressure is still applied to one side of the actuator and the wheels would continue to rotate to the hard-over position. To counter this, a feedback assembly on the gear signals the ECM to move the spool back to the centered position and hold the wheels at the appropriate steering angle). In this manner the steering angle is proportional to the input current (to the torque motor) from the ECM.

Linear Variable Differential Transformer

The position of the second stage spool is monitored by a LVDT which gives this position information to the ECM. If the torque motor input signal and spool position do not agree (within a short time interval) the ECM will automatically disable the steering system.

Transfer Valve

The transfer valve is used to hydraulically remove control of nose wheel steering from the SCV and place it in the free castoring mode. With hydraulic pressure (> 800 psi) available to the steering manifold, the transfer valve is forced to the closed position. This allows control of the steering actuator to be provided by the SCV. When hydraulic pressure drops (system pressure drops or is shut-off by closing the SSV or AV) to less than 800 psi (approximately), the spring in the transfer valve forces its spool to a position such that both sides of the steering actuator are connected to return via the compensator (explained fully later on). The transfer valve causes hydraulic pressure to bypass the SCV and uses compensator pressure (250 psi) in a shimmy damping mode. When hydraulic pressure is restored (? 800 psi) the transfer valve closes all its ports and control of steering is resumed by the SCV.

One-Way Restrictor Valves (Figure 41)

Both sides of the steering actuator are supplied with hydraulic pressure via one-way restrictor valves. They provide shimmy dampening and prevent cavitation of the actuator when in the free castoring mode.

Figure 41   One-Way Restrictors and Feedback Assembly

Movement transmitted from the nose landing gear forces the actuator to move in either direction. Fluid flow from one side is restricted via the orifice in the one-way restrictor, thereby dampening movement. Fluid flows through the transfer valve and free flows to the other end of the actuator via the check valve in the one-way restrictor. If a countermovement comes from the gear, fluid flow reverses and the function of the one-way restrictor valves reverses.

Feedback Assembly

A feedback assembly is mounted on the nose gear strut and via linkages senses gear position to provide the ECM with feedback information. The feedback assembly contains 2 rotary variable differential transformers (RVDT) designated as (FB1 and FB2).

Steering Actuator (Figure 42)

The steering actuator contains two free-floating pistons, one on either end of a steering rack. Linear movement of the rack drives the pinion (and steering cuff) via the torque links to rotate the wheels.

When pressurized, the piston is prevented from moving more than 55° (steering angle) by a mechanical stop inside the actuator. In this way nose wheel steering command from the cockpit is limited to 55° left or right.

If the nose wheels are castored beyond 55°, the pinion will move the rack until it reaches 68° steering angle. At this point the rack will bottom out and the rack and pinion separate. As long as the rack and pinion are engaged shimmy dampening is provided. (If during nose wheel steering the wheels exceed $56 + 2 - 0°$, the ECM automatically disables the system. The system cannot be re-engaged until the steering angle is less than 55° and the ARM switch is selected off, then on).

If the nose wheels are castored beyond 68°, the pinion will continue to rotate (not shimmy dampened) until a stop tooth on the steering cuff abuts the rack at 99°. During free castoring the baulk ring prevents the rack from moving, in order to prevent jamming or misalignment of the rack and pinion when they re-engage.

With reversal of direction, the baulk ring will rotate to allow the pinion to automatically mesh with and re-engage the rack.

Compensator (Figure 43)

The compensator ensures positive protection against cavitation and provides a reservoir of fluid in case of pressure loss. The compensator is basically an accumulator and relief valve. The relief valve makes sure that hydraulic pressure in the return side of the steering system does not drop below 250 psi.

The accumulator is continuously charged via a restrictor from the arming valve (providing, of course, hydraulic pressure is available and the NLG selector valve is energized) and has a capacity of 2 cu. in. Should pressure drop, the relief valve will close and provide sufficient pressure to prevent shimmy and cavitation of the system.

AT MAX. STEER 55°

Figure 42A Steering and Castor—Steering Operation

RIGHT   LEFT

BAULK RING RESTRAINING
RACK DURING CASTORING

**RACK DISENGAGED AND FREE TO
CASTOR BEYOND STEERING RANGE**

RIGHT   LEFT

CASTOR STOP

**CASTORED 99°
(CASTOR STOP ABUTS THE RACK)**

Figure 42B   Steering Operation

PRESSURE LESS THAN
250 PSI

PRESSURE GREATER THAN
250 PSI

PISTON

VALVE

INNER
SPRING

OUTER
SPRING

OUTLET

OUTLET

Figure 43   Compensator

Figure 44 Electronic Control Module

Electronic Control Module (ECM) (Figure 44)

The ECM is an electronic unit designed to perform the following functions.

- To control the SCV in accordance with the command received from HW1 and/or R1.

- To enable or disable the steering system hydraulically by controlling the steering selector valve (SSV). The SSV is enabled when:

  a) The steering switch is set to ARM and the nose gear is down and locked.

  b) Both WOW channels indicate aircraft on ground and

  c) No faults exist

- To monitor for any failure condition. Should a failure occur, the SBW system is disabled automatically and turns on the N/W STEER FAIL light on the pilot's instrument panel.

- To perform a pre-landing built-in-test-equipment (BITE) check. If a malfunction of any component or circuit is detected the SBW system is automatically disabled and the N/W STEER FAIL light illuminates.

- To provide a diagnostic BITE test.

Operation (Figures 45 and 46)

Control of the current to the steering control valve (and thus nose wheel steering angle) is provided by a servo amplifier in the ECM. HW_1 and R_1 inputs are summed to arrive at a steering command angle. For example, if 10° of steer right is demanded by the handwheel and 7° of steer left is demanded by the rudder, the ECM will demand 3° of right steering. It is not possible, however, to achieve more than 55° of steering by summing the handwheel and rudder inputs in the same direction, as the steering actuator cannot mechanically achieve more than 55°.

HW1/R1 input is then summed with FB1 in the servo amplifier, which gives a direction signal opposite to the steering command in order to nullify the steering command. (So that the wheels only turn the angle selected and not more). With all three inputs at null (7.6V) the output of the servo amplifier is null (7.6V). The two ends of the SCV coil will be at 7.6V and no current flows. If the rudder, for example, should command left, the input to the servo amplifier would vary and correspondingly the output to the torque motor varies. As the steering system responds, FB1 will input an opposite steering input such that when the steering command angle is reached the sum of the inputs to the servo amplifier is again at null. (For example, the rudder demands 3° steer left: R1 inputs a signal of − x volts. As the steer angle is reached the output of FBl reach + x volts and the sum is then null).

Figure 45   Nose Wheel Steering Control—Block Diagram

Simultaneously, 2 monitoring functions are performed. The output of the servo amplifier and the LVDT signal (from the SCV) input into a circuit that determines if the spool position (as detected by the LVDT) and the servo amplifier signal are in agreement. If they are not, an error signal is generated that will close the SSV and illuminate the N/W STEER FAIL light. The steering system is thus disabled.

The other monitoring function is provided by HW2, R2 and FB2 which input into the second channel of the ECM. The inputs from these controls are summed as described under steering control (HW1, R1 and RB1). If any discrepancy exists, the steering system is disabled (as described above).

The system thus incorporates 2 checks of any steering command. One ascertains that the command is valid by ensuring that it is seen on both channels and the other verifies that the SCV is doing what it was told to do.

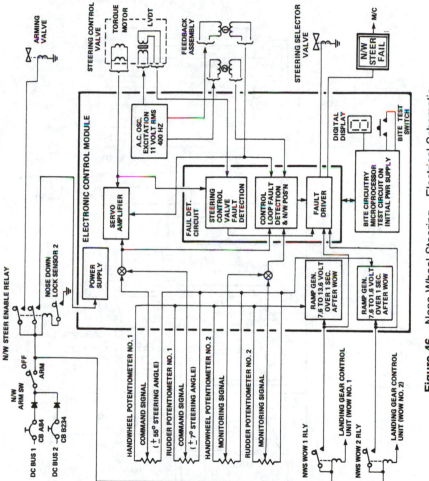

Figure 46 Nose Wheel Steering—Electrical Schematic

425

Figure 47A   Nose Wheel Steering Hydraulic Schematic

To make sure that no steering inputs are applied in-flight, the ECM has 2 independent "ramp generator" circuits, one supplying each end of all 4 potentiometers (HW1, HW2, R and R2). One WOW channel supplies each ramp generator circuit, which, in the "airborne" condition, holds the ramp output at null (7.6V).

When the WOW signal indicates "on ground", one ramp generator produces an increasing signal and the other a corresponding and equal falling signal for 1 second. After 1 second control reverts back to the normal steering mode. In this manner steering command inputs are inhibited in flight and transition to steering control comes on smoothly when the aircraft touches down.

Monitoring

Any failure in the steering system automatically disables the system by closing the SSV and turns on the N/W STEER FAIL light. The remaining failures that will do this are:

a) ECM fault (internal circuitry) and

b) if the max steering angle exceeds $56 + 2\text{-}0°$ ($56\text{--}58°$). This would occur if, in a $55°$ turn the crew, through differential braking, caused the steering angle to exceed this limit.

Once disabled, the system can only be re-engaged if the fault is cleared and the system is reset. (ARM switch ON-OFF).

Built in Test Equipment (BITE)

The ECM Incorporates self-test functions which monitor the condition of the system components.

Pre-Take-Off Check

With the aircraft on the ground (WOW), setting the arm switch to ARM causes the ECM to do a system check. The ECM gives a cursory check of all inputs as well as making sure that the steering selector valve is energized. If not the system is disabled.

Pre-Landing Check

In flight, with nose wheel steering armed, the action of the nose gear becoming down and locked causes the ECM also to perform a system check as well as ensuring that the SSV is not energized (i.e. steering not operational). If the test is not satisfactory the system is disabled.

Diagnostic BITE Check

A diagnostic BITE check can be performed on the ECM itself (Figure 44). Removing the cover provides access to a test button and a digital display.

When the test is initiated the SSV is de-energized for 15 seconds while the ECM performs an internal check. After 15 seconds the SSV is energized and the test now requires handwheel and rudder inputs.

Procedure

- Aircraft must be on the ground (WOW)
- Hydraulic pump 3A or 38 on
- N/W steering arm switch set to ARM

NOTE: Failure to adhere to the following sequence will disable the ECM. The system must be reset in order to check again.

a) Push BITE button and hold
   - ECM displays "0" for 1 second, then "1" for 1.5 seconds
b) Release button
   - ECM displays "2" for 1 second, then "3" for 1.5 seconds
c) Push button during "3" display and release
   - ECM performs a software check
   - turns off SSV (turns on N/W Steer Fail Light) and begins 15 second BITE check. If any ECM faults are found a "1" is displayed. If no faults are found an "8" appears. The N/W Steer Fail light should go out and the SSV is energized.
d) During the 5 minutes after the "8" appears the operator must enter the cockpit and input a rapid hardover handwheel movement, hold for 3 seconds and release.
e) Next, a rapid hardover rudder movement is entered, held for 3 seconds then released.

NOTE: The steering actuator must move during this check.

If the test is not completed within 5 minutes after the "8" appears, a "1" is displayed and the ECM must be reset.

If a fault is found during the check, the assigned number code will be displayed. (It is possible to have several numbers displayed alternately if the fault cannot be determined.) The N/W Steer Fail light will also illuminate.

If no faults are found a "0" is displayed. Whether a fault is found or not the ECM will be latched and must be reset before nose wheel steering operation can resume.

The numbers assigned to certain faults are:

0 – NO FAULT

1 – ELECTRONIC CONTROL MODULE

2 – STEERING SELECTOR VALVE

3 – STEERING CONTROL VALVE

4 – HANDWHEEL POTENTIOMETER

5 – FEEDBACK ASSEMBLY

6 – RUDDER POTENTIOMETER

7 – SHORT CIRCUIT

8 – INSTRUCTION TO INPUT HANDWHEEL AND RUDDER SIGNALS

This BITE test could also be used at specific intervals to determine system serviceability.

WHEELS AND BRAKES

Main Wheel Assembly

The four main wheel assemblies are identical and are designed for use with 26 x 6.6 size tubeless tires. Each wheel consists of a hub, a tire, two bearings, three blowout plugs and a tire inflation valve.

The wheel hub is of the removable flange type which enables fast and easy tire changes. The flange is bolted to the hub and a preformed packing prevents air leaks at the hub-to-flange joint. The tire inflation valve is located in the web of the wheel hub.

Two taper roller bearings are located in the wheel hub, the outer race of each bearing being shrunk into the hub. A moulded rubber seal protects the inboard bearing against loss of lubricant or ingress of foreign matter. The outboard bearing is protected by a metal bearing retainer. Lugs and recesses on the flange enable the mounting of the wheel on its brake during installation. The wheel is held in place by an axle nut and washer.

Three blowout plugs with an inner core of fusible metal are installed in the wheel to protect it and the tire from damage should the heat generated by the brakes become excessive.

Nose Wheel Assembly (Figure 49)

The two interchangeable nose wheel assemblies are designed for use with 18 x 4.4 size tubeless tires. Each wheel consists of a hub, a wheel, two bearings and a tire inflation valve. Each hub consists of two halves made from magnesium alloy sandcastings. The halves are bolted together and a preformed seal in a retaining groove prevents air leaks at the hub-joint. Two Tyseal taper roller bearings are installed in their housings on the hub. The tire inflation valve is fitted to the web of the wheel hub and the wheel is secured on the axle by an axle nut and washer.

ROLLER BEARING
INNER RACE AND
CAGE

SEAL

ROLLER BEARING
OUTER RACE

ROLLER BEARING
INNER RACE AND
CAGE

VALVE CAP
INFLATION VALVE

Figure 49 Nose Wheel Assembly

Main Brake System

General

Each main wheel is fitted with a hydraulically powered carbon composite disc brake unit. The inboard brakes are powered by No. 3 hydraulic system and the outboard brakes by No.2 hydraulic system. Application of brakes is by mechanical operation of the pilot's or co-pilot's brake pedals. The pressure to the brakes is normally modulated by an anti-skid system that provides optimum braking under all runway conditions. The anti-skid system provides individual brake control and provides deceleration detection, touchdown and locked wheel protection and built in system test. Provision is also made for the use of brakes without the anti-skid protection.

A brake accumulator is installed in each hydraulic system to provide a reserve of pressure in the event of hydraulic power failure. A parking brake lever mechanically locks the brake control valve in the on position.

Brake Assembly (Figure 50)

The brake assembly consists of a forged aluminum housing, titanium torque tube and a carbon composite disc stack. A bleeder valve and two inlet ports are provided for each brake. The brake assembly can be used as a right or left-hand brake by using alternative inlet port connections.

Five aluminum cylinder sleeves threaded into the housing contain the brake pistons. Each sleeve is sealed against leakage by preformed packings and packing retainers. An insulator is installed in the end of each piston to reduce the transfer of brake heat to the housing.

The torque tube is held between the back plate and brake housing by bolts, washers and self-locking nuts. The bolts are installed through holes in the back plate, slots in the torque keys, and bolts holes in the housing.

The carbon-composite disc stack consists of a pressure plate located against the brake pistons, three rotating discs, two stationary discs, a stationary end plate and a steel back plate.

The built-in clearance of the brake stack is maintained at all times by an automatic adjustment mechanism within each brake piston.

A wear indicator provides a visual indication of the wear remaining in the disc stack. When the end of the wear indicator pin is flush with the top of the indicator spring holder, the disc stack must be removed and replaced as a unit.

Braking force is transmitted to the wheel by the three rotating discs.

BLEED ADAPTER

BRAKE HOUSING

BRAKE WEAR INDICATOR

TORQUE TUBE

PRESSURE PLATE

ROTATING DISC

STATIONARY DISC

ROTATING DISC

STATIONARY DISC

ROTATING DISC

END PLATE

BACK PLATE

INSULATOR

OPERATING PISTON

Figure 50 Brake Assembly

433

The rotating discs are separated by two stationary discs which are keyed to the torque tube. The rotating and stationary discs are centered between the pressure plate and end plate which are also keyed to the torque tube. The back plate is bolted to the torque tube and housing. During operation, hydraulic fluid enters the housing inlet port and fluid passages and forces the pistons against the pressure plate. The movement of the pressure plate compresses the disc stack against the back plate, causing friction between the contacting surfaces. This friction retards the rotating discs, which provide braking action.

Operation (Figure 51)

The pressure and return lines of hydraulic system No.3 are connected to the inboard brake metering valve. Likewise the No.2 system is connected to the outboard valve. A metered pressure line on the brake metering valve routes its output to the respective anti-skid valve.

The spools of each dual brake metering valve receive mechanical inputs via push-pull controls and the dual brake valve control mechanism from both pairs of brake pedals mounted on the pilot's and co-pilot's rudder pedals. When a pedal is depressed the spool of the brake metering valve moves and meters hydraulic pressure to the anti-skid control valve which modulates brake pressure to eliminate wheel skid. When the pedal is released, the spool of the metering valve moves to direct brake pressure to the return line of the metering valve.

Wheel velocity signals from each Wheel speed sensor are fed to the anti-skid control unit. A skid detector circuit extracts wheel deceleration information which is compared to a pre-programmed reference signal level. When wheel deceleration signal level exceeds reference signal level, a difference signal, indicative of an incipient skid, is generated. This signal, amplified, is applied to the spool of the appropriate anti-skid control valve. The spool moves to a point where brake pressure is fully or partly connected (for a programmed brief interval of time) to return line on the anti-skid valve. In this state, brake pressure is dumped to prevent the wheel skidding.

The brake accumulator in each hydraulic system provides a reserve of pressure in the event of hydraulic power failure, sufficient for six normal brake applications. The pressure transducer in the hydraulic line adjacent to each accumulator, provides the signals to a dual pressure indicator. This indicator is installed on the right side of the pilot's instrument panel, and enables a continuous readout of accumulator pressure in each system.

If the anti-skid is off or inoperative, metered pressure output is routed, unaltered, through the anti-skid valves to enable a more direct control of brake pressure from the brake pedals.

Figure 51 Brake System—Schematic

435

The hydraulic fuse immediately upstream of each hydraulic swivel assembly protects the system against fluid loss, should a component on the main landing gear be damaged or ruptured. Each fuse is fitted with a lever that (when selected) holds the fuse in an open position to allow for bleeding of the brakes. When the lever is released the fuse will automatically reset.

Both dual brake metering valves are connected to the nose landing gear up line, so that on selecting landing gear Up, metering valve spools are moved to the brake on position and stop the rotating main wheels. After retraction the pressure to the brake metering valves is removed allowing the spools to move back to the off position and release the brakes.

Parking Brake

Description

The parking brake system consists of a parking brake handle mounted at the lower right edge of the pilot's instrument panel connected via a push-pull cable assembly to the parking brake lever of the dual brake valve control mechanism. Both inboard and outboard brakes will hold when No. 2 and No. 3 hydraulic system power is available. When the hydraulic systems are OFF, only the inboard brakes will hold parking brake pressure for prolonged periods.

Operation

To apply the parking brake, fully depress both brake pedals on either the pilot's or co-pilot's rudder pedals and pull the parking brake handle out. pulling the parking brake handle causes a pair of latches in the brake valve control mechanism to engage, securing the control valves in the on position. To lock the parking brake handle in the ON position, it must rotate 90° while the pedals are still depressed. To release, fully depress pedals, rotate the brake handle back 90° and push the handle in.

When the parking brake is set, a multi-contact micro-switch (Figure 55-Anti Skid) is closed, with the following results:

- The red light marked PARKING BRAKE illuminates at the lower left corner of the center instrument panel.

- The anti-skid control relays lose power; this causes the INBD FAIL and OUTBD FAIL lights on the anti-skid panel to come on.

NOTE: With the parking brake set the ANTI-SKID system Master Caution annunciator is inhibited.

- A parking brake shut off valve located in the inboard anti-skid return line closes. This prevents any of the anti-skid control valve fluid from returning to the reservoir, thereby trapping brake pressure.

When the parking brake is released the red light will go out.

- Should the parking brake shut-off valve fail to close, the inboard ANTI-SKID FAIL light will illuminate.
- Since only the inboard brakes are equipped with a parking brake shut-off valve, only the inboard brakes will hold for prolonged parking.
- The outboard brake pressure will slowly leak down via the anti-skid valves unless the No. 2 hydraulic pumps are running.

The position of the parking brake shut-off valve is signaled by a proximity sensor in the valve. The condition of this sensor is monitored and checked by the flight control monitoring unit in the avionics bay.

When testing the integrity of the proximity sensor, select channel 12 on the selector and position the test switch to S1 and then S2. Each position of the test switch should illuminate the green light on the monitor panel.

For further information on flight control monitoring refer to the Flight Controls Chapter.

ANTI-SKID

General

The anti-skid system consists of an anti-skid unit, two dual anti-skid control valves and wheel speed sensors located in the axle of each main wheel (Figure 52). The system independently controls the braking of each main wheel by automatically varying the hydraulic pressure output of each dual anti-skid control valve to the respective brake.

The anti-skid system incorporates the following features:

- Modulated skid protection of each wheel via the primary anti-skid circuits.
- Locked wheel protection which provides a pressure dump signal in the event of a deep skid or failure of a wheel to spin-up at touchdown and at the same time provides a coarse back-up circuit in the event of failure of the primary anti-skid circuit.
- Touchdown protection, which, via input from the weight on wheels circuitry, dumps brake pressure from all wheels while the aircraft is airborne, but is overridden to allow normal skid-controlled braking as soon as the wheels have spun-up.
- Built in test equipment to provide a check of virtually all the system circuits, both on the ground (pre-takeoff) and in the air (pre-landing).

Description and Operation

Anti-Skid Control Panel (Figure 53)

A panel marked ANTI-SKID is located at the right-hand bottom of the center instrument panel. Mounted on this panel are a switch with ARM

Figure 52   Anti-Skid—Components

and OFF positions, two split-legend annunciators marked INBD FAIL
(amber)/INBD TEST (white) OUTBD FAIL (amber)/OUTBD TEST
(white), and a TEST button. The arming switch applies power to the anti-
skid relays from the DC Buses 1 and 2, provided that the parking brake
is released and the nose gear is down and locked. These relays connect
the anti skid valves and the FAIL lamps to the anti skid unit.

Figure 53   Anti-Skid System—Block Diagram

Wheel Speed Sensor

The wheel speed sensor is an electrical signal generating device that provides wheel speed information for the anti-skid control unit.

One such sensor mounted on each end of each main wheel axle is engaged through a wheel drive cap to the associated main wheel. As the Wheel turns, the rotor of the sensor rotates about the stator, varying the magnetic field of the stator and generating an AC signal in the stator coil. The frequency of the AC signal is directly proportional to the wheel speed.

Anti-Skid Control Valve (Figure 54)

The valve is a dual, two stage, flapper-nozzle type pressure control valve. The valve is connected in the hydraulic lines between the brake metering valves and aircraft brakes. One dual valve controls pressure to the inboard brakes, the other dual valve controls pressure to the outboard brakes. Each half of the dual valve operates independently in controlling pressure to its associated brake. Check valves permit the use of a common return for both valves of the dual valve.

When the anti-skid system is armed and the wheels are being braked during a landing roll, the dual control valves route the metered brake pressure unchanged to the respective brakes. However, if an approaching skid or an actual skid is sensed by the control unit, the resultant command signal output will move the flapper towards the first stage nozzle.

The first stage pressure immediately becomes greater than the second stage pressure, forcing the second stage spool to move to a point where brake pressure is open to the return line. In this state, brake pressure applied at the associated brake is dumped to prevent the wheel from skidding. Opening the brake pressure to the return line also opens the end of the auxiliary piston chamber to the return line. The resultant unequal pressure on the auxiliary piston forces the main spool back towards the center only when the command signal is removed. The metered pressures are once more open to brake pressures, and feedback pressures applied to the auxiliary piston are once more in balance. They remain in that condition until the next command signal to the valve is received.

By design, there is a small continuous internal fluid flow from the flapper-nozzle to system return.

This is of no consequence while the hydraulic pumps are in operation, but becomes significant when only accumulator fluid is available, since the internal leakage flow would discharge the accumulator in some 15 seconds. To prevent this, when the hydraulic systems are shut-down for parking, a solenoid-operated shut-off valve is installed in the return line from the anti-skid valve of No.3 hydraulic system. Therefore only the inboard brakes are held for an extended length of time.

Anti-Skid Control Unit (Figure 55)

This unit is organized in four channels, one for each wheel. Each channel receives information from its own wheel speed sensor and controls its own

Figure 54 Anti-Skid Valve

anti-skid control valve. For simplicity, only one channel (left outboard) is shown in detail in the schematic.

For power supply and monitoring purposes the channels are paired within the control unit. Each pair of channels (inboard or outboard) has its own dual DC supply (Bus 1 and Bus 2) and supplies its own FAIL light on the anti-skid control panel. The anti-skid control unit is powered

Figure 55 Anti-Skid System with Parking Brake-Schematic

443

anytime DC Bus 1 and 2 are powered. This is necessary because the wheel spin up output is used to arm the ground spoiler circuit regardless of anti-skid selection.

The anti-skid unit monitors wheel velocity information from each wheel speed sensor. The AC signal from the sensor is applied to the input of the converter circuit, which produces a DC voltage proportional to the frequency of the input signal. The resultant DC voltage is then applied to the inputs of the skid detector and the locked wheel detector.

The skid detector circuit is a rate detector that extracts wheel deceleration information from the converter output. The information obtained is compared to an internally generated reference signal level. When the actual wheel deceleration signal level exceeds the reference signal level, a difference signal is generated that is indicative of an incipient skid. The difference signal, is then amplified by the skid detector circuit and applied to the inputs of the summer.

During normal anti-skid operation the modulator circuit controls the valve current and provides neither large nor quick changes in pressure. Each time an incipient skid condition is reached, the skid detector circuit sends a signal to the summer, which provides the required momentary reduction of brake pressure to halt the skid tendency.

After each incipient skid, the modulator again allows brake pressure to increase at a controlled rate. Thus a cyclicaction occurs during which the modulator repeatedly allows pressure to rise to the incipient skid threshold and each subsequent incipient skid causes brake pressure to again fall slightly below the incipient skid threshold. The frequency of this cyclic action is often greater than 10 cycles per second. The actual frequency depends upon many factors, including runway conditions and hydraulic system response. This adaptive characteristic of the anti-skid system ensures proper brake pressure for all combinations of runway conditions and pilot-applied pressures.

The signals that are applied to the summer are transformed into a valve current that is proportional to the voltage level of the summer output. The valve current controls the skid control valve, providing the maximum braking pressure while minimizing the tendency toward the development of deep skids.

The modulator is desensitized or limited in its capability to dump brake pressure when the modulator desensitizer circuit is activated.

This circuit provides protection by preventing excessive dumping of brake pressure which can occur by the charging up of the modulator circuit during gear oscillation induced by rough runway conditions.

Each modulator desensitizer circuit is activated by a dual contact relay which is de-energized closed when airborne or when the shock strut is not adequately compressed, due to lack of weight-on-wheels. The relays supply a ground, via a resistor, to the desensitizer circuit which reduces the signal applied to the modulator.

Each relay is energized open when it receives a weight on wheels signal from its own WOW prox. switch. This de-activates the modulator desensitizer circuits thereby restoring the full authority of the modulator.

The modulator desensitizer relays are paired Lt. & Rt. inboard and Lt. & Rt. outboard. If one of the pair fails to be energized while the other is de-energized, a fail light will illuminate when the anti-skid system is tested.

In addition when the control unit is tested the appropriate sensor fail light on the face of the unit will illuminate.

A 10-knot cutout circuit disables the anti-skid at speeds below 10 knots.

The touchdown protection circuit is armed when aircraft wheel speed is above 35 knots or when the weight-on-wheels switch indicates an airborne condition.

Prior to touchdown, it is imperative that no brake pressure reaches the brakes. Small amounts of pedal pressure can hold the wheels locked at touchdown, resulting in flat spotted or blown tires. The touchdown protection feature of the anti-skid system prevents any pressure at the brakes prior to wheel spin-up at touchdown. The skid control valves are fully energized, which completely dumps the pressure to the brakes. This condition will remain until either wheel spin up exceeds 35kts or the aircraft has weight-on-wheels.

The locked wheel detector circuit receives the wheel speed input from the converter. This circuit is activated when wheel speeds are above 35kts. When the detector senses a rapid deceleration or a wheel lock up, it removes brake pressure until the wheel speed returns to approximately the speed before the wheel lock up.

Normal reapplication of pressure would be too abrupt, so the pressure is slowly reapplied at a controlled rate.

The locked wheel protection provides a coarse back-up circuit in the event of a failure of the normal anti-skid circuit.

Immediate operation of the weight on wheels status to the on-ground mode is not critical, as long as it occurs before aircraft ground speed drops to 35 knots. If a weight on wheels switch fails in the airborne mode and does not switch to the on-ground mode, braking on the associated pair of wheels will be lost at speeds below 35 knots until the anti-skid system is manually switched off.

The built-in test (BITE) is a pilot initiated "ring" test that makes an end-to-end check of the skid control system.

The test button is on the anti-skid panel.

In order to test the system the following conditions must be met.

- System "armed'
- Nose gear downlock switches 1 and 2 must sense down and locked.
- Parking brake off
- Wheel speed below 17 knots.

Pressing the test button activates the test circuits which cause the inboard and outboard test and fail lights to illuminate. If the pre-test conditions are not met, or a fault exists within the anti-skid unit's circuits, then the lights will not come on.

On releasing the test button, the four lights should go out. If a failure light remains on, it indicates a failure in the system.

A failure in the system can be isolated by using the fault isolation circuit within the anti-skid unit. On the face of the control unit are two amber lights, one labeled SENSOR and the other VALVE and a six position rotary switch.

The OFF position turns test circuit off.

In the TEST position a lamp test is made and both lights should illuminate.

The other four positions refer to the anti-skid channels LT. and RT. inboard and LT. and RT. outboard.

Should a light illuminate in any of these test positions, it indicates a failure in either an anti-skid valve, a wheel speed sensor or the anti-skid circuit.

The fail lights may illuminate for the following reasons:

- Both fail lights when nose gear is down and locked and system is not armed.
- Both fail lights when parking brake is 'on'.
- INBD FAIL light only if parking brake shut off valve fails to open when gear is down and locked and system is armed.
- INBD FAIL light illuminates only after system is tested when nose landing gear downlock No. 1 sensor fails to indicate locked with the gear down and locked.
- OUTBD FAIL light illuminates only after system is tested when nose landing gear downlock No. 2 sensor fails to indicate locked with the gear down and locked.
- INBD FAIL light illuminates after system is tested: Indicates a failure in the inboard system.
- OUTBD FAIL light illuminates after system test: indicates a failure in the outboard system.

Anti-skid Relays

The inboard and outboard anti-skid relays activate the anti-skid system when energized by connecting the anti-skid valves and the fail lights to the control unit.

In addition the inboard anti-skid relay, when energized, powers the parking brake shut off valve to release the parking brake.

When de-energized these relays supply grounds to illuminate the fail lights from the nose downlock sensors if the gear is down and locked. This reminds the flight crew to arm the anti-skid system on approach.

The anti-skid relays are energized when anti-skid is armed, the parking brake is selected off and the nose downlock switches indicate gear is down and locked.

Spin Up Relays

These relays energize to provide an arming signal to the ground spoiler circuit when wheel speed exceeds 17kts. (See Flight Controls) The anti-skid control unit provides a "wheel speed greater than 17kts" signal during test and in consequence a disable relay is added to prevent inadvertent ground spoiler deployment during anti-skid test.

The spin up relays are energized when wheel speed exceeds 17kts and anti-skid test is not depressed.

Spin Up Disable Relays

These relays energize during anti-skid system test to prevent the wheel spin up signal moving the ground spoilers at this time, by removing power from the spin up relay coil.

Power is applied to the spin up disable relays from the anti-skid test button when depressed. Grounds are supplied from the "wheel spin up greater than 17kts" circuits to energize the relays. When the test button is released the spin up signal remains for a short time. To prevent the disable relays de-energizing prior to loss of wheel spin up the relays have a power hold-on latch.

CONTENTS

INTRODUCTION

The Challenger flight controls are divided into 6 main systems incorporating the following controls:

- Roll Control
    - ailerons
- Pitch Control
    - elevators
- Yaw Control
    - rudder
- Flight Control Monitoring
- Lift Modulation
    - flaps
        - flight spoilers
        - ground spoilers
- Stall Protection System

Roll, pitch and yaw controls are called primary controls while lift controls are called secondary controls (Figure 1).

Pilot inputs to operate the different control surfaces are given from the following commands:

- Ailerons: Handwheels
- Elevators: Control Columns
- Rudder: Rudder Pedals
- Flaps: Flap Control Lever
- Flight Spoilers: Spoiler Control Lever
- Ground Spoilers: Spoiler Control Lever
- Aileron Trim: Switch on center pedestal.

Figure 1   General Arrangement

• Rudder Trim: Switch on center pedestal.
• Pitch Trim: Switches on pilot's and
                                  co-pilot's hand-wheels.

The roll, pitch and yaw controls are of the dual type, i.e. the pilot's
and co-pilot's handwheels, control columns and rudder pedals are interconnected and working in unison.

The roll and pitch control systems can be individually disconnected by
the roll disconnect and pitch disconnect handles in the event of a control
run jam. This system allows the control of one aileron and/or one elevator
should the other jam. In the case of a rudder control jam, a breakout
mechanism is provided which will allow control to be maintained.

With the exception of the flaps and the trim controls, all the flight
control surfaces are hydraulically actuated from pilot inputs through a
network of cable pulleys and push/pull rods.

No. 1, 2 and 3 hydraulic systems are used to supply hydraulic power to the components operating the flight control surfaces.

The hydraulically actuated control surfaces are each powered by at least two hydraulic systems. The systems are fully independent from each other, and one alone is sufficient for operation. System logic ensures that loss of one hydraulic system will not affect or prevent the operation of any other control surface. Hydraulic power distribution is shown in figure 2.

The flaps are actuated from pilot input through an electronic control unit and two electric motors.

The trim controls are actuated from pilot input switches through electrically driven actuators.

Each flight control surface power control unit (PCU) is monitored for failure by the servo monitor system. Failure detection is either internal to

Figure 2 Hydraulic Distribution

the PCU (aileron and rudder PCU's) or external as part of the input linkage (elevators). A proximity switch is used to detect failures which are displayed on the servo monitor panel on the cockpit center pedestal.

A stall protection system prevents the aircraft from entering an attitude where a deep stall may occur.

ROLL CONTROL

General

Roll control is provided by two hydraulically operated ailerons hinged on the rear spar of the wings between W. S. 282 and 353 (Figure 3).

Aileron control is achieved through a cable and pulley system operated from two interconnected handwheels mounted on the control columns.

The two handwheels are linked by a cable system and an interconnecting shaft that incorporates a disconnect mechanism (roll disconnect), which allows the pilot to isolate the L/H or R/H aileron control circuit should either circuit become jammed. A spring loaded artificial feel unit is incorporated in each circuit aft quadrant.

A power control unit (PCU) is associated with each aileron. Each PCU is a dual unit consisting of two equal and parallel power components with a common interconnecting input linkage. The outboard power components are connected to hydraulic system 3 while the inboard ones are supplied by system 1 on L/H and system 2 on R/H.

Aileron trim is achieved through an electrically driven actuator linked to the aft quadrants by a rod/bell crank system.

Description

Starting from the cockpit, the aileron control system contains the following sub-assemblies. Pilot's and co-pilot's system being identical, only the components of one system will be listed below:

- Handwheel Assembly
- Roll Disconnect Mechanism
- Forward Cable Quadrant
- Aft Quadrant/Feel Mechanism
- Aileron PCU's

Figure 3 Aileron Control

458

- Torsion Bar
- Position Indicator and Transmitter
- Pressure and Return Hydraulic Lines
- Aileron Flutter Damper

Handwheel Assembly

Installed on the upper part of the control column, the handwheel contains the cable driving the forward aileron quadrant (axially installed at the end of the interconnecting shaft). Two stops are also incorporated limiting the handwheel angular travel.

Roll Disconnect Mechanism

The roll disconnect mechanism ensures, by means of a spring loaded locking pin, the connection between the two halves of the interconnecting shaft. In the event of a jamming condition in one of the systems, this system can be isolated from the other by disengaging the locking pin. This is achieved by pulling and rotating 90° the roll disconnect handle located on the center console. When the two half shafts have been disconnected, only the aileron of the unjammed circuit will remain operational from its corresponding handwheel (L/H aileron for pilot's handwheel or R/H aileron for co-pilot's).

Aft Quadrant/Feel Mechanism (Figure 4)

Located in the main landing wheel well, the aft quadrants are double grooved pulleys. The quadrant sub-assemblies include:

- a lever receiving the inputs from the trim mechanism
- an artificial feel unit consisting of a spring loaded roller held into a cam fixed on the quadrant. This mechanism is also used to center the input controls.

NOTE: In addition, the R/H quadrant has a third groove receiving the cable from the autopilot servo.

Power Control Unit (PCU) (Figure 5).

The hydraulic actuation of the ailerons is accomplished by identical aileron PCU's. Each PCU consists of two identical, parallel working ac-

AUTO PILOT
SERVO INPUT

TRIM ACTUATOR

AUTO PILOT
SERVO

AFT CABLE
QUADRANT (RH)

AFT CABLE
QUADRANT (LH)

TO LH QUADRANT

COMMAND INPUT

TRIM ACTUATOR

CAM AND QUADRANT ROTATES
WITH COMMAND INPUT. SPRING
LOADED BELLCRANK RIDES UP
ON CAM TENDING TO COUNTERACT
QUADRANT ROTATION.

ARTIFICIAL FEEL MECHANISM

Figure 4   Aileron Control—Aft Quadrant

tuators. The actuators contain double acting, equal area cylinders and are attached to a common mounting plate.

Each of the dual power controls contain a manifold which in turn houses a combination control and anti-jam valve, a failure monitoring sensor, a damping valve, a compensator, two anti-cavitation valves, a relief valve and a pressure differential indicator.

Figure 5   Aileron PCU Schematic

A summing and feedback feature is incorporated as part of the input linkage to null the system when the aileron position corresponds to pilot's input demands.

The dual actuators are mounted on a common base and are powered from independent hydraulic systems. The L/H and R/H outboard actuators are powered by the No. 3 hydraulic system whereas the L/H and R/H inboard actuators are powered by the No. 1 and No. 2 system respectively.

The pressure differential indicator indicates the presence or absence of adequate pressure drop across the fluid compensator. Indication is by means of a pin in the manifold which will extend, revealing its green painted end if the required pressure drop is present (10–25 psid). Exposure of the green pin indicates that the PCU is charged with fluid and that some hydraulic pressure is available. If the green pin is not visible, this will indicate that either there is insufficient fluid in the PCU or insufficient pressure.

The relief valve located in the manifold retract line provides pressure relief should the ram retract pressure exceed 3400 psi.

The anti-cavitation valves prevent cavitation in the extend or retract chambers of the main ram, and open if the pressure in the chambers drops below return pressure.

Two filters installed in the inlet ports prevent foreign material from being introduced into the main ram and/or the aircraft system.

The fluid compensator is located in the manifold return line. Its purposes are:

- to prevent the loss of fluid from the PCU when the hydraulic system is depressurized.
- to hold the return line of the PCU positively closed until the PCU is filled with fluid.

The control valve consists of a primary and a secondary spool.

Control input is transmitted via the quadrant and drive hub to the PCU linkage. The quadrant includes a cable tension regulator which is made of two quadrants mounted on a drive hub housing, a locking shaft and a compensation mechanism.

Torsion Bar

Installed on the outermost WS353 wing rib and attached to the aileron by a rotating link, the torsion bar will in case of hydraulic failure subject the upward movement of the aileron to an increasing load, preventing upfloat. Downward movement is not affected by the torsion bar.

Flutter Damper (Figure 6)

Each aileron is equipped with a flutter damper. It is a simple hydraulic double acting linear shock absorber mounted just outboard of the aileron PCUs. It is mounted to the wing box structure, and connected to the aileron front spar by an idler lever and a breakaway link.

The purpose of this installation is to provide flutter damping in case of failure of *BOTH* PCU's. The breakaway link provides jam protection in case of damper seizure.

See figure 7 for details.

SERVICEABILITY
INDICATOR

TYPICAL FLUTTER DAMPER
(ELEVATOR SHOWN)

Figure 6   Flutter Damper

Position Indicator

A position transmitter installed on the rear spar and linked to the aileron provides visual indication of the aileron angular movement to a position indicator located on the center instrument panel.

MOVE PISTON ROD IN FRONT OF WINDOW

INDICATIONS AT 20° ± 15° C FLUID TEMPERATURE

Figure 7   Aileron and Elevator Flutter Damper

Operation (Figure 3)

Rotation of the handwheel is transmitted via a splined shaft to a quadrant mounted at the top of the control column.

From the upper quadrant the column circuit is routed down and out of the control column and terminated at the forward aileron quadrant on the interconnecting shaft. The aileron fuselage cable run commences at the forward aileron quadrant on the interconnecting shaft.

From the forward quadrant the fuselage cable circuit is routed to the aft quadrant. The aft quadrant provides the function of aileron centering, artificial feel, trim input, and autopilot input.

The artificial feel unit forms part of the aft quadrant and is a spring loaded roller which is held into a cam fixed to the aft quadrant. Movement of the quadrant and cam causes the roller to ride up the cam. Since the cam is fixed to the quadrant, the latter's movement will be opposed by

Figure 8 Aileron Trim

the spring force which attempts to retain the roller in the center of the cam.

From the aft quadrant a cable circuit is connected to the aileron quadrant/tension regulator, which now operates the PCU input linkage.

Aileron Trim (Figure 8)

Aileron trim is applied via push rods and bell cranks from the trim actuator to the roller arm segment of the artificial feel unit. Activation of aileron trim will displace the roller arm and roller. The cam, however, will retain the roller centered and so move the quadrant and hence the aileron. Since the trim causes the aft quadrant of each cable run (L/H and R/H) to move, both pilot's and co-pilot's handwheels will also move when trim is applied. The autopilot servo when operating causes rotation of the co-pilot's aft quadrant only and would, therefore, move only the R/H aileron should the roll disconnect be activated.

PITCH CONTROL

General

Pitch control is provided by a set of hydraulically operated elevators hinged to the rear spar of the horizontal stabilizer with no mechanical interconnection.

Their displacement is controlled by fore and aft movement of the control columns which through mechanical cables and linkages is transmitted to the power control units (PCU's) installed in the horizontal stabilizer.

The two control columns are linked by an interconnecting shaft that incorporates a disconnect mechanism (pitch disconnect), which allows the pilot to isolate the L/H or R/H control circuit should either circuit become jammed.

A pitch feel simulator (artificial feel) unit provides the control column with the required "stick" force, which is varied relative to the horizontal stabilizer position.

Each elevator is driven by two identical power control units (PCU's) powered as follows:

Hydraulic system No. 1 operates the L/H elevator outboard PCU.

Hydraulic system No. 2 operates the R/H elevator outboard PCU.

Hydraulic system No. 3 operates the inboard PCU's of each elevator.

Each PCU contains a servo valve distributing hydraulic pressure on either side of a cylinder operating the elevator.

Pitch trim control is achieved by varying the angular position of the horizontal stabilizer leading edge from command switches located on the pilot's and co-pilot's handwheels.

Description (Figure 9)

Starting from the cockpit, the elevator control system contains the following sub-assemblies. Pilot's and co-pilot's systems being identical only the components of one system will be listed below.

Figure 9 Elevator Control

468

- one Pitch Disconnect Assembly (the only sub-assembly common to both systems).
- one Control Column
- one Fwd Cable Quadrant
- one Aft Cable Quadrant
- one Pitch Feel Simulator Unit
- one Gain Change Mechanism
- one Load Limiter
- one Aft Linkage Balance Spring
- two Jam-Tolerant Input Rods
- two Power Control Units
- two Auxiliary Centering Mechanisms
- two Flutter Dampers

Pitch Disconnect

The pitch disconnect mechanism ensures, by means of spring loaded locking pin, the connection between the two half shafts linking the control columns. In the event of a jammed condition in one of the systems, this system can be isolated from the other by disengaging the locking pin. Disconnect is achieved by pulling and rotating 90° the pitch disconnect handle located on the center console. When the shafts are disconnected the elevator of the unjammed system will remain operational from its corresponding control column (L/H elevator by pilot's column or R/H elevator by co-pilot's column).

Control Column

Each control column pivots about the center line of the interconnecting shaft. Its upper end receives the aileron handwheel with its associated cables running through the column and the stick shaker motor. Its lower end has a fork to receive one end of the forward quadrant push/pull rod.

NOTE: The R/H control column also includes a balance spring, which compensates the static weight of the control columns in the neutral position.

With the system properly rigged and the elevators in neutral, the control column should be 4.5° forward. Column forward and aft travel, including overtravel, is limited by two stop bolts located in the lower end of the column.

Forward Cable Quadrant

The base of the control column provides an attachment point for the pull/push rod connecting the control column to the forward cable quadrant.

The L/H and R/H fwd quadrants are identical with the exception of a stick pusher input installed on the R/H quadrant. The stick pusher is part of the stall protection system and is described later in this section.

The forward cable quadrants transmit the command cable movement to the aft cable quadrants.

Aft Cable Quadrant (Figure 10)

Located inside the vertical stabilizer, the aft cable quadrants transmit the command cable movement to:

- the gain change mechanism
- the pitch feel simulator unit

The L/H aft quadrant also receives inputs from the autopilot servo.

NOTE: Should the autopilot be engaged with the pitch disconnect handle pulled, only the L/H surface would respond.

Pitch Feel Simulator Unit (Figure 11)

The pitch feel simulator unit provides an artificial "stick" force to the control column when the elevators are moved. This force is varied relative to horizontal stabilizer position.

The L/H and R/H feel simulators are attached together but not mechanically linked. Input from the horizontal stabilizer is transmitted by two push/pull rods (one for each unit) attached to the input levers of the simulator units. The output levers are connected to the two aft quadrants.

Gain Change Mechanism

The gain change mechanism is located in the vertical stabilizer.

It is a variable ratio geometry bell crank and linkage assembly that modifies the input signal from the aft quadrant so that the elevator movement vs control column position adheres to a pre-determined response curve.

Load Limiter (Figure 9)

The load limiter is a control rod with a spring-loaded rod end. Installed between the gain change mechanism and the PCU's input mechanism, its

Figure 10   Aft Cable Quadrant and Gain Change Mechanism

purpose is to protect the input mechanism from excessive load, e.g. when the system is operated without hydraulic power or overtravel is induced.

Aft Linkage Balance Spring

The upper end of the load limiter is attached to a bell crank mounted on top of the vertical stabilizer. Attached to the bell crank is an adjustable balance spring which, should the load limiter or the downstream control rod become detached, prevents their static weight initiating unwanted command inputs to the PCU's.

TRIM
ACTUATOR

PITCH FEEL
SIMULATOR
UNIT

Figure 11   Pitch Feel Simulator Unit

Jam-Tolerant PCU Input Rods (Figure 12)

These input rods, located between the input torque tube and the PCU input linkage, will collapse in case of a PCU control valve jam and thus allow continued operation of the adjacent PCU. A proximity switch

Figure 12   Jam-Tolerant PCU Input Rod

mounted on the rod will detect such a condition and display it on the servo monitor panel. The inboard rods are of a fixed length, while the outboard rods are adjustable.

NOTE: The adjustment of these rods is *critical*-consult the maintenance manual for adjustment procedure.

Power Control Unit (Figures 13 & 14)

Each elevator is operated by two identical power control units (PCU's). In operation, fluid is applied to the PCU PRESS port and then to a 100

Figure 13 Elevator P. C. U.

micron (absolute) filter. From the filter hydraulic pressure is directed via a check valve to the control valve and to the bypass valve. This control valve directs fluid flow to the actuator to move the piston.

Centering Mechanism

Auxiliary centering devices are mounted under the upper skin of the horizontal stabilizer, and are provided to return the elevators to neutral

Figure 14 Elevator P. C. U.—Schematic

from the "up" position in case of disconnected control cables or rods. Adjustment is provided by three slotted holes on their mounting plate.

NOTE: Recentering to neutral of the elevator from the down position is by a system integral to the PCU.

Flutter Dampers

Each elevator is flutter protected by two flutter dampers. They are simple hydraulic double acting linear shock absorbers similar to those used for the ailerons.

They are mounted inside the horizontal stabilizer just outboard of the PCU and mechanically connected to the elevator front spar. For details see figures 6 & 7.

Hydraulic Lines

The pressure and return lines of system No. 1 and 2 are routed forward of the vertical stabilizer mid-spar. System No. 3 lines are routed on the aft face of the rear spar.

From the vertical stabilizer, flexible lines direct fluid to the rigid lines mounted in the horizontal stabilizer. No. 1 and No. 2 system pressure and return lines are directed to the L/H and R/H outboard PCU respectively. The No. 3 system pressure and return lines are teed off to both L/H and R/H inboard PCU.

At the inlet and outlet ports to each PCU the rigid lines are coiled to allow for some movement during operation.

Operation

The fwd and aft movement of the control columns is transmitted to the L/H and R/H push/pull rod linked to the forward quadrants.

From the forward quadrants the L/H and R/H cable runs each terminate at an aft cable quadrant which is mounted on the rear face of the vertical stabilizer forward spar.

The aft cable quadrants transmit the command cable movement to:

- the gain change mechanism for further transmission
- the pitch feel simulator unit.

The L/H aft cable quadrant also receives an input from the autopilot servo. Activation of the servo will result in movement of the aft quadrant and therefore, will control the control column and the elevator. Should the autopilot be activated with the pitch disconnect activated, the L/H surface only would respond.

The output from the gain change mechanism is directed to the PCU input mechanism at the top of the vertical stabilizer via the load limiter.

The function of the gain change mechanism is to vary the geometry so that the elevator response vs control column movement adheres to the necessary response curve. In order to achieve the required response, the gain changer converts the rotation command input from the aft quadrant to a linear output through a series of bell cranks and adjustable push rods.

The second output from the aft quadrant is to the pitch feel simulator unit. This unit provides the required stick force relative to elevator movement, and is varied also according to horizontal stabilizer position.

Pitch Trim (Figures 15 & 16)

Pitch trim is accomplished by varying the angle of incidence of the horizontal stabilizer. The system moves the leading edge of the horizontal stabilizer between 0° and 9° down, at controlled and defined rates of movement, in response to various command inputs from the pilot's manual controls and the automatic flight control system (AFCS).

The command inputs are fed into the horizontal stabilizer trim control unit (HSTCU) which operates an electromechanical linear actuator attached to the stabilizer.

Horizontal Stabilizer Trim Control Unit (Figure 17)

The HSTCU unit is a two-channel unit featuring fail-safe operation. The controller senses input signals from the pilot's control switches, the velocity and position sensors of the trim actuator, and the automatic flight control system. Output signals are transmitted to the trim actuator. Channels are automatically changed in the event of a power failure to the controller, and simultaneous up/down commands received by the unit are ignored.

The system is electrically powered from A.C. power, channel No. 1 from AC Bus 1 and channel No. 2 from the AC Essential bus.

Trim Actuator

The trim actuator is located at the top of the vertical stabilizer. The electrically driven screw actuator is mounted on double gimbals to accommodate normal motion of the unit as well as deflections of the airframe. The actuator contains twin motors, one being a back-up unit and each having high and low-speed windings. The motors are connected to a screw jack through a gear drive; an electric brake is provided to preclude runaway conditions. All elements of the actuator are dual-channel so that the system continues to function in the event of a failure in one of the

Figure 15   Pitch Trim System Components

channels. The actuator includes four velocity sensors and two position sensors. High speed is used for manual trim commands and variable speed rates are used for commands from the AFCS and are achieved by the combination of low and high speed windings.

Figure 16 Pitch Trim—Block Diagram

Manual Trim Control Switches

A dual-pole, dual-actuation type UP/DOWN manual trim control switch is located on each of the control column wheels. Commands from the pilot's switch override those from the co-pilot's and the automatic flight control system. Commands from the co-pilot's switch override only those from the automatic flight control system.

Emergency Disconnect Switches

An emergency disconnect switch is located on each of the control column wheels. The emergency disconnect switches may be independently ac-

Figure 17 Pitch Trim—Simplified Schematic

480

tuated to remove power from the system and brake the actuator. Following actuation of either emergency disconnect switch, the system must be re-engaged by pushing the two switch/lights of the trim control panel on the center console.

Trim Position Indication

The trim position sensors receive signals from the actuator. One of the trim position sensors supplies the automatic flight control system with stabilizer angle data. Both position sensors provide travel limit signals for the controller.

The position indicator located on the center instrument panel, gives the amount of stabilizer trim, up or down, and is calibrated in degrees. It receives its signal from an independent position transmitter mounted on the top end of the aft vert. stab. spar.

Control and Indication

A panel mounted on the center pedestal contains a split lens switch/light identified as CHAN 1 INOP and CHAN 2 INOP, that indicates failure of the respective channel. Normally, channel 1 is engaged and both lights are out. A combined OVERSPEED caution light/CHANGE CHANNEL switch is also located on the panel. For test purposes, this button can be used to switch the system from one channel to the other.

Both the CHAN INOP and the OVSP/CHANGE CHANNEL switch/lights must be pushed to engage the system, and to re-engage in the event that the pilot's or co-pilot's wheel mounted disconnect switch has been actuated. The OVSP switch/light illuminates amber in case of an overspeed condition in the actuator.

Pitch Trim Operation

Manual trim command inputs are initiated by the pilots by means of the control column switches, and automatic inputs are initiated by the automatic flight control system (autopilot or Mach Trim).

System logic is such that the pilot's control switch has priority over any other input source, while the co-pilot's switch has priority over the automatic flight control system. The trim controller also receives feed-back information from the actuator on direction and rate of movement as well as position information.

Manual inputs go to the high speed windings of the motor, while inputs from the AFCS are variable according to airspeed inputs from the air data computer.

Mach Trim inputs, which are present whenever Mach Trim is engaged but the autopilot is not, come from the stability augmentation computer and are relayed to the actuator which automatically compensates for aircraft attitude at higher Mach numbers.

For pre-flight testing, channel 1 can be operated using the manual trim switches and monitoring the position indicator. By pressing the OVSPD/ CHANGE CHANNEL button, the pilot effects a transfer to channel 2 which is similarly operated and monitored. In this case, the CHAN 1 INOP light will come on to indicate that the transfer has been completed. Pressing the OVSP/CHNG CHAN button a second time reverts the system back to channel 1, and the CHAN 1 INOP light goes out. CHAN 2 INOP light stays off.

Normally, channel 1 is engaged. In the event of a single electrical failure, except an overspeed condition, the CHAN 1 INOP light comes on and the trim control unit automatically transfers the commands to the back-up channel 2.

In the event of an overspeed condition, the OVERSPEED amber light comes on and the channel is shut-down. In this case a manual transfer to the other channel is required by pushing the OVSP/CHANGE CHANNEL button.

YAW CONTROL

General

Yaw control is provided by an hydraulically actuated rudder hinged on the rear spar of the vertical stabilizer.

Two anti-jam breakout mechanisms (L/H and R/H) ensure that jamming of a system does not affect normal rudder control through the remaining system.

The rudder surface is driven by three identical power units (PCUs) and each PCU is powered by one of the three hydraulic systems.

Each PCU contains a control valve distributing hydraulic pressure on either side of a cylinder operating the rudder.

Rudder trim is achieved with an electrically driven actuator connected via the yaw dampers to the PCU input torque tube. The actuator is controlled by a switch located on the center pedestal.

Description

Starting from the cockpit the rudder control system contains the following sub-assemblies. Pilot's and co-pilot's systems being identical, and common from the summing mechanism, only the components of one system will be listed below (figure 18).

- one Rudder Pedal Assembly
- one Primary Feel Unit (R/H only)
- one Anti-Jam Breakout Mechanism
- one Aft Quadrant
- one Summing Mechanism
- two Load Limiters
- one Secondary Feel Mechanism

483

Figure 18 Rudder Control

484

- one Yaw Damper Sub-Assembly
- three Auxiliary Centering Mechanisms
- three PCUs
- three PCU Input Load Limiters
- Hydraulic Pressure and Return Lines
- all Associated Cables, Pulleys and Control Push/Pull Rods

Rudder Pedals

The pilot's and co-pilot's input is via two crosscoupled sets of rudder pedals. Each set of pedals is individually mounted below the cockpit floor.

Pilot's or co-pilot's input is transmitted from the rudder pedal to a forward pivot assembly by a push rod. The rudder pedals are adjustable fore and aft with an adjustment knob located between each of the pedals. The R/H pivot assembly also contains the primary feel mechanism which consists of a cam with a spring-loaded follower.

A lower bellcrank on each pivot assembly translates pedal movement into fore and aft movement of a push/pull rod which in turn is connected to the forward cable quadrant. The second arm of the bellcrank provides the mounting point for the connecting push/pull rod between each of the pedal sets.

Anti-Jam Breakout Mechanism (Figure 19)

Part of each forward quadrant is an anti-jam breakout mechanism which, should one cable run become jammed, allows the other to continue. A cross coupling cable synchronizes the movement of the breakout mechanism and, by adjusting the bellcrank pivot point on the free quadrant, will ensure that the degree of rudder movement will be unimpaired.

Aft Quadrant (Figure 20)

At the aft section, each cable run terminates at its own quadrant. The two quadrants rotate in opposite directions under normal circumstances. Associated with each quadrant is a lever which provides an attachment point for a push/pull rod connected to the summing mechanism.

Summing Mechanism

The summing mechanism accepts the quadrant inputs at the upper and lower ends of a rigid link. The R/H quadrant is connected to the upper end, and the L/H quadrant to the lower end.

PUSH ROD INPUT

A

B

NO JAM CONDITION

A

B

FWD

FORWARD
QUADRANT   JAMMED CONDITION

IN OPERATION THE COMMAND INPUT DRIVES A
BELLCRANK WHICH IS ATTACHED TO THE CABLE
PULLEY AT POINT A AND VIA THE CONNECTING
ROD TO THE BREAKOUT BUNGEE AT POINT B.

IN A NO–JAM STATE THE BELLCRANK PIVOTS AT
POINT B CAUSING ROTATION OF THE PULLEY
THROUGH THE ATTACHING POINT A.

SHOULD A CABLE JAM OCCUR, POINT A BECOMES THE
PIVOT POINT AND THE BELLCRANK IS ALLOWED TO
ROTATE AGAINST THE BUNGEE SPRING FORCE.

Figure 19   Rudder Anti-Jam Breakout Mechanism

The summing mechanism is itself attached to two supporting links which
are pivot mounted at the top to the airframe structure. The summing
mechanism transmits pilot pedal inputs to a bellcrank via a push/pull rod.

Incorporated within the summing mechanism is a load limiter which
functions only in the case of system failure to compensate for asymmetric
loading in the cable control run. In the event that either of the rudder
cable circuits is cut, the load limiter acts as a rigid link to maintain the
summing mechanism in the required geometric relationship, preventing it
from collapsing, thus providing for continued control of the rudder.

Figure 20 Rudder PCU Control

The reverse is true for a jammed circuit. To operate in this mode it is essential that the limiter collapses to permit the extra travel of the summing linkage, and so still provide full rudder travel.

Secondary Feel Mechanism

Installed at the output of the summing mechanism is a secondary feel mechanism similar to the primary feel. Its function is to assist in centering of the rudder and prevent backlash in the control runs.

Load Limiter

Installed upstream between the secondary feel mechanism and the trim/ yaw damper input link, the function of this load limiter is to limit the load applied to PCU inputs when the system is operated without hydraulic power.

The upper end of the load limiter is attached to a bell crank assembly which will translate the manual input to the power control unit input torque tube. A balance spring is attached to the same bellcrank as the load limiter and prevents an inadvertent command input from being applied at the PCU input should the load limiter become detached at its lower end.

Power Control Units (Figures 21 & 22)

The operation of the PCUs is identical to that of the elevator PCUs. With the exception of some internal dimensional differences the units are the same. Failure detection is by means of a proximity sensor installed in each PCU, which feeds a signal to the servo monitor.

Auxiliary Centering Mechanisms (Figure 20)

Each PCU input lever is connected through a control rod to an auxiliary centering mechanism. It is a spring loaded, hinged stop which will center the PCU should the input mechanism become disconnected.

Rudder PCU Input Load Limiters (Figure 20)

Each rudder PCU input link is connected to the input torque tube by a load limiter. Its purpose is to permit continued input movement to the other PCUs should one of them fail or jam.

The center (No. 3 hydraulic system) input load limiter is of a fixed length, while the No. 1 and No. 2 PCU input load limiters are adjustable for force fight elimination & centering.

NOTE: The adjustment of these load limiters is *critical*-consult the corresponding chapter of the maintenance manual for adjustment procedure.

Operation

The forward and aft movement of the rudder pedals is transmitted through a push/pull rod to the forward quadrant/anti-jam breakout mechanism.

NO. 1 SYSTEM & NO. 2 SYSTEM SIMILAR

LEGEND

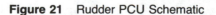

━━━━━ SUPPLY LINE
━━━━━ RETURN LINE
━━━━━ SUPPLY & RETURN LINE

Figure 21 Rudder PCU Schematic

Figure 22 Hydraulic Schematic of Rudder PCU

From the forward quadrant the movement is transmitted to the aft quadrant by cables.

The aft quadrant input is transmitted to the summing mechanism by a pair of push/pull rods (one for each quadrant).

The summing mechanism movement is transmitted to the secondary feel unit through a push/pull rod and the load limiter connected in parallel to the feel unit.

The upper side of the secondary feel unit bell cran connected to the input load limiter which operates the PCU input mechanism. At the upper end of the load limiter is a bell crank which is connected to the torque tube control rod. Attached to this bell crank is a spring which, should the load limiter or the down controls become detached will prevent their static weight from causing an unwanted command input to the PCUs.

Rudder Trim (Figure 23)

Rudder trim is commanded by rotation of the knob on the trim control panel located on the center console. The trim actuator will, when selected, raise or lower the yaw damper walking beam to which both dampers are

Figure 23 Rudder Trim

attached, and through the same linkage as the manual input, activate the PCU. (Operation of the yaw dampers will be covered in Chapter 10 Automatic Flight Control System).

The trim actuator contains an integral position transmitter which drives a pointer in the trim position indicator.

Flight Control Monitoring

General

Flight control monitoring is accomplished by the flight control monitor, the control surface position indicator, the trim position indicator and the flap position indicator.

The flight control monitor receives inputs from aileron elevator and rudder sensors from which it can detect jam conditions and alert the pilot with the appropriate caution.

The control surface and trim position indicators display actual position of the corresponding surfaces on the center instrument panel.

Flight Control Monitor

This system consists of jam proximity sensors located in each PCU, a flight control monitor unit and four warning lights on the stability augmentation/servo monitor panel as shown in Figure 24.

In addition to the flight controls the flight control monitor unit contains a single channel for parking brake shut-off valve sensing.

The system is testable from the flight control monitor unit front face.

Jam Proximity Sensors

Each PCU has a proximity sensor mounted on it, for a total of eleven PCU sensors. These sensors and the parking brake shut-off valve sensor are identical in operation-they differ from the proximity switches used in the landing gear, flaps and spoilers since they simply contain a sensing coil without any switching circuitry. This switching is accomplished inside the flight control monitor and operates when a metal target comes within close proximity of the sensing coil.

Figure 24   Flight Control Monitor—Components

The sensors are installed on the PCUs in two different ways. In the rudder (YAW) and aileron (ROLL) PCUs the sensors are installed in the PCU itself and consequently 'target in proximity' indicates a PCU jam or lack of hydraulic pressure. However, the elevator (PITCH) sensors are mounted on the input rod and in this case 'target in proximity' indicates a PCU jam condition only.

The sensor on the parking brake shut off valve senses whether the valve is open or closed.

Flight Control Monitor Unit

This unit, located in the avionics bay, receives inputs of PCU status and uses this information to control four lights on the stab aug/servo monitor panel as shown in figure 25. Mounted on the front of the unit are four LEDs (repeaters of those in the flight deck), a test switch, a test lamp and a thirteen position rotary channel selector switch.

The logic is configured, as shown in figure 26, such that a flight deck warning will annunciate if a jam occurs in any PCU and a check of this circuitry will illuminate a lamp in the flight deck when all PCUs lack hydraulic pressure. However, since the elevator PCU sensors do not monitor hydraulic pressure, these four inputs must be inverted in order to illuminate the green MON SAFE light with no hydraulic pressure available. Also since the rudder and aileron PCU sensors monitor hydraulic pressure, the amber ROLL and YAW warnings will illuminate for lack of hydraulic pressure as well as a jam condition.

The parking brake circuit in the flight control monitor will illuminate the anti-skid INBD FAIL lamp if the parking brake shut-off valve fails to open when power is applied to it (anti-skid selected to ARM and parking brake off).

The flight control monitor unit comprises twelve channels each monitoring a single proximity sensor as listed below:

Channel Number	Proximity Sensor
1	Left outboard elevator PCU
2	Left inboard elevator PCU
3	Right inboard elevator PCU
4	Right outboard elevator PCU
5	Upper rudder PCU
6	Center rudder PCU
7	Lower rudder PCU
8	Left inboard aileron PCU
9	Left outboard aileron PCU
10	Right outboard aileron PCU
11	Right inboard aileron PCU
12	Parking brake shut-off valve

In addition to these twelve channels the unit contains built-in test circuitry operated and monitored from the front face of the unit. A suspect

Figure 25 Flight Control Monitor—Block Diagram

channel may be verified by selecting the rotary channel selector to the correct channel number, setting S1 to A and B respectively and checking the appropriate lamps illuminate (L1, L2, L3 etc).

Stability Augmentation/Servo Monitor Panel

This panel contains the four annunciators associated with the flight control monitor-PITCH, ROLL, YAW and MON SAFE.

PITCH illuminates amber, with accompanying master caution FLT

Figure 26   Flight Control Monitor—Schematic

CONT annunciator, when any elevator PCU (left inbd, left outbd, right outbd or right inbd) indicates a jam condition.

ROLL illuminates amber, with accompanying master caution FLT CONT annunciator, when any aileron PCU (left inbd, left outbd, right outbd or right inbd) indicates a jam condition

OR

any aileron PCU has no hydraulic pressure-in practice when any hydraulic system (1, 2 or 3) is unpressurized.

YAW illuminates amber, with accompanying master caution FLT CONT annunciator, when any rudder PCU (upper, center or lower) indicates a jam condition

OR

any rudder PCU has no hydraulic pressure-in practice when any hydraulic system (1, 2 or 3) is unpressurized.

Figure 27 Control Surface Position Indication—Components

MON SAFE illuminates green only when ALL aileron and rudder PCUs have no hydraulic pressure (hydraulic systems 1, 2 and 3 are unpressurized) and all elevator PCUs are unjammed. MON SAFE must always be accompanied by ROLL and YAW annunciators and never by the PITCH annunciator.

FLAP POSITION INDICATOR

FLAP POSITION TRANSMITTER
(R/H INBOARD FLAP HINGE)

Figure 31   Flap Position Indication

Control Surface Position

The control surface position indicator relays to the flight crew a readout of the actual position of the following control surfaces:

Position Transmitters

Each of the three transmitters is a potentiometer fed from a reference voltage and ground by the trim position indicator. The wiper voltage, representative of position is fed to the trim position indicator to drive the corresponding pointer.

Trim Position Indicator

This instrument, located on the center instrument panel immediately below the surface position indicator, contains three pointers, each driven from the respective trim position transmitter.

This unit receives 28 VDC power from Bus 1. This power supplies the pointer drive circuitry as well as providing the reference voltage for each of the transmitter potentiometers.

Flap Position Indication

This system comprises a flap position potentiometer located on the right hand inboard flap hinge and an indicator located on the co-pilots instrument panel.

Power is supplied from the battery bus as shown in figure 31.

Lift Modulation

General

Lift modulation is accomplished by the deployment of any one or a combination of the spoilers and flaps.

The flight spoilers consist of a single panel hinged to the upper surface of each wing. They are hydraulically powered from systems No. 1 and No. 2, but mechanically controlled by a lever on the center console. The flight spoilers can be deployed by the flight crew up to a maximum of 40°.

The ground spoilers consist of a panel hinged forward of each inboard flap on the upper trailing edge. They are electrically controlled and powered from hydraulic system No. 1.

The flap system consists of four flap panels operated by a dual flap motor, screw jacks and connecting flex drives. Flap deployment is adjustable to 20°, 30°, or 45° by a selector switch on the center console.

The flaps are of the double slotted type, the outboard panels having a fixed leading edge vane, and the inboard a movable vane which extends as the flaps are lowered. Extension and retraction of the flap system is controlled by the flap control unit which also provides outputs to other aircraft systems.

Flight Spoilers (Figures 32 & 33)

The command input is from a lever located on the center console. Movement of the spoiler control lever is transmitted via a push/pull rod to a torque shaft, which in turn transmits the command to a forward cable quadrant.

The control lever is prevented from inadvertent movement by a series of detents, which must be overcome as the handle is moved.

Figure 32 Flight Spoilers—Components

The cable run is routed aft and terminates at an aft cable quadrant which is mounted between the aft aileron cable quadrants.

The aft quadrant provides a mounting point for two Controlex cables. These transmit command movement along the L/H and R/H wing rear spar to a bell crank and then through a load limiter to the power control

**FLIGHT SPOILER LH
(SPOILER RH IDENTICAL)**

CONTR
VALVE

CONTR.
VALVE

PILOT INPUT

NO. 1 SYSTEM

NO. 2 SYSTEM

LEGEND

SUPPLY LINE
RETURN LINE
SUPPLY & RETURN LINE

Figure 33   Flight Spoiler Hydraulic Schematic

units. The load limiter is incorporated to protect the PCU input mechanism from the excessive loads should the hydraulic power be off.

To prevent extreme asymmetry of the flight spoilers in the unlikely case of a disconnected input linkage, a detent mechanism is installed on the rear spar near to the outboard PCU.

The PCU control valves are spring loaded down, but the spring loaded detent mechanism, connected to the input linkage, applies force to position it in the mid-position.

A micro switch on each mechanism provides a signal to the corresponding left or right flight spoiler light on the center pedestal beside the spoiler lever. These lights illuminate green whenever the spoilers are deployed more than 20°, and indicate that the detent mechanism is operating.

Each flight spoiler surface is actuated by two identical PCUs. The PCUs are independent and powered by the No. 1 and No. 2 hydraulic system as follows: Inboard-system No. 1 and Outboard-system No. 2.

Spoiler position is reflected on an indicator in the center instrument panel. The position for each spoiler is detected by a surface position transmitter mounted on the rear wing spar (Figure 28).

Proximity switches-one per spoiler, located between the center hinges, provide position signals to corresponding left and right caution lights on the glareshield.

These lights, marked LH FLT SPLR and RH FLT SPLR, illuminate amber whenever the flight spoilers are not down. These proximity sensors also supply inputs to the take-off configuration warning.

Operation

Flight spoiler deployment is initiated by pulling the spoiler control lever aft through a series of eight detents, with position markings for 0, 1/4, 1/2, 3/4 and full.

The control linkage moves the control valves on the PCUs, which move the spoilers proportionally as the handle is moved.

When the spoilers start moving, their proximity switches illuminate the amber LH and RH FLT SPLR lights on the glareshield, and the position transmitters feed signals to the spoiler pointers on the control surface position indicator on the center instrument panel.

When the spoilers move past the 1/2 (20°) position, the micro switches on the spring loaded detents on the PCUs are activated, and illuminate the green LEFT and RIGHT flight spoiler lights on the center pedestal.

To retract the flight spoilers, the handle is moved forward. The green lights extinguish as the spoilers retract below the mid-position, and the amber lights extinguish when the spoilers are fully stowed.

Ground Spoilers

Description

The ground spoilers consist of a single panel hinged to the upper wing surface just forward of the inboard flaps. The ground spoilers have only two operating positions: 0° and 45°. The "not down" position is indicated with amber lights located on the glareshield. The spoilers are operated each by a single actuator powered from the No. 1 hydraulic system.

The main components of the system are: (Figure 34)

- the Spoiler Control Lever, which actuates two switches in the fully aft position (an aft position beyond full flight spoiler selection).
- the Spoiler Control Unit, located in the avionics bay.
- the Dual Hydraulic Selector Valve, located in the MLG bay.
- two Hydraulic Spoiler Actuators with internal locks.
- two Proximity Switches that send a deployed signal to the glareshield indicator lights.

The ground spoiler actuator (Figure 35) has an internal mechanical locking device that locks the spoiler in the down position. Hydraulic pressure is required to release this lock before the actuator can extend.

Operation

Ground spoiler operation is controlled by the spoiler control lever in the cockpit, which must be placed in the fully aft EXTEND position by pushing a button on the handle and simultaneously lifting the handle aft. Thus, the ground spoilers can only be extended when the flight spoilers are already fully extended.

The spoiler control lever activates two switches, which direct an extend command from the spoiler control unit to the valve solenoids. The spoiler control unit receives inputs from power lever position switches, weight-on-wheels information from the landing gear control unit, wheel spinup information from the anti-skid control unit, and power from the Ground Spoiler Panel ON/OFF/TEST switch. (Figure 37)

The spoiler control unit will extend the ground spoilers only if:

- the ON/OFF/TEST switch on the Ground Spoiler Panel is in the ON position.
- the spoiler control lever is in the aft position.

Figure 34 Ground Spoiler Control

NOTE
ACTUATOR PISTON SHOWN
FULLY RETRACTED AND
LOCKED

Figure 35   Ground Spoiler Actuator

- both power levers are at the idle position.
- a weight-on-wheels and/or wheel spin-up above 17 kts signal
  is present.
- the solenoid valves are in the same position.

When this logic is correct, electrical power from the spoiler control unit
will energize a dual hydraulic selector valve, which operates in series to
extend, and in parallel to retract the spoilers (Figure 36).

The two parts of the valve are hydraulically interconnected to ensure

Figure 36   Ground Spoiler—Hydraulic Schematic

simultaneous operation of the spoilers. Neither spoiler actuator can be pressured to extend unless both valves are energized.

With both solenoid valves de-energized hydraulic pressure is supplied to the 'retract' port of both actuators powering the spoilers to retract.

With both solenoid valves energized hydraulic pressure is routed through the No. 1 valve to the No. 2 valve and then to the "extend" port of both actuators causing both spoilers to deploy.

If, for any reason, either solenoid fails to operate, both spoilers will be locked or powered into the retracted position.

To prevent inadvertent deployment of the ground spoilers, a separate

Figure 37 Spoilers—Electrical Schematic

508

circuit in the spoiler control unit monitors and compares the position of the two valves in the dual hydraulic selector valve.

If a dissimilar condition is detected for more than one half second, the spoiler control unit de-energizes the solenoids (stows the spoilers) and illuminates the ground SPLRS INOP light on the center pedestal.

A proximity switch located beneath the surface of each ground spoiler panel sends a signal to illuminate the amber GND SPLR lamp on the glareshield anytime the spoiler is not stowed. These same proximity switches also supply inputs to the take-off configuration warning.

In addition to indicating ground spoiler deployment on the ground, the amber GND SPLR lights also indicate the presence of a false output when the system is airborne with the spoiler handle not in the "ground spoiler deploy position". A two second delay is present in this circuit to prevent nuisance "blips" at touchdown if WOW and wheel speed signals are not stable.

Testing

The system is tested by selecting the ON/OFF/TEST switch on the ground spoiler panel to the TEST position and holding it there, with the spoilers selected to the stowed position. The indications are as follows:

- no indication for 2 seconds
- LH and RH GND SPLR lights illuminated for 3 seconds-triggered by the deploy command through the false output detector relay.
- ground SPLRS INOP light illumination coincident with loss of both amber GND SPLR lamps
- all light(s) extinguish when TEST is released. Setting the switch to ON through the OFF position resets the ground spoiler unit.

GLOSSARY

Definition of Hydraulic and Related Terms

ACCUMULATOR—A container in which fluid is stored under pressure as a source of fluid power.

ACTUATOR—A device for converting hydraulic energy into mechanical energy. A motor or cylinder.

AERATION—Air in the hydraulic fluid. Excessive aeration causes the fluid to appear milky and components to operate erratically because of the compressibility of the air trapped in the fluid.

AREA—The number of square units in a surface.

BACK PRESSURE—A pressure in series. Usually refers to pressure existing on the discharge side of a load. It addes to the pressure required to move the load.

BAFFLE—A device, usually a plate, installed in a reservoir to separate the pump inlet from return lines.

BALANCED ACTUATOR—A hydraulic or pneumatic actuator having the same area on both sides of the piston.

BUTYL—The trade name of a synthetic rubber product made by the polymerization of isobutylene. It withstands such potent chemicals as Skydrol hydraulic fluid.

BY-PASS—A secondary passage for fluid flow.

CASE PRESSURE—A low pressure maintained inside the case of a hydraulic pump. In the event of a damaged seal, fluid will be forced out of the pump rather than allowing air to be drawn in.

CAVITATION—A localized gaseous condition within a liquid stream which occurs where the pressure is reduced to the vapor pressure.

CHARGE (supercharge)—1) To replenish a hydraulic system above atmospheric pressure. 2) To fill an accumulator with fluid under pressure (see Precharge Pressure).

CHARGE PRESSURE—The pressure at which replenishing fluid is forced into the hydraulic system (above atmospheric pressure).

CHECK VALVE—A valve which permits flow of fluid in one direction only.

CLOSED CENTER VALVE—One in which all ports are blocked in the center or neutral position.

CLOSED CENTER CIRCUIT—One in which flow through the system is blocked in neutral and pressure is maintained at the maximum pressure control setting.

COMPENSATOR CONTROL—A displacement control for variable pumps and motors which alters displacement in response to pressure changes in the system as related to its adjusted pressure setting.

COMPONENT—A single hydraulic unit.

COMPRESSIBILITY—The change in volume of a unit volume of a fluid when it is subjected to a unit change in pressure.

CONSTANT DISPLACEMENT PUMP—A pump which displaces a constant amount of fluid each time it turns. The faster it turns, the more it puts out.

CONTROL—A device used to regulate the function of a unit (see Hydraulic Control, Manual Control, and Compensator Control). Compensator Control).

COOLER—A heat exchanger used to remove heat from the hydraulic fluid.

CRACKING PRESSURE—The pressure at which a pressure actuated valve begins to pass fluid.

CUNO FILTER—The proprietary name of a fluid filter made up of a stack of discs separated by scraper blades. Contaminants collect on the edge of the discs and are periodically scraped out and collected in the bottom of the filter case.

CUSHION—A device sometimes built into the ends of a hydraulic cylinder which restricts the flow of fluid at the outlet port, thereby arresting the motion of the piston rod.

CYLINDER—A device which converts fluid power into linear mechanical force and motion. It usually consists of a movable element such as a piston and piston rod, plunger rod, plunger or ram, operating within a cylindrical bore.

DEADBAND—The region or band of no response where an error signal will not cause a corresponding actuation of the controlled variable.

DELIVERY—The volume of fluid discharged by a pump in a given time, usually expressed in gallons per minute (gpm).

DIFFERENTIAL CYLINDER—Any cylinder in which the two opposed piston areas are not equal.

DIRECTIONAL VALVE—A valve which selectively directs or prevents fluid flow to desired channels.

DISPLACEMENT—The quantity of fluid which can pass through a pump, motor or cylinder in a single revolution or stroke.

DOUBLE-ACTING ACTUATOR—A linear actuator which is moved in both directions by fluid power.

DOUBLE-ACTING CYLINDER—A cylinder in which fluid force can be applied to the movable element in either direction.

ELECTRO-HYDRAULIC SERVO VALVE—A directional type valve which receives a variable or controlled electrical signal and which controls or meters hydraulic flow.

ENERGY—The ability or capacity to do work. Measured in units of work.

FILTER—A device whose primary function is the retention by a porous media of insoluble contaminants from a fluid.

FLOW CONTROL VALVE—A valve which controls the rate of oil flow.

FLUID—1) A liquid or gas. 2) A liquid that is specially compounded for use as a power-transmitting medium in a hydraulic system.

FLUID POWER—The transmission of force by the movement of a fluid. The best examples are hydraulics and pneumatics.

FORCE—Any push or pull measured in units of weight. In hydraulics, total force is expressed by the product P (force per unit area) and the area of the surface on which the pressure acts. $F = P \times A$.

FOUR-WAY VALVE—A directional valve having four flow paths.

FULL FLOW—In a filter, the condition where all the fluid must pass through the filter element or medium.

GALLING—Fretting or pulling out chunks of a surface by sliding contact with another surface or body.

GAUGE PRESSURE—A pressure scale which ignores atmospheric pressure. Its zero point is 14.7 psi absolute.

GEROTOR PUMP—A form of gear pump which uses an external spur gear, inside of and driving an internal gear having one more tooth space than the drive gear. As the gears rotate, the space between two of the teeth increases, while that on the opposite side of the pump decreases.

HEAD—The height of a column or body of fluid above a given point expressed in linear units. Head is often used to indicate gage pressure. Pressure is equal to then eight times the density of the fluid.

HEAT EXCHANGER—A device which transfers heat through a conducting wall from one fluid to another.

HORSEPOWER—(HP)—The power required to lift 550 pounds one foot in one second or 33,000 pounds one foot in one minute. A horsepower is equal to 746 watts or to 42.4 British Thermal Units per minute.

HYDRAULIC BALANCE—A condition of equal opposed hydraulic forces acting on a part in a hydraulic component.

HYDRAULIC CONTROL—A control which is actuated by hydraulically induced forces.

HYDRAULICS—Engineering science pertaining to liquid pressure and flow.

KINETIC ENERGY—Energy that a substance or body has by virtue of its mass (weight) and velocity.

LINE—A tube, pipe or hose which acts as a conductor of hydraulic fluid.

LINEAR ACTUATOR—A device for converting hydraulic energy into linear motion—a cylinder or ram.

MANIFOLD—A fluid conductor which provides multiple connection ports.

MANUAL CONTROL—A control actuated by the operator, regardless of the means of actuation. Example: Lever or foot pedal control for directional valves.

MICRON—One millionth of a meter. It is normally used to donate the effectiveness of a filter.

MICRONIC FILTER—The trade name of a filter having a porous paper element.

MICRON RATING—The size of the particles a filter will remove.

MOTOR—A device which converts hydraulic fluid power into mechanical motion.

NAPHTHA—A volatile and flammable hydrocarbon liquid used chiefly as a solvent or cleaning agent.

OPEN CENTER CIRCUIT—One in which pump delivery flows freely through the system and back to the reservoir in neutral.

OPEN CENTER VALVE—One in which all ports are interconnected and open to each other in the center or neutral position.

ORIFICE—A restriction, the length of which is small in respect to its cross-sectional dimensions.

ORIFICE CHECK VALVE—A component in a hydraulic or pneumatic system that allows unrestricted flow in one direction, and restricted flow in the opposite direction.

PASCAL'S LAW—A basic law of fluid power which states that pressure in an enclosed container is transmitted equally and undiminished to all points of the container and acts at right angles to the enclosing walls.

PILOT PRESSURE—Auxiliary pressure used to actuate or control hydraulic components.

PILOT VALVE—An auxiliary valve used to control the operation of another valve. The controlling stage of a 2-stage valve.

PISTON—A cylindrically shaped part which fits within a cylinder and transmits or receives motion by means of a connecting rod.

PNEUMATICS—That system of fluid power which transmits force by the use of a compressible fluid.

POPPET—That part of certain valves which prevents flow when it closes against a seat.

PORT—An internal or external terminus of a passage in a component.

POSITIVE DISPLACEMENT—A characteristic of a pump or motor which has the inlet positively sealed from the outlet so that fluid cannot recirculate in the component.

POWER—Work per unit of time. Measured in horsepower (hp) or watts.

POWER PACK—An integral power supply unit usually containing a pump, reservoir, relief valve and directional control.

PRECHARGE PRESSURE—The pressure of compressed gas in an accumulator prior to the admission of liquid.

PRESSURE—Force per unit area; usually expressed in pounds per square inch (psi).

PRESSURE DROP—The difference in pressure between any two points or a component.

PRESSURE LINE—The line carrying the fluid from the pump outlet to the pressurized port of the actuator.

PRESSURE REDJCING VALVE—A valve which limits the maximum pressure at its outlet regardless of the inlet pressure.

PRESSURE SWITCH—An electric switch operated by fluid pressure.

PUMP—A device which converts mechanical force and motion into hydraulic fluid power.

RACK AND PINION ACTUATOR—A form of rotary, actuator where the fluid acts on a piston on which a rack of gear teeth is cut. As the piston moves, it rotates a mating pinion gear.

RECIPROCATING—Back-and-forth straight line motion or oscillation.

RELIEF VALVE—A pressure operated valve which by-passes pump delivery to the reservoir, limiting system pressure to a predetermined maximum value.

REPLENISH—To add fluid to maintain a full hydraulic system.

RESERVOIR—A container for storage of liquid in a fluid power system.

RESTRICTION—A reduced cross-sectional area in a line or passage which produces a pressure drop.

RETURN LINE—A line used to carry exhaust fluid from the actuator back to sump.

ROTARY ACTUATOR—A device for converting hydraulic energy into rotary motion—a hydraulic motor.

SEQUENCE—1) The order of a series of operations or movements. 2) To divert flow to accomplish a subsequent operation or movement.

SEQUENCE VALVE—A pressure operated valve which, at its setting, diverts flow to a secondary line while holding a predetermined minimum pressure in the primary line.

SERVO MECHANISM (servo)—A mechanism subjected to the action of a controlling device which will operate as if it were directly actuated by the controlling device, but capable of supplying power output many times that of the controlling device, this power being derived from an external and independent source.

SERVO VALVE—1) A valve which modulates output as a function of an input command. 2) A follow valve.

SHUTTLE VALVE—A valve mounted on critical components which directs system pressure into the actuator for normal operation, but emergency fluid when the emergency system is actuated.

SILICONE RUBBER—An elastic material made from silicone elastomers. It is used with fluids which attack other natural or synthetic rubbers.

SINGLE ACTING CYLINDER—A cylinder in which hydraulic energy can produce thrust or motion in only one direction. (May be mechanically or gravity returned.)

SINTERED METAL—A porous material made up by fusing powdered metal under heat and pressure.

SKYDROL HYDRAULIC FLUID—A synthetic, nonflammable, ester base hydraulic fluid used in modern high-temperature hydraulic systems.

SPOOL—A term loosely applied to almost any moving cylindrically shaped part of a hydraulic component which moves to direct flow through the component.

STATIC—Still; not moving.

STODDARD SOLVENT—A petroleum product similar to naphtha, used as a solvent or cleaning agent.

STRAINER—A course filter.

STROKE—1) The length of travel of a piston or plunger. 2) To change the displacement of a variable displacement pump or motor.

SUCTION LINE—The hydraulic line connecting the pump inlet port to the reservoir or sump.

SUMP—A reservoir.

SURGE—A transient rise of pressure or flow.

SWASH PLATE—A stationary canted plate in an axial type piston pump which causes the pistons to reciprocate as the cylinder barrel rotates.

TANK—The reservoir or sump.

TEFLON—A proprietary name for a fluorocarbon resin used to make hydraulic and pneumatic seals and backup rings.

TORQUE—A rotary thrust. The turning effort of a fluid motor usually expressed in inch pounds.

TWO-WAY VALVE—A directional control valve with two flow paths.

UNLOAD—To release flow (usually directly to the reservoir), to prevent pressure being imposed on the system or portion of the system.

UNLOADING VALVE—A valve which by-passes flow to tank when a set pressure is maintained on its pilot port.

VALVE—A device which controls fluid flow direction, pressure, or flow rate.

VARIABLE DISPLACEMENT PUMP—A pump whose output may be varied by the pressure on the system. For high-pressure applications, this is usually done by varying the stroke, either actual or effective, or a piston-type pump.

VARSOL—A petroleum product similar to naphtha, used as a solvent.

VELOCITY—The speed of flow through a hydraulic line. Expressed in feet per second (fps) or inches per second (ips).

VENT—1) To permit opening of a pressure control valve by opening its pilot port (vent connection) to atmospheric pressure. 2) An air breathing device on a fluid reservoir.

VISCOSITY—A measure of the internal friction or the resistance of a fluid to flow.

VOLUME—1) The size of a space or chamber in cubic units. 2) Loosely applied to the output of a pump in gallons per minute (gpm).

WOBBLE PLATE—A rotating canted plate in an axial type piston pump which pushes the pistons into their bores as it "wobbles".

WORK—Exerting a force through a definite distance. Work is measured in units of force multiplied by distance; for example pound-foot.